Edite Vieira, whose married name is Edite Phillips, was born in Portugal and spent the early years of her life there. She then went to live in Mozambique where she began a career in radio. She worked as an announcer/translator for Spanish National Radio for five years, where she met her husband, and was also secretary to the Portuguese Ambassador in Madrid for two years.

In 1964 she moved to London with her family and now works for BBC radio as a journalist and announcer of programmes in Portuguese. Edite Vieira is the author of many books in Portuguese including a collection of her own poetry and a book on cooking for our times. She has two children, a son and a daughter, and still finds time for her most absorbing hobby which is, of course, cooking.

The Taste of
PORTUGAL

Traditional Portuguese Cuisine

EDITE VIEIRA

ROBINSON PUBLISHING
LONDON

Robinson Publishing
11 Shepherd House
5 Shepherd Street
London W1Y 7LD

First published by Robert Hale Ltd., 1988
First Robinson Publishing edition 1989

Printed by The Guernsey Press Co. Ltd., Guernsey, Channel Islands

To Diana and Paul

Contents

Acknowledgements   viii
Foreword by João Hall-Themido   ix
Author's Preface   xi

Introduction   1
   A Flavour of the Country   1
   Food and Tradition   3
   Preparing to Cook   19

Soups   38

Bread Dishes   56
   Açordas   58
   Migas   62
   Ensopados   64
   Dry Soups   65
   Gaspachos   67

Fish, Shellfish and Seafood   71
   Salted Cod Dishes   72
   Sardines   79
   Fish Stews   81
   Other Fish Dishes   84
   Lampreys   87
   Shellfish   90
   Seafood   94

Meat   97
   Beefsteak   97
   Stews   100
   Kid   104
   Other Meat Dishes   106
   Pork   109
   Poultry and Game   121

Sauces   135

Vegetables and Accompaniments   139

Sweet Things   147
  Puddings 147
  Sweets 170
  Pastries 178
  Small Cakes 187
  Fried Cakes 190
  Biscuits 197
  Buns 199
  Large Cakes 203
  Fancy Bread 209
  Jams and Jellies 211
  Fillings 216

Drinks   220
  Portuguese Wines 220
  Liqueurs and Fortified Drinks 228

Appendix: Vegetarian Recipes   233
Index   236

Map: Provinces and Demarcated Wine Regions of Portugal   4

Acknowledgements

This list would be far too long if I were to mention the names of all the kind friends and relations who, in one way or another, helped me with their support and suggestions. A book of this sort inevitably entails the co-operation of many people and I am really grateful for having been able to count on their understanding and practical help.

After this general thank you, however, a very special one to: Maria Antónia de Vasconcelos, Chief Editor of *Reader's Digest* in Portugal who was in fact instrumental in my doing this book and enthusiastically provided me with lots of material and encouragement; Maria Rolim Ramos; Eugénio Lisboa; Luís de Sousa Rebelo; Maria do Rosário Cunha; Helena Guerreiro Klinowsky; Manuela da Luz Chaplin; Maria Adosinda Torgal Ferreira; my daughter Diana for the lovely drawings in the preliminary pages and Maggie Redfern for the delightful chapter-opening illustrations; Abílio Simões, from the Caravela Restaurant in London, for his generous contribution; and, of course, my mother, who had the insight of initiating me into her cookery secrets from an early age.

Foreword

by João Hall-Themido
Ambassador of Portugal to Great Britain

As the author of this excellent and comprehensive book on traditional Portuguese cuisine states right at the beginning, there are not many books on the subject in English, and even less of sufficiently high quality. This in itself would justify the present publication, all the more so since the Portuguese art of cooking has been widely recognized as one of the most valued for its variety, richness and quite distinct character among the cuisines that the Western world may be proud of.

Eating is not similarly important in different countries. To the Portuguese *it is* important. Not only eating but eating well and speaking about it. There is nothing to be ashamed of in this love for one of the great pleasures of life. A notable French philosopher, Michel de Montaigne, once stated that 'the art of dining well is no slight art, the pleasure not a slight pleasure'. No Portuguese, I am sure, would disagree with the author of the famous *Essays*.

Eating well helps shape a better and happier view of life. No one and certainly no Portuguese sees the world quite in the same colours *before* and *after* a good meal. In this we are probably not vastly different from other peoples. Aldous Huxley, who is widely translated and appreciated in Portugal, once stated that 'a man may be a pessimistic determinist before lunch and an optimistic believer in the will's freedom after it'.

In different but not less striking words, the great gourmet and connoisseur Brillat-Savarin used to say that the discovery of a new dish does more for the happiness of mankind than the discovery of a star. Having read with unmitigated pleasure and profit Ms Vieira's book, I was left in no doubt that this useful and vivacious contribution to a better knowledge of the Portuguese art of cooking will do more than a little for the happiness of mankind – at least the mankind of the English-speaking kind.

J. H-T.

Author's Preface

It seems that not much – or at least not enough – has so far been published in English on the subject of Portuguese cookery. I was therefore thrilled to be asked to give my contribution in order to help narrow this gap.

I include in the book some background information on Portugal (some customs, a few snippets of history and so on) to enhance and, as it were, frame the subject, so that the reader may have some idea of the setting in which the dishes were created. So even if you do not dash immediately into the kitchen to cook Portuguese style, I hope the book will provide a good read.

Until quite recently I thought that reading cookery books was just a mania of mine, but I have now discovered that many people use them even as bed-time reading matter. I would, however, prefer that you use this book not so much as a sleeping-pill as a guide for cooking.

When preparing Portuguese dishes I am, mainly, *matando saudades* of Portuguese food. Those who understand Portuguese will know that *saudade* is something like nostalgia, but somehow not quite the same and very difficult to define, and that the Portuguese are forever referring to *saudades*, meaning they miss this or that, or someone, most desperately. To relieve this painful feeling they must *matar saudades* (*matar* means to kill, hence to kill that deep nostalgia) by doing whatever is needed for the purpose. In this case ... cooking.

I remember that when my children were small (after we came to live in London) they were always eager for their meals. For a while I wasn't working and had plenty of time for the kitchen, and they were delighted with my cooking. In their innocence they said once that surely the Queen of England did not have on her table such good food as we did. It is always a pleasure to prepare them such typical dishes as *caldo verde* (green broth), *fatias douradas* (golden slices), rice pudding and other delicious everyday Portuguese dishes. And they beg me to prepare 'my soups', each time they come home for a visit.

I used to take for granted the food I grew up with. It was only when I left Portugal, first to live in Africa, then in Spain and afterwards in Britain, that I began to realize how wonderful my childhood meals really had been and how much effort and care my mother lavished on the food she prepared for the family, day in and day out. Christmas, especially, was always something I longed for, as a child, partly because of the magnificent fried turnovers (*azevias*) she made, filled with a *compôte* of sweet potato spiced with cinnamon – my favourite flavouring. I shall always remember them as something unique and, alas, quite lost in the past, for I do not think I could ever again taste sweet-potato turnovers as good as those.

My mother used to have a very dab hand for soups and stews as well. Stews are much favoured by the Portuguese, and you will find exquisite ones made with fish, beef, chicken, lamb or almost anything. The basic preparation for the stew consists of the *refogado*, which I explain on p.31, and it is good to eat even by itself, especially if you have a piece of homemade bread at hand.

I have been 'commuting' quite a lot between London and Lisbon for the last few years, and find it fascinating to observe how Portuguese customs regarding food have been evolving. People are now much more open to international cuisine but, at the same time, are also more aware of the authentic fare still offered at many restaurants, particularly in rural areas.

Much basic Portuguese fare is simple, wholesome food, using straightforward ingredients, and if you are at all 'into' whole foods and/or vegetarianism, you will find quite a lot that will appeal to you in the Portuguese way of eating. Inclined towards vegetarianism myself, I have included an appendix referring to the vegetarian recipes, but you will see many others which can easily be adapted by omitting the animal products.

There are so many national and regional specialities in Portugal (not all of them available at restaurants, by any means) that it would be out of the question to cover in one single book more than a fraction of them, so I have had to pick some of the most popular or representative. Some dishes demand an acquired taste, perhaps, but I am sure you will be adventurous and try them. And, when you are eating, don't forget to ask others, as the Portuguese do: '*É servido?*' ('Would you like some?'), to which they will say: '*Não obrigado, bom proveito*' ('No, thanks, enjoy it'). And so I hope you do.

Introduction

A Flavour of the Country

The remarkable thing about Portugal is that despite being so small – only 350 miles (561 km) long and 140 miles (218 km) wide – it embraces so much variety, both in climate, geography, people, food, crafts and so on.

Many races have amalgamated to produce strikingly different types of people, some tall, blondish, sometimes blue-eyed; others rather short, stocky, almost olive-skinned, with dark eyes and hair. This is the legacy of so many invaders and settlers in the territory (Greeks, Phoenicians, Carthaginians, Iberians, Celts, Swabians, Visigoths, Romans, Muslims from North Africa) before it finally became a nation in 1143 AD.

While being generally considered a Mediterranean country and sharing some of its characteristics, Portugal is quite a separate entity, set out into the Atlantic and, as it were, turning its back to Europe and opening itself to the sea. This, of course, brought the Portuguese to their great adventure of discovery and expansion, right back in the fifteenth century, when Prince Henry 'the Navigator' surrounded himself with sailors and scholars and planned the first expeditions to the unknown worlds only heard of in fantastic tales and legends. It was the start of an empire which lasted five hundred years and spread the Portuguese language throughout the world. It is at present among the six most widely-spoken languages and the official

1

one of eight different countries.

Continental Portugal can be roughly divided into two main and contrasting regions: one to the north of the River Tagus (where highlands and the central range of mountains dominate) and the other to the south of the river, where the land never reaches great altitudes except when the plains of the Alentejo give way to the Algarve. Between the coast and the inland provinces there is a similar contrast, where the coastal lowlands, mainly sandy beaches, are followed by a steady increase in altitude, towards the interior, especially in the north. These characteristics, allied to the wind system and the influence of the Gulf Stream, give Portugal a temperate climate, though again the north is more rainy and colder. It bears more Atlantic features, while south of the Tagus a Mediterranean-type climate is more prevalent, with less rain and much higher temperatures in summer.

Although agriculture occupies about a quarter of the active population and almost half of the land, production far from covers the needs of the people. The main crops are wheat, maize, rice, potatoes, wine and olive oil.

In the lush and picturesque Minho and Douro Litoral provinces every inch is cultivated or covered by forests. The region is densely populated by vivacious and industrious people, much given to folk-religious festivities. Here originated many dishes later adopted by the whole country. Oporto is its proud and beautiful main city – the *Invicta* (Invincible) – resenting the attentions given to Lisbon, the capital. The region is dotted with old palaces and manor houses still lived in or converted into inns, lending an air of dignified elegance with their simple white façades where doors and windows stand out as frames of granite.

In the north-east lie the most remote and sparsely populated provinces – Trás-os-Montes (behind the Mountains) and the Beiras – a rugged, spectacular and austere landscape becoming more colourful along the deep Douro river valley which crosses the region and looks up to the vines from which the port wine is made. These are planted in almost inaccessible terraces. Here all is sobriety and tradition, underlined by the warmth of the people.

The Beira Litoral province is noted for its sparkling wines, spas, suckling pig, marvellous beaches, with the old and romantic city of Coimbra at its centre. On the other hand, the heart of the country is the land of rolling hills and vast plains – the Ribatejo and Alentejo provinces – with an intensely rural life, where pure-bred horses and fighting bulls are reared and the cork forests and the wheat tinge the land with yellow and ochre.

The Estremadura province and the majestic Setúbal peninsula are bustling regions, geared to serving the capital. Like Rome, Lisbon is built on seven hills. Its immense port at the estuary of the Tagus once attracted all the European merchants, but today it is still a very important port of call – just as it had been for the Romans, for over six centuries, under the name Olissipum Felicitas Julia.

Down south is the Algarve which is now becoming renowned the world over for its glorious beaches and almost non-existent winters. It is a paradise of figs, almonds, oranges, honey and beautiful fish and is much more tuned to tourism than any other region except perhaps Madeira.

The archipelagos of Madeira and Azores are also part of Portugal and have been – quite rightly – compared to jewels in the sea. Their traditions, food, crafts and festivities are deeply rooted and maintained with zeal and love. In Madeira (a land popular with the English and a favourite haunt of Churchill's on his painting trips) agriculture is taken seriously in man-made terraces covering the island, growing tropical flowers, bananas and all sorts of fruit and vegetables, as well as the famous vines for the madeira wine. The more remote and mysterious Azores are green and blue with wild hydrangeas and lakes filling old craters. Here too agriculture is important and includes the cultivation of fragrant pineapples. It is said that the Azores were once part of the lost kingdom of Atlantis – a legend quite easy to believe in that spectacular and beautiful string of islands.

Food and Tradition

What is a national dish? How best to classify an authentic regional delicacy?

Fialho de Almeida in *Os Gatos* (*The Cats*, 1893) had no difficulty in expressing what he thought: 'It is a culinary creation which resents being written down in manuals; it is characteristic, incapable of being expressed in amounts of ingredients, fractions of time and the quick or slow action of cold, heat, water, ice, the use of a strainer, a food-mill, a knife or spoon.... Like a national legend, a national dish is the product of collective genius: no one in particular invented it – it has been invented by all. When one is born, one is already crying for it, and when one is travelling very far from the country, it is what one remembers first – before even remembering father and mother.'

Having stated so eloquently what he considered to be

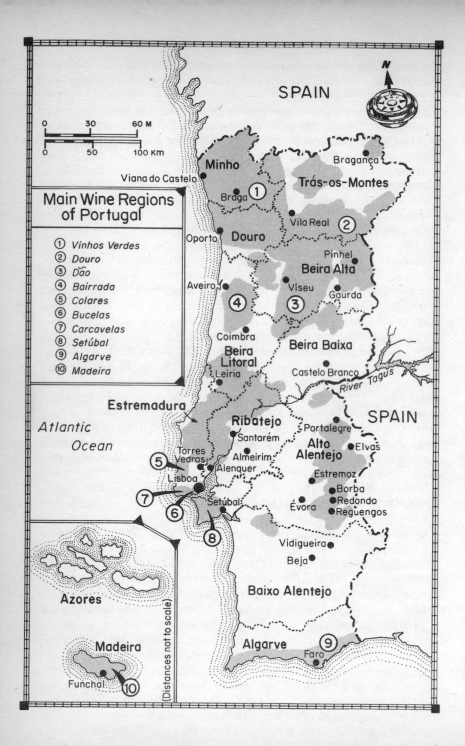

N

SPAIN

Bragança

Minho

Viana do Castelo

Braga (1)

Trás-os-Montes

Vila Real (2)

Main Wine Regions
of Portugal

Oporto

Douro

Pinhel

(1) *Vinhos Verdes*
(2) *Douro*
(3) *Dão*
(4) *Bairrada*
(5) *Colares*
(6) *Bucelas*
(7) *Carcavelas*
(8) *Setúbal*
(9) *Algarve*
(10) *Madeira*

Aveiro

Beira Alta

Viseu   Gaurda

(4)   (3)

Coimbra   **Beira Baixa**

**Beira
Litoral**

Leiria   Castelo Branco

River Tagus

Estremadura

SPAIN

Atlantic

Ocean

Ribatejo   Portalegre

Santarém   **Alto
Alentejo**   Elvas

Torres
Vedras   Almeirim   Estremoz

(5)   Alenquer   Borba

Lisboa   Redondo

(7)   Setúbal   Évora   Reguengos

(6)

(8)   Vidigueira

Beja

Azores

Baixo Alentejo

Madeira   **Algarve**   (9)

Funchal   Faro

(10)

(Distances not to scale)

0   30   60 M

0   50   100 Km

Provinces and demarcated wine regions of Portugal

authentic food, he then complains bitterly about loss of standards: 'Among us the art of cooking and eating is degenerating, like everything else at present. It is a lack of cohesion in people's tastes and it is also the fault of brainless innovators, for whom our national traditions never attain the level of the most uninteresting Anglo-French concoctions ... I hope you will agree that this matter is well deserving of a patriotic crusade to reinstate the country to its former high standards. Defending their national cuisine, the people will be defending the territory. Armed invasion starts in the kitchen.'

Fialho de Almeida most emphatically declared that, '... without a shadow of doubt the Portuguese is the most refined, the most voluptuous and succulent cuisine in the world ...', because, 'It is true to say that we had excellent masters, having for instance inherited from the Arabs the casserole and the art of frying, which was a lot; and that our voyages of discovery meant more than an outlet for the fighting moods and bad habits of those rowdy noblemen who were going bankrupt in the metropolis. We did acquire – thanks to the spices from the Orient, the tangy bits from Brazil and the art of using sugar from sweet-toothed countries, Turkey, India and the Moors of northern Africa – culinary skills, foods, delicacies, recipes, which turned us into a foremost gastronomic people. There is no other country that can boast such an array of national dishes.'

On a different note Almeida Garrett, another classic writer (1799–1854) in *Introduction to the Pilgrim* also demands fidelity to tradition: 'Let's be ourselves; let's see by ourselves; copy from ourselves – and forget about imitating Greeks, Romans or anybody else', and again, 'I have more faith in popular traditions than in all the books by chroniclers, archaeologists or commentators put together.' (*St Ana's Arch*)

These were the feelings of many patriots at the time, faced with the intrusion of foreign (mainly French) culture and customs in Portugal. They needn't have worried, though. One century later tradition is very much in people's minds, especially as far as food is concerned.

The richness of the gastronomic heritage of a country may not be an appropriate yardstick for that country's whole culture, but it is an important aspect of it. Eating is a basic need, yes, but eating well is an art. It is said that someone who does not care much about food – or, rather, who does not have much appreciation for really good food – is insensitive in other areas too. I wouldn't be surprised if that is true.

In Portugal, a separate country for well over 800 years (since 1143) and with the oldest established frontiers in Europe (since

1267), we would be right to expect a rich legacy of culinary treasures and talents, and indeed, despite its small size, Portugal does have a refreshingly versatile cuisine.

A good deal of printed matter and manuscripts regarding Portugal's traditional cookery was lost when Lisbon suffered a major earthquake in 1755. The city was practically destroyed, over 15,000 lives were lost and amid the destruction many books disappeared forever. So it was particularly lucky that Portuguese documents dating from the sixteenth century containing medieval recipes were found (only a few years ago) at Naples National Library, in Italy – when, in 1565, the Portuguese Princess Maria (1538–77) married the Duke of Parma, she took with her to Italy her personal library, including notebooks containing recipes and useful advice for the home. This material has now been transcribed into modern Portuguese (though keeping the savour of the archaic descriptions) and it suggests clearly that at least some of the recipes had already been handed down, pushing back their original date and thus making them all the more intriguing from the scholar's point of view. As far as we are concerned, they have the virtue of confirming the really old roots of many traditional Portuguese recipes.

However, recipes in documents such as these probably mirror the customs of nobility and royalty more than those of ordinary people. That would explain, for example, the use of Oriental spices (notably cinnamon and cloves) in a great number of these recipes. Many spices were available in medieval Portugal through *especieiros* – spice-men or spice-traders – but they fetched prices beyond the pocket of the man in the street, even after Portuguese explorers had reached India and the Far East by sea.

The cookery booklets belonging to Princess Maria are methodically and neatly divided into recipes for meat, eggs, milk and preserves. There are also some remarkable hints for the home, which I am sure would still apply – for example, a hearty version of chicken broth (p. 40) was recommended for many lung sufferers of the time, and the following formula to treat *esquinecia* (*angina tonsilar* in modern Portuguese, *quinsy* in English). Take cinnamon, ginger and nutmeg, ½ oz (15 g) of each; 4 or 5 cloves; 1 oz (30 g) sugar, all pounded to a very fine powder. The patient must take as much of the powder as can be held between three fingers and push it through his 'gullet', as far as possible. Drink some cold water and repeat three times on three to four consecutive days.

A colourful recipe for milk tartlets, which might well be the precursor of the much loved cream tarts (p.178), says: 'Take a pan and put it over the fire with an amount of water equal to about ½ pint (300 ml) and no salt. After reaching boiling point, add the milk and sugar – which should be 8 oz (225 g), if you want half a dozen tartlets. If this amount is not enough, add some more. Then take the flour, put it in a container with one dozen eggs, yolks and whites, and after it is all well beaten add to the milk; it should not be too thin. Pour this into the pan. Boil until cooked and remove from the heat, then prepare the dough, which must include a little sugar and 2 egg yolks and butter, all well beaten. Shape the tartlets and put them into the oven. They must not be overcooked. Then pour the boiled milk cream into them and when full pour butter on top. Return them to the oven. When cooked on top, remove.' The introduction of egg custard in Italy is credited to the Portuguese, and perhaps recipes like this one had something to do with it.

The few cookery books from the sixteenth century onwards which did survive the earthquake also give extremely interesting recipes. As in Maria's notebooks, they call for the use of cinnamon and, curiously enough, mix sugar with chicken, something still found in some regions. Here is a recipe for 'egg-coated chicken': 'Prepare the chicken and roast it, and after it is well roasted cut it into pieces. Coat each piece with beaten eggs, yolks and whites together. When the chicken is well coated in these beaten eggs, fry it in butter, in a frying pan which you must have over the fire. Using the same butter, afterwards fry slices of bread also coated in the beaten eggs. Dip the chicken and bread into a sugar syrup. Then put everything on a platter with the bread under the chicken and pounded cinnamon and the syrup on top.' Another sweet made with chicken breasts, cooked and pounded, mixed with ground rice and sugar, was very popular in the Middle Ages not only in Portugal but also in Spain and Italy (at least). An old recipe still followed in Coimbra is practically the same, step by step, and still given the same name, *manjar branco* – blancmange (p.165).

Things which are common in Portugal today, such as quince jam (*marmelada*), sponge cake (*pão-de ló*) and cheese tarts (*queijadas*), as well as the use of marinades for rabbit and other meats, are all included in these medieval recipe books, which were, remember, themselves collections of old, traditional material.

Food – if not recipes proper – was the subject of various other surviving chronicles, reflecting Portuguese eating habits from the nation's earliest days and giving a vivid description of the seriousness of this matter, even then.

Kings, nobles and high-ranking military men would choose with great care the various servants whose task it was to wait at the table, serve the wine and keep an eye on the quality (and amount) of the food that went into their master's larder. These servants were accorded special privileges for their devotion and efficiency, and of course their work kept them busy all day, for they had also to care for the many cups, trays, basins and other implements (many of them made of silver) needed for the great number of guests normally present – with the ladies usually eating at separate tables.

Bread was an important item in the Middle Ages, and the best was made with wheat flour. Maize bread (p.57) commonly called *broa* nowadays, was then known as *borona* and is mentioned in documents dating as far back as 1258. It was made with millet and similar cereals, as corn arrived from South America only towards the end of the fifteenth century, subsequently completely replacing the cultivation of millet in Portugal.

Before the advent of metal or ceramic plates, rounds of bread would hold the solid food (meat, fish), and the rich would sometimes discard the bread which had become soaked in tasty gravy, giving it either to their dogs or to the many beggars crowding outside their doors. Cutlery was not much used in those days. Spoons had been around for a long time, but their main function was as a kitchen implement. The first 'tool' to make a regular appearance at table was the pointed knife, used for cutting meat and to spear food as a fork does now. Although two-pronged forks had long since been invented and used, albeit rarely, in some countries, most Europeans did not use them, in conjunction with the knife and spoon, until the seventeenth century. The more advanced three- and four-pronged forks were not in general use until the nineteenth century.

The advantange – if one can call it that – of not using cutlery was that people felt more obliged to wash their hands both before and after eating, which they did not always think necessary when its use was finally established.

What did they eat with their fingers? Mainly meat. There was apparently plenty of it around – at least for the higher classes. They ate it fresh, salted and cured: pork, beef, sheep, lots of poultry and an infinite variety of game. People felt deprived if they did not eat meat at every meal (a view still prevailing among many, even today). Fish was eaten mainly by the less affluent, as well as shellfish and plenty of eggs. People of means limited their fish intake to the days prescribed by the Church for that purpose. Vegetables were also regarded as food for the poor, but everybody seems to have consumed fruit, fresh and dried, especially as a snack, complemented by a large cup of wine. Wine was produced all over Portugal in the Middle Ages (see p.220) and was exported in large quantities, England being the main customer. Even nuns in the convents were quite free to drink wine (this was not discouraged until later), and an old document shows that in some convents they consumed something like 2½ pints (1.5 l) of 'daily wine'.

During the Middle Ages, the Portuguese had two main meals: dinner (the heavier of the two) started between 10 and 11 a.m. and would be finished by noon, followed by a 'siesta'; supper was around 7 p.m. Also, according to various chronicles, a drink of wine and some light food were taken on rising, and the same between meals and in the evening.

For the higher classes dinner would include soup, two or three (most likely three) meat courses, accompaniments and desserts. Supper was generally a version of the same but perhaps on a more reduced scale. Less affluent people would fashion their meals in the same way but with less variety and with just one or two meat courses per meal, and also some fish. The populace often had to content themselves with vegetables, pulses, chestnuts and large quantities of bread, all of it washed down with copious wine.

It is thought that the amount of food consumed in medieval Portugal was quite gargantuan, by our present standards, as it led to laws being passed, occasionally, to regulate the number of meat courses in proportion to the eater's station in life. King Duarte (r. 1433–7), who was called 'The Eloquent' for his culture and intelligence, wrote several books, in two of which (*How To Be a Good Horseman* and *Loyal Counsellor*) he advised, among other things, that people be frugal at table, have an interval of eight hours between the two main meals, and water down their wine. Duarte was one of the five outstanding sons of King João I and his English Queen, Philippa of Lancaster (daughter of John of Gaunt), and it seems that they all had moderate eating habits. That Fasting was practised by at least some of the princes may have been due to the influence of their pious mother.

Prince Henry 'the Navigator', who promoted the Portuguese voyages of discovery from which stemmed Europe's maritime expansion and colonization of new lands, was thus responsible for enterprises which were not only radically to change the course of Portugal's history but also initiated the study of the products of these strange lands. New plants and seeds were brought back from these voyages and some successfully adapted to the European climate. Others such as tea, coffee, cocoa, peanuts and tropical fruit were transplanted from one new territory to another.

The exodus of large numbers of settlers started with the colonization of the Atlantic Islands (Madeira and the Azores) in 1425 and 1439. Curiously enough, it was from these islands that some of the biggest contingents of Portuguese emigrants would, in time, go to the United States and Canada, and to South America (Venezuela, Argentina and, mainly, Brazil). From Portugal itself over the centuries scores of people followed in the footsteps of the early pioneers. They established themselves not only in Brazil but also in Africa, India and many other places besides. In fact, it is calculated that at present over 3½ million Portuguese live abroad (though recent emigration has been within Europe, seeking work). That does not include second and third generations who have been assimilated into their host countries, especially in Brazil, Canada and the United States. In the United States alone the first and second generations of Portuguese total some 1½ million.

The Portuguese are extremely adaptable. If they were not, there would not be so many of them in all corners of the earth. But when it comes to food, they are forever complaining, when abroad. So, if they live as a family, they continue cooking Portuguese dishes, at least on special occasions, and get together with fellow-countrymen whenever possible, to share hearty meals and drink Portuguese wine, listening to and singing folk songs and the melancholy *fado* and talking with *saudades* about their country. Even the second and third generations keep at least some of the food traditions handed down from their parents and, when they visit Portugal, one of the main attractions is sampling traditional dishes at their source.

Of all the religious and secular celebrations in Portugal, Christmas is the most important as a family gathering occasion, an excellent excuse and opportunity for the enjoyment of good food, prepared with love, time and the co-operation of all.

Christmas Eve supper is the real highlight of the season, a long drawn-out affair, after Midnight Mass. The classic writer Ramalho Ortigão (1836–1915) states in *The Arrows* (*As Farpas*): 'There is a kind of Portuguese banquet which completely surpasses any dinners you may have in Paris, and that is Christmas Eve supper ...' Everybody is hungry, the smells from the kitchen are tempting, platters laden with food compete with each other for space on the table and spill over to sideboards and dressers, with fresh and dried fruit, nuts, the ever-present rice pudding and the many fried and baked cakes especially concocted for the season, all in lavish proportions, to last through to the end of the year.

A typical menu for Christmas Eve supper in Minho (the most celebrated of all and followed in many parts of the country, with variations) would include the following:

'Salted Cod with Everything' (*Bacalhau com todos* or *Bacalhau de Consoada*, p.72)
Octopus with Rice (p.95)
Salted Cod Cakes (p.76)
Golden Soup (a dessert, p.157)
Rice Pudding (p.147)
Fried Cakes (p.190)
Punch – Mulled Port (p.228)

Christmas lunch will probably start with a homely and fragrant chicken broth (*canja*, p.40) or, in northern provinces, with the salted cod mixture left over from supper and reheated with an olive-oil sauce. Then comes the turkey or one or two capons, with their trimmings. Desserts will be the remains of the Christmas Eve meal.

Seasonal or celebratory dishes typical of Portugal's regions are indicated in the respective sections, but many of them are also prepared for other occasions, such as the Christmas fried cakes which are also made for Carnival or Easter, at least in the northern provinces. Carnival is still celebrated with great pomp in most Portuguese regions, and food specially prepared for this occasion reflects the care given to this kind of festivity. It follows the pig-killing season, so pork dishes naturally figure on the menu. The Trás-os-Montes province includes *Cozido à Portuguesa* (Boiled Meats, Portuguese Style, p.100), even though this is an otherwise everyday dish.

In the Madeira and Azores archipelagos Carnival is celebrated with street festivities, with young people in fancy dress, music, 'battles of flowers' and general amusements. The Azores reserves its 'fluffy cakes' (*fofas*, p.185) for this occasion. The Carnival is also celebrated with lively parades all over the Algarve province.

For Easter the custom is not so much to prepare special menus as to make sure there are plenty of sugared almonds in the house to eat and to give as presents to all the children in the family, as well as the Easter fancybreads (*folares*) decorated with eggs. In Braga (Minho province) Easter is celebrated with the most solemnity. One of the oldest cities in the country, it was 'Bracara Augusta' to the Romans and capital city for the Swabians. Its beautiful shrines, the cathedral and various important churches give Braga the name 'Portuguese Rome'.

Soon after the Holy Week, in the first days of May, Guimarães (birthplace of the first Portuguese king) and Barcelos – both in Minho – celebrate the Cross Festival, dedicated to the Passion of Christ. Pilgrimages are followed, as usual, by fireworks and a noisy country fair. Barcelos is a delightful Roman town, with many medieval buildings, an important centre for local crafts whose markets attract people from miles around, to sell and buy pottery and the region's traditional handicrafts, such as wood carvings, silver and copperware, embroidery and lace. Barcelos has become famous also for its cockerel, which many consider the symbol of Portugal (legend has it that a man wrongly accused of some terrible crime declared that to prove his innocence a roast fowl on the judge's table would crow. To the judge's great surprise the cooked cockerel got up and crowed – hence the man was pardoned.)

In popular festivities religion and pagan customs are apt to get mixed. All over Portugal, in old rites associated with Christian celebrations, saints are given certain protective roles as if they were pagan gods. All the year round, but especially in summer, and mainly in the north-west of the country, there is hardly a Sunday without a *romaria* (a saint's day) here or there, with song and dance, food and wine, after the particular saint of each town or village has been honoured and asked to perform specific miracles.

St Anthony (born in Lisbon, 1195; died in Padua, Italy 1231) is the patron saint of sweethearts. He must be one of the most burdened saints, pestered with requests for finding lost things and, especially, for finding husbands for single girls. St Anthony is celebrated all over Portugal but in Lisbon nobody fails to honour him and the other two so-called 'popular' saints: St John and St Peter. The festivities commence on 13 June and go on until the 29, coinciding with bygone pagan solstice celebrations. Altars are erected in suitable places in the old districts of Lisbon, and the whole night people sing, dance and eat grilled sardines. Everywhere little pots of fragrant basil are sold, to give as presents and to take home, as a sweet-scented souvenir.

At night young people make bonfires and leap over them, singeing thistles afterwards, to see whether they will flower the following day: a 'love divination' of old. Similar solstice festivities coinciding with St John's feast are held in other localities, the most famous of them being Vila do Conde, Braga and Oporto. St John's are, in fact, Oporto's greatest festivities of this kind. Everybody comes out onto the streets, saluting each other, holding a leek or lemon balm in their hands. Altars with various images are arranged throughout the city, and people dance and sing all night. Vinho verde goes well, then, with the roast kid traditionally eaten.

In the country, religious festivities and fairs demand those lovely pasties (*fogaças*) which are also made as offerings as well as sweet buns, fancy breads and bread pies, All Saints Day buns and cakes and other sweets.

Cake-shops and tea-houses thrive all over Portugal, for it is a Portuguese habit to eat cakes with coffee, tea or any other beverage. In Lisbon there are streets where almost every other entrance leads to a cake-shop, which also serves light lunches of savoury pastries, pies and prawn rissoles, generally eaten standing. For a more leisurely meal many of these shops do have tables, where people meet to chat, for business or to do their courting and where sometimes one is permitted to spend hours, having bought only a cake or two and a coffee or tea.

But eating out in Portugal does not consist only of going to pastry-shops. Not only big cities but even small towns and villages have a good number of eating-houses of various standards. The best policy is to choose those which seem to be preferred by the locals and to watch for the dishes they ask for. Generally each restaurant will indicate on its menu the *pratos do dia* (dishes of the day) which always include typical Portuguese fare. People do not mind travelling long distances to a restaurant specializing in some particular regional dish. Some dishes are available only in their authentic version in the areas where they originated.

There is now a movement to revive the traditional cuisine of Portugal, with more care lavished at restaurants and with many national competitions between professional cooks from the different regions. The media also endeavour to stimulate this interest.

The fact that many Portuguese traditional dishes, to be at their best, should be eaten straight from the oven or stove explains why, normally, the Portuguese wait patiently for food to be served. But, in any case, whenever possible mealtimes are protracted, while family and friends exchange views on the food they are eating, reminisce about other dishes and talk of many other things until, with an alarmed look at the clock, they realize how late it is.

In keeping with their Latin traits, Portuguese people tend to talk a lot. They have a saying, '*As palavras são como as cerejas*' – 'Words are like cherries', meaning that they become entangled with one another and cannot be stopped. Popular sayings in Portugal show that food is much in people's minds in all situations. For example, *'Temos o caldo entornado'* and *'Cheira-me a esturro'* – 'The broth has overflowed', and 'I can smell burnt food', both meaning that things are not what they should be, or that some kind of blunder has been made. And calling somebody a *'papa-açorda'* ('pap-bread soup') means that he or she is a slow-moving, lazy person.

Most good restaurants in Portugal used to have on their menus a good choice of *hors d'œuvres*. The idea was to pick and choose just a small portion from the many dishes presented – a difficult proposition, since they all look so inviting. Indeed, I know of at least one restaurant in Setúbal (south of Lisbon) where they used to have such *hors d'œuvres* beautifully displayed on a large trolley which one could have as a meal in themselves – and what a sumptuous meal!

There are still a few restaurants where these 'interesting' goodies are served, and one can always find them at parties and receptions. But, of course, why not prepare them at home?

These are just some of the most traditional *hors-d'œuvres* one is likely to find at the Portuguese table and which can also be served as snacks. Try to display them artistically, on well-decorated platters or trays.

Cod cakes (p.76) – indispensable. They must be made small (shaped with a dessertspoon or even a teaspoon, before frying).

Prawn rissoles (p.90) also made small.

Fried almonds. Fry whole peeled almonds in a little vegetable oil until golden. Cover the frying-pan, to avoid splashing, but remember the almonds will be ready in a couple of minutes. Do shake the pan, to give them an even 'tan'. Sprinkle with salt, after keeping them for a while in kitchen paper, to absorb excess fat.

Whole canned sardines – straight from the can, well drained, of course (in either their oil or tomato version).

Chunks of canned tuna or any other canned fish other than sardines (squid, anchovies and so on).

Prawn (or shrimp, or lobster) salad. Mix some prepared shellfish with home-made mayonnaise (p.138) and decorate with black olives and sliced hard-boiled eggs. Surround with lettuce leaves.

Black-eyed beans salad. This is delicious cold and a must for this table (p.140).

Stuffed eggs. Boil the eggs for 10 minutes, plunge them in cold water before shelling and allow to cool. Then slice them in half lengthwise and scoop out the yolks. Mix these into a paste with some mayonnaise and canned sardines or tuna (a teaspoonful of each ingredient for each yolk used). Cut a small slice off the bottom of each egg 'boat' so they will stand, and refill them with the prepared paste. Top each mound with a stoned black olive and a little parsley. Decorate the plate with a frill of lettuce leaves and tomato slices.

Variation: Instead of fish, you can bulk up the pureéd yolks with chopped tomato flesh. Mix the mayonnaise and refill as before.

Vegetable salad. Cook some potatoes, carrots and green beans, drain and cut into small cubes after cooling. Add some cooked peas and mix the vegetables with mayonnaise.

Fish savoury butters. These are excellent for the *hors-d'œuvres* table or for snacks. They keep well in the fridge for a few days or can be frozen. Fish butters are versatile and have a distinctive taste very welcome as a change from other flavours. To prepare, mix thoroughly equal amounts of very good butter with the chosen canned fish, which can be either sardines (in oil, well drained and then skinned and mashed), canned tuna (drained and mashed) or anchovies. The sardines in oil seem to give the best result, however. Season the mixture with a little lemon juice and a dusting of pepper. Serve spread on pieces of thin toast, small crackers or small sandwiches, or as a filling for tomatoes or boiled eggs. It can also be served as a kind of dip, with a side dish full of *crudités* (raw tender vegetables cut into small sticks).

Other savoury butters. Minced garlic or chopped parsley are also popular ingredients to mix with butter.

Cold meat. Use any cold meat available, thinly sliced. A favourite in Portugal is *presunto* (smoked ham – see p.22), a delicate, slightly salty cold meat also served with slices of melon as a starter in many Portuguese restaurants (a sweet-salty contrast, very good as an appetizer).

As the pace of living changes and the commuter belt spreads around the main urban areas, eating habits have also to change, of necessity.

Lunch, for instance, used to be taken at home, but nowadays very few are able to return home at lunch time and then go back to work again. However, many people enjoy a 1½- to two-hour lunch-break, so, whether in restaurants, canteens or cafeterias, a sit-down lunch can be enjoyed with a certain degree of leisure. But increasingly more people opt for a quick but nourishing snack, at least occasionally, as a lunch.

Dinner is a more relaxed and substantial meal, though again some recognize that it may be wiser to have a good lunch and a light evening meal or, at least, just one big meal a day, making the other a light one, be it at lunch-time or in the evening (around 8 p.m.).

All these patterns are really in the melting-pot of change at present, with each family making its own arrangements. The interest in healthy patterns of eating is also very much in evidence all over Portugal and is influencing these changes.

Breakfast is normally a very light meal. Many take nothing at all until mid-morning, very few people have cereals, eggs or anything else, apart from a large cup of milky coffee and perhaps a roll and butter. Mid-morning and mid-afternoon snacks are taken by practically everyone.

Main meals are generally well thought out, which means a succession of dishes for each meal. A starter, generally a soup (Portugal has wonderful soups), a main course (meat or fish), a dessert (pudding, baked apple, rice pudding, fresh fruit, mousse etc), maybe cheese and finally coffee. Not long ago all those who could afford it always had two courses (fish *and* meat) after the soup, at least at one of their main meals or whenever there were guests. In more elaborate meals, such as banquets or special occasions, this still applies.

Everyday menus rather depend on the purse, of course, but beefsteak and salt cod dishes (not cheap, nowadays) are included as often as possible. Middle-of-the-road everyday meals might include a combination of the following dishes:

Soups	*Fish*	*Meat*	*Other Dishes*
Fish	Salt cod	Beefsteak	Bean stew
Green broth	Sardines	Beef stew	Bread soups
Vegetable purée	Fish stews	Boiled meats	Broad beans
Bean and cabbage	Baked fish	Chicken stew	Peas and poached
Green bean	Grilled fish	Hunter's rabbit	eggs
Chicken broth	Hake 'with	Liver 'with Them'	
Turnip-tops	everything'		
Chickpea			

Those dishes fall within the traditional category, but naturally enough many Portuguese people also adopt *nouvelle cuisine* dishes and international cookery, at least now and then. However, the staple diet is a good soup followed by a meat or fish course, accompanied by potatoes or rice (or pasta) and perhaps a salad, with fruit afterwards.

Portuguese cuisine does not offer a great variety of side dishes of vegetables or salads, perhaps because it is felt that the dishes, or at least the soups, already include enough greens and legumes. It will also be noted that the range of vegetables used in traditional recipes is not very wide, due no doubt to the fact that old-fashioned cooking was based on local produce in season.

Entertaining at home, except for special occasions, is becoming less common in Portugal. Maids are not available as before, not only because there are fewer women willing to do the job but because those who do demand wages which place them out of reach for many people. Also, as there are many more women going out to work and as men do not, as a rule, help much in the kitchen, except when they fancy, it becomes less practical to organize social meals at home. So they are much more spaced out nowadays and supplemented or substituted by restaurant meals.

When entertaining at home, though, Portuguese families like to provide a large variety of savoury and sweet dishes, and the buffet-table, at which people help themselves, has been adopted in some homes as a compromise to enable the housewife without a maid to invite a largish party of friends and still be able to mingle with them, having prepared things in advance, perhaps with some outside help. I am referring here to urban homes, because in the country entertaining still follows old patterns, with everyone sitting down at a large table, with members of the family serving each other.

The Portuguese word *chá* means 'tea' — *cha* being the word used where tea originated, in China, Japan, Indochina, India and Ceylon. The navigators brought the plant back and established it in some of Portugal's African colonies, in Brazil and in the Azores archipelago.

By the end of the seventeenth century tea was already being drunk — and much appreciated – by the Portuguese nobility, and it was popularized at the English Court by Catherine of Braganza when she married Charles II. One can only imagine the circle the Queen must have created around her, probably exchanging Court secrets while sipping tea, during the many idle moments palace life afforded. Catherine was an unhappy, barren Queen and, although the King did not repudiate her for this reason and had great respect for her, their married life was far from easy. But this had been a marriage of some considerable convenience, consolidating a then much needed alliance and affording England a vast dowry, consisting of a large sum of money, plus Tangiers, in northern Africa, and the Indian port of Bombay, a starting-point for subsequent English expansion in India.

Nowadays tea is still widely drunk in Portugal, served rather weak and without milk or lemon. Afternoon tea and cakes are offered to visitors calling at the house and in pastry-shops. Tea and toast are a favourite snack for the ladies, especially the older generations.

Coffee, however, is the choice hot drink in Portugal. For breakfast, after meals and as a snack, coffee is drunk throughout the day, with or without milk. Cream is not used.

Coffee originated, it seems, in the Abyssinian mountains. It is said that a shepherd happened to notice that his goats became unusually lively when feeding on a certain plant. Word spread around and later the beans were also tried by the people. Eventually, as we all know, the whole world had the chance of sharing the goats' experience!

Although already taken in many eastern countries since the fifteenth century, it was only in the sixteenth that the first coffee-houses were opened, in Mecca. Europe acquired a taste for coffee in the seventeenth century, and it soon became well established. Portugal had the plant cultivated in her former colonies in Africa and Brazil and has enjoyed excellent coffee ever since.

The Portuguese are very particular about their coffee and always demand the best. Coffee is served in various ways, which are given peculiar names: *galão* (gallon) is a large glass full of milky coffee; *garoto* ('little boy') is a small cup or glass, again with milky coffee – one can ask for a *garoto escuro* ('dark little boy') if less milk is preferred; *bica* ('spout'), the most popular, is a small cup of strong black coffee, while *carioca* (the name given to a native of Rio de Janeiro) is a *bica* slightly watered down, for those who dislike too much caffeine.

People go to cafés, cafeterias and pastry-shops at all times of day, to drink their coffee, on its own or with cakes (or rolls, filled with ham, cheese, beef or omelette).

A popular drink for those who want to avoid caffeine is the *carioca de limão* (a lemon *carioca*) which consists simply of boiling water poured over lemon rind and allowed to stand in it all the while one is drinking the fragrant liquid. Very pleasant and refreshing as a change.

As a cool drink for quenching thirst, however, nothing is better than a *limonada* made with cool water mixed with lemon juice (½ small lemon for each tumbler), some lemon rind and sugar to taste.

Much as the Portuguese love their wine (and their coffee and tea), they are also much inclined towards mineral water, of which the country offers a wide range, from the many celebrated and ancient spas dotting the north and centre of the country. In the south there is only one famous mineral water, that from the excellent and beautiful Monchique Spa, in the Algarve. The Azores archipelago also has two important spas, Varadouro and Furnas.

Throughout the country there are some forty-four healing

waters competing, some of them bottled – such as the Vimeiro, Luso, Pedras Salgadas and Vidago. These waters are taken for health or just for pleasure. Some have to be taken on the spot itself, where treatment can be had for a variety of complaints, from liver conditions to skin and metabolic ailments. In Portugal it is very common to spend a regular spell at 'the waters' – a therapeutic holiday, combining treatment and rest, amid a beautiful landscape. And both at home and in restaurants the drink to have at the table is mineral water, when wine is not liked or advisable, for some reason. 'What are you having for drink?' the waiter will ask. If wine is refused, he will automatically suggest various mineral waters.

'The valet brought in, on a silver tray, two bottles of Vidago water, just opened,' wrote Eça de Queiroz in *The Remarkable House of Ramires* (*A Ilustre Casa de Ramires*). 'Not wanting to miss the marvellous fizz, Gonçalo immediately filled a big crystal glass: "What delicious water, man!" he exclaimed.'

Preparing to Cook

Ingredients

BASIC CONDIMENTS AND SEASONINGS

From the fifteenth century Portuguese seamen were instrumental in bringing to Europe, from the Orient, rich loads of spices which, up to that time, were available only via the traditional overland routes and across the Red Sea, being then distributed by Italy throughout the Western World. As the Portuguese had the advantage of carrying and selling the goods direct, they were able to offer them at a cheaper price, and this caused the market for spices to shift from Genoa and Venice to Lisbon.

In those times spices were quite indispensable, especially pepper, to disguise the taste of meats badly cured or salted, yet Portugal, as a whole, remained impervious to over-much influence from this outside invasion of flavours, except for the already used pepper and just a few other spices, notably cinnamon.

So, as it will be seen in the recipes, not many exotic ingredients occur in traditional Portuguese cookery, whose hallmark is simplicity.

Curries and such-like dishes were – and are – appreciated by those with experience of the East or Africa, but back home they never cut much ice. And in spite of the old Empire, spread over the five continents of the earth, only in recent times has there been interest in Indian and Far Eastern restaurants in Lisbon, though Chinese cuisine has had some representation there for longer. As to African-style cooking, its absence is almost total. All this may be a pity, but it shows how satisfying the Portuguese find their own gastronomic repertoire.

The range of herbs normally used is not wide (though it depends a little on the region), and therefore the variety of fresh herbs on sale at markets and greengrocers' often comprises only parsley, mint, coriander and bay leaf. But many other aromatic herbs grow in Portugal, of course, and are obtainable by anyone wishing to use them for specific dishes and for medicinal purposes. I give below a list of most herbs, spices and flavourings used in Portuguese cookery.

aniseed (seed and powder)
basil (fresh leaves)
bay leaf (fresh or dried)
chillies (whole or powder)
cinnamon (stick and powder)
cloves (whole and powder)
coriander (fresh leaves and
    stalks)
cumin (seed and powder)
garlic
lemon (rind and juice)
mandarin (rind and juice)
mint (fresh sprigs)
nutmeg
onions

orange (rind and juice)
oregano (fresh or dried)
paprika
parsley (fresh leaves and
    stalks)
pepper
rosemary (fresh and dried)
saffron
sage (fresh or dried)
tarragon (fresh or dried)
vanilla (essence and pod)
wine (white and red, port and
    madeira)
wine vinegar
winter savory

Most of these ingredients can be had anywhere, of course. The most difficult to obtain would be fresh basil (which can be grown from seed and which makes a fragrant little plant) and fresh coriander (obtainable at Indian, Greek, Cypriot and Chinese greengrocers, though it can also be grown in the garden or in boxes, just like parsley). From these two, however, only coriander is a real must for Portuguese cookery. I have indicated 'paprika' for *colorau* (made from powdered mild peppers) because it is the nearest in taste and, after all, made from the same thing.

I have already mentioned onion and garlic in the list but they do deserve a separate note with regard to Portuguese cookery. In fact, we might not have any Portuguese cookery at all without these two vital ingredients. An old Portuguese adage states that, 'Salt cod wants garlic.' The truth is, most traditional recipes, cod or not, want garlic. As to onions, it will be seen that the basic procedure for *refogado* (the first step to so many Portuguese dishes) is precisely to fry onions in oil. (See p.31.)

COOKING FATS AND OIL
'Olive oil, wine and friendship, the older the better', says a Portuguese proverb.

Olive oil – still the most important cooking medium used in Portugal and is an essential 'typical' flavour in many dishes. Being one of the main products of the country (Portugal is the fourth world producer), it is only natural that olive oil is used for preference in peasant cooking. Nevertheless, as olive oil is an acquired taste, there is no problem at all in replacing it with milder vegetable oils, such as groundnut, sunflower and so on. Nowadays, some urban Portuguese cooks also prefer these oils, or a mixture of olive oil with a milder one. For frying, olive oil is perhaps too strong, and in most Portuguese homes other vegetable oils are now used for this purpose. But the love of olive oil leads to its being used even for many cakes, of which it is an essential part.

Lard – sometimes half lard and half oil (any oil that may be preferred) – is the second most used cooking medium in Portugal. It is generally sold already processed, or it can be prepared at home, by rendering down fresh lard.

Butter – or a mixture of butter and margarine/lard/oil – is also used, especially for frying steaks and seasoning grilled meats and grilled fish.

SALTED DRIED COD
So widespread and basic is the use of salt cod in Portugal that it is known as 'the faithful friend' (*fiel amigo*) a rather forceful way of expressing such a preference but one which shows the deep esteem and almost reverence felt for it. It would be unthinkable to find a Portuguese who did not like salt cod, in its immensely varied concoctions.

Salt cod lends itself to being cooked in many different ways, and there are literally dozens of different recipes in use, all over Portugal. Taking into account all these, plus variations, it is possible not too far fetched to accept, as it is said, that one could have a different salt cod dish every day of the year. This is an extraordinary and curious situation in a small country where the use of fresh fish is such an outstanding feature (it is calculated that some forty per cent of the protein consumed in Portugal derives from fish).

During the fifteenth and especially in the sixteenth century fishing vessels started leaving Portugal's shores to catch cod in distant Newfoundland, which was discovered by the Corte Real brothers in 1500. Other nationalities fished there too, but the Portuguese fleet predominated, and their catch was useful for providing a 'convenience food' for the men who, at that time, were engaged in the great voyages of discovery and, when fridges and freezers were still centuries away, was also a boon for those on terra firma.

The trawlers used to unload their cod catches around the Aveiro area and in Viana do Castelo (north-west), to be dried until the fish acquired a creamy-grey colour. They were then ready to hang from hooks or be layered on shelves, at grocers' or in specialist shops, as it is done to this day. The annual, rather arduous cod fishing went on for centuries. Unfortunately the present fleet of trawlers has been allowed to fall into disrepair, and only a few still venture to sea. Most of the salt cod consumed in Portugal nowadays is imported from Nordic countries, notably from Iceland and Norway.

In Britain good-quality salt cod is generally available at Portuguese, Spanish, Italian, Greek, some Asian and West Indian grocers' and, of course, in very good stores. It is sold by weight, and the attendant will slice it for you in a special kind of 'guillotine'. It keeps well but one should take the precaution of wrapping it and storing it in a dry cupboard, well aired and away from other foods, because of its strong smell. If you find this objectionable, you may like to keep it, as I do, in the cool drawer of the refrigerator, provided it is well wrapped and then protected by two layers of plastic. This will prevent its drying and will also ensure that there is no unpleasant odour permeating the fridge.

Salt cod is not cheap, but it does go a long way, because it more than doubles in volume after soaking, and it is very nourishing.

See Methods, p.31, for the preparation of salt cod, prior to cooking.

PORK AND PORK PRODUCTS
Pork being such popular meat in Portugal, the art of curing ham and making sausages has developed to a quite remarkable degree.

Presunto is smoked ham, laboriously prepared, extremely tasty – though generally on the salty side – and used both as a raw snack (and for super-special sandwiches) and to add to certain dishes, in which case the fattier and cheaper cuts can be used.

Presunto is made from whole legs of pork preserved in a mixture which includes a paste made with plenty of salt, paprika, wine and crushed garlic, which must cover the raw meat very thickly. (This mixture can vary from region to region.) The meat is then left between layers of salt for several weeks, after which the salt is scrubbed off and the legs of pork are hung in the *fumeiro* (smoking place), following traditional methods. The smoking can be prolonged for up to two months, but once again it varies from region to region. Once the smoking is finished, the ham is brushed with olive oil, paprika and a little borax (which acts as a preservative). At this stage the *presunto* is not yet at its best, though it can be consumed. Nevertheless, any *presunto* worth having must have been cured for a year.

The best Portuguese *presuntos* come from the Lamego and Chaves regions (in the northern province of Trás-os-Montes). Outside Portugal look for *presunto* at Portuguese shops, or make do with Italian *prosciutto*, which is similar and can be had at any good delicatessen.

There are various kinds of sausages found only in Portugal, and even there varying from region to region. In the main, they are very rich and intended, in many cases, as the chief part of a meal, though some kinds (*paio, chouriço*) are eaten also as snacks and sandwich-fillers. Some are eaten fresh, others smoked just for a few days and others (the majority) cured for a long time, before eating. They can be grilled, fried, baked or boiled, according to their kind, and are generally accompanied by plainly cooked vegetables (potatoes and cabbage), rice or pulses. They can also be used as the 'main attraction' at a barbecue, where family and friends gather around the open fire, in unsophisticated, noisy and delightful parties, in the countryside.

Chouriço is the most popular of Portuguese sausages, highly seasoned and flavoursome. A few slices of it will improve some dishes enormously. When of good quality, it is beautiful eaten raw, as a tasty morsel or as a filling for sandwiches.

There are many varieties of *chouriço* in Portugal, depending on the regions. In each region the seasonings and methods can vary, producing different kinds.

Basically, *chouriços* are sausages about 1 inch (2.5 cm) in diameter and either short, 5–7 inches (13–18 cm) in length, or double that size, in which case they will be tied up in a loop. They are filled with lean and fat pork meat and seasonings (mainly garlic and red-pepper paste) and are thoroughly smoked.

Linguiça is another variety of *chouriço*, narrower and longer.

Although similar sausages are made in various countries, none seems to be exactly like *chouriço*, which does stand out and is therefore difficult to replace. In recipes calling for *chouriço* as a flavouring, it is better to replace it with good smoked bacon or *presunto* than to risk mixing other kinds of sausages. Or try some good salami.

Paio and *Salpicão* are not unlike *chouriço*, as far as taste is concerned, but these much thicker sausages are made almost exclusively with loin of pork in big chunks and are therefore much meatier and nicer still. The difference between *paio* and *salpicão* resides more in the spices used than in the type of meat (though the *salpicão* includes more fat).

Chouriço de Sangue (blood sausages) are very rich versions of black pudding, filled with cooked pork meat (lean and fat), blood, bread, oil, wine and a great variety of seasonings. They can also include various other cooked meats, such as chicken, veal, cured ham.

Morcelas' main ingredient is also blood, with bread and pork meat in equal amounts, wine and plenty of seasonings. In some regions rice is used as a binder, instead of bread.

Alheiras are rich sausages made from a variety of meats (the more, the better, obviously) and eaten grilled or fried, with potatoes and greens. Their composition includes poultry meats (chicken, duck, rabbit), game, pork (lean and fat), bread (which acts as a binder), olive oil, garlic and various spices.

'*Farinheiras'* comes from *farinha*, the Portuguese word for flour, which betrays the main ingredient of this sausage. The other most important components are pork fat (no meat at all in this recipe though the Alentejo has a version including some), wine and seasonings. The resulting sausage is surprisingly tasty, though not everyone's cup of tea. It is generally added to *cozido à portuguese* (p.100) together with *chouriço* and other meats, fresh and cured.

Outside Portugal, and unless there is a Portuguese shop somewhere, it is very difficult indeed to find any of these specialities. Therefore any recipe relying too heavily on any of these is best put aside for better times when they are available, or experimented with using other ingredients but without hoping to get the real taste of the dish.

Many recipes include a piece of pork fat, sliced, cubed or whole. This is called *toucinho* and consists of salted or cured pork fat with some lean – or simply the fat. Nowadays bacon proper (smoked rashers) is also available in Portugal. Either way, fatty bacon can be substituted where pork fat is required, cutting it according to the instructions in the recipes.

WINES AND WINE VINEGAR
Many Portuguese dishes rely heavily on marinades made with

wine (generally white wine, but sometimes red) and also wine vinegar – see wine and garlic marinade, p.32. Wine is also used in various recipes, even if there is no marinade involved. Almost all meat dishes improve with the addition of a little wine and/or some wine vinegar (diluted in water), and some fish recipes include wine and vinegar, as well.

When it is difficult to find the right wine, vinegars made with wine or even cider can be substituted, halving the amount called for and topping up with water, to dilute the strong vinegar taste. Do not use kinds of vinegar other than those indicated. Cider is a good replacement for wine, in marinades, adding perhaps a little vinegar, for sharpness.

Port and madeira wines (almost always the dry versions) are also used to enrich some dishes. Naturally a little dry sherry will do, if port or madeira is not available, and in the absence of all three you can make do with ordinary wine or even cider.

The chapter on wines (p.220) gives an overall view of Portuguese wines and other alcoholic drinks.

MAIZE FLOUR (COARSE CORNMEAL)
Maize (corn) grows profusely in Portugal and is used for much more than just feeding chickens and pigs. Maize bread is a speciality (p.57), as are a kind of soup, maize porridge (*papas de milho*, p.54), and a pudding, sweet maize porridge (*papas doces*, p.169). Some cakes also include cornmeal (pp.189, 190). Maize meal is also a good soup thickener and goes well with spinach, watercress and turnip-tops. Other traditional dishes using cornmeal include *sarrabulho* (p.117). If cooked until it is really thick (mashed potato consistency), it can serve as an accompaniment to grilled fish – especially charcoal-grilled sardines.

Buy coarse cornmeal (or maize meal, or maize flour – it can have either name, according to local customs) at health-food shops or from Italian grocers, to guarantee freshness, but make sure it is not the very fine ordinary cornflour, used for thickening sauces etc.

CITRUS FRUITS
These precious fruits were introduced into the Iberian peninsula by the Moors who had themselves brought them from eastern countries. They grow all over Portugal but are cultivated mainly in the Setúbal and Algarve regions. Oranges from the Algarve are the best for the table: big, seedless navels, fragrant, juicy and very sweet. Oranges from Setúbal are smaller and used both for the table and for jams and preserves.

Citrus fruits are widely adopted as a flavouring for cakes and pudding and for delicious homemade liqueurs (see wines, p.220). Both lemons and oranges are cut into wedges or slices to garnish fish or meat dishes at the table. Their peel can be candied and is very popular for cakes (especially *Bolo-Rei*, King's Cake, p.208) or to eat as a sweet, together with candied *abóbora* (white pumpkin) and candied cherries, small whole mandarins, figs, pears, apricots and plums. Candying fruit is perhaps too laborious to be attempted at home, but candying orange peel is not very difficult, and many Portuguese housewives still do it (p.177).

ALMONDS

Almond trees grow quite freely in Portugal, especially in the Algarve province, where they cover extensive areas, although lately other trees have been substituted, as agriculture in the Algarve becomes more diversified.

Almonds are eaten as a snack, either roasted or fried and sprinkled with salt (see the *Hors d'œuvres*, p.14), and covered with a hard sugar coating for the Easter table, but mainly they are used in confectionery, after being ground. Many beautiful sweets include ground almonds, together with egg yolks and sugar. In the Algarve marzipan sweets are a speciality (p.170).

A delightfully romantic legend tells of a Nordic princess who came to the Algarve, having married its Moorish ruler. Winter arrived and, missing the snow-covered fields of her distant native country, she became sad, pensive and tearful. Then her loving husband had an idea: he would have the land covered with almond trees, and at blossom time (around February) they would look like snow. And so it was done. When the trees blossomed, the princess gazed through the window – and lo and behold, the fields seemed to be covered in snow! She clapped her hands and laughed – something she had not done for a long time, and she lived happy ever after.

COCKLES

The nearest to *ameijoas* are cockles (or clams). They are very common all along the Portuguese coast, so they appear in many recipes, on their own or mixed with other ingredients – such as the pork and *ameijoas* dishes from the Algarve.

Like any other shellfish, they must be impeccably fresh. Should it be difficult to obtain them, mussels can be substituted in most recipes, and although the flavour may vary, it will be quite acceptable.

Remember that all shellfish is at its best during cold months (the *r* months – as tradition puts it).

They should be left in salt water (about 5–6 tablespoons salt for each 2 pints/1.2 l of water) for a few hours, to help remove all the sand. Before cooking wash them very thoroughly. They should open while cooking. Those which do not must be discarded.

When it is not at all possible to buy fresh cockles (or clams or mussels), the cooked version will be the only alternative. Buy only from a very good source and cook as indicated in the recipe but reducing the boiling time.

CHESTNUTS

'Caetana, once she thought of eating many chestnuts and black pudding, foods she was particularly partial to, immediately started putting on weight.'
Camilo Castelo Branco (1825–90), *Lamego Nights* (*Noites de Lamego*)

The northern inland provinces have many chestnut trees and provide chestnuts for the whole country, when in season (some of them also exported, in recent years). Chestnuts are very popular as a dessert or snack, boiled in water flavoured with salt and a handful of aniseed (which imparts a wonderful fragrance to them), baked in the oven or roasted over charcoal in special earthenware pots full of holes. Many chestnuts are dried and then eaten as a snack, or soaked and used in savoury dishes.

In olden times, when there were no potatoes around, chestnuts were used as an accompaniment to many dishes. In Trás-os-Montes this custom is still in evidence. I am told by my friend Maria de Lourdes Paixão, whose family comes from that province, that in certain remote villages they still follow the old habit of burying fresh chestnuts – it seems that they last much longer that way.

It is possible to buy excellent dried chestnuts at health-food shops, and it is worth getting used to their mildly sweet texture.

For cooking, dried chestnuts are best soaked for twenty-four hours and then boiled for about one hour, using the soaking water (having drained it of any loose skins).

TURNIP-TOPS

It is sad to see how some vegetables do not seem to be acceptable for the table in some countries. Turnip-tops fall into this category in Britain. In Portugal they are much appreciated as a delicate vegetable for soups and for accompaniments. They must, of course, be very tender, otherwise they will be suitable only for soups which are to be blended and sieved.

The best turnip-tops are gathered before the turnips are

actually formed, looking like the larger radish leaves. If you cannot get any grower to supply you with this vegetable, try to grow it yourself, if you have a garden. They grow very easily and are ready to eat within three to four weeks. Sow the turnip seeds thinly on well-prepared soil and watch the results. Small turnip-tops cook in six to eight minutes.

The leaves of fully grown turnips are also good to eat, at least the smaller ones, and can be used like those above, although they will have to be boiled for longer, like cabbage leaves. They enhance vegetable soups and should not be thrown away.

Just before the turnip-tops go to seed, they present handsome tops, *grelos*, like little bunches of flowers ready to bloom. They are similar but less compact than broccoli heads.

At this stage, the bigger leaves have become a bit tough, but the pinnacles of sprouts and smaller leaves, surrounding them, are tender and delicate; they have long been a favourite green with the Portuguese. They are prepared just by boiling in salted water, to accompany any fish or meat dish, just as one would prepare boiled cabbage or spring greens. They go well with poached fish or salted cod. (See the recipes for 'Hake with Everything', 'Cod with Everything' and 'Christmas Eve Cod', pp.84, 72 and 72.)

If you have a chance to cultivate or buy this vegetable, I am sure you will agree how good it is.

SWEET POTATO
Sweet potatoes have been cultivated in the mild climates of Madeira and the Algarve since they were first brought to Europe by the discoverers of South America. They have become a staple food in both these regions, especially in Madeira, and there are many ways of cooking them, both to complement savoury dishes and as a main ingredient for cakes.

QUINCES
Quinces have been used for jams and jellies for centuries, and in Portugal they have never lost favour, unlike in some other countries, especially in northern Europe.

There are two distinct kinds of quince trees in Portugal (the Japanese quince bush is not known there). One is the *marmeleiro*, which gives *marmelos* – hence the name *marmelada* given to the jam ('marmalade', the word used in English for bitter orange jam, may be derived from *marmelada*, quince jam in Portuguese) and the other is *gamboeira*, whose fruit is a variety of *marmelo*, called *gamboa*, which is bigger, smoother and sweeter than its counterpart but which has the same kind of flavour and perfume. Both are used for jellies and jams, and once in this form they are indistinguishable one from the other.

'Quince cheese' is the name given in English to Portugal's *marmelada*, because quince jam, once dried, can be cut like cheese. Quinces are also nice just boiled with sugar and some water, as a dessert (cooked as you would apples) or baked in the oven (whole and unpeeled), sprinkled with sugar at the table (after peeling, once baked) and eaten still slightly warm.

Marmelos are more acid than *gamboas* (though not half as acid as Japanese quinces) and tend to become more reddish when cooked. All these fruits oxidize rapidly while they are being peeled and cut, which helps to give a good colour to the preserves. *Marmelada* does not follow exactly the same procedure as ordinary jam. See quince jams, p.211.

Quince trees grow quite freely and almost wild in mild climates, and the fruits are exported from places like Cyprus and Turkey. I always thought that they would not grow in Britain, but they do. I have one quince tree, in my garden, in London, which was brought to me a few years ago by my late father, last time he visited us here. He planted it himself, with great care and a sense of relief, for to his way of thinking I had been terribly deprived by not having some quinces handy, every year. I am sure he would rejoice if he were to see how that tree has grown, producing a lot of fragrant quinces, albeit on the small side (through lack of strong sunshine).

CHEESES
Dairy products do not rank very high in Portuguese priorities, at least as far as traditional cuisine is concerned, for the country's climate does not favour a great variety of cheeses. However, there are a few outstanding ones, such as those small cheeses made with ewes' and goats' milk (or a mixture of both) and sold both fresh and dried. These delicious cheeses follow their own 'season', so at times one may not find a particular kind still fresh or already dried, but rather half-dried – which is fine, too. These cheeses are generally soft and creamy and extremely tasty, either on their own or with fruit or bread, but they would not be suitable for cooking, and indeed it would be a pity to melt away in a pot their rich, mild texture.

Although the basic ingredients are the same, the proportions and preparation methods vary between regions, and so one gets variations on the same theme, each with a distinctive quality. Those made with goats' milk alone become brittle and crumbly when dried and are perhaps more salty, good with wine, as a snack. The saying 'bread and cheese – and the table is laid' means that one does not need anything else for a meal.

Another maxim of peasant wisdom declares, 'Cheese and bread keep a man healthy.'

Some small cheeses, after being well dried, are kept in wide jars and covered with olive oil, and are much sought-after for their pronounced flavour. These kinds of cheese are made all over Portugal, mainly as a 'cottage industry' business, not in big factories. Some of the most famous are from the Alentejo and Ribatejo regions. The small fresh cheeses sold in Lisbon during the winter months are generally made in nearby Mafra and Sintra. A bigger version, sold by the kilo, is also available during the same months and, lately, for most of the year.

The king of Portuguese cheeses, however, is the splendid *Serra* (the Mountain), about 7 inches (18 cm) in diameter, which comes from Serra da Estrela, in the Beira region. It used to be made exclusively on a non-industrialized basis – not so now. The Serra cheese is made from pure ewes' milk and therefore has a unique creaminess, which makes it possible to spread it almost like butter, during winter (hence its name, *amanteigado* – buttery). Later on it hardens and becomes semi-cured and finally cured, when it can be sliced easily, although still keeping a creamy texture and a characteristic taste.

Widely available in the country all the year round and much favoured also is the cheese from the Azores (*Queijo da Ilha/* Island Cheese) made with cows' milk and quite similar to strong farmhouse Cheddar. This cheese is, of course, suitable for cooking and is used for that purpose, especially when grated cheese is called for.

However, in both price and suitability for certain recipes (mainly sweet) the *requeijão* is the prime cheese. It is actually a by-product, made with the whey of milk, boiled and moulded into round shapes of about 3½ inches (9 cm) and sold fresh on Portuguese market stalls, in grocers' shops and in delicatessens, in little baskets or on a cabbage or fig leaf. It has a close texture and is excellent to eat on its own, with bread or fruit, or as a sweet, mashed up with sugar (or honey, or jam) and perhaps a sprinkling of cinnamon. It is ideal for cheese cakes and savouries. *Requeijão* is probably unobtainable outside Portugal but it can very successfully be substituted by cream, curds or good cottage cheese (or, better still, a mixture of these). I find that the Italian fresh *ricotta* cheese sold in many good delicatessens and specialist cheese shops is extremely similar to *requeijão* in both taste and texture (although *ricotta* does not have any salt added, while *requeijão* has a little). When available, *ricotta* replaces *requeijão* to perfection for any cheese tarts or puddings one may want to prepare, Portuguese style.

Hard cheeses combine very well with *marmelada* – quince

(p.211), and in Portugal it is common to serve little squares of both, together, as a snack or dessert.

I have referred here to the basic traditional types of cheese, but there are other kinds which follow foreign procedures, resulting in very good local versions of, for instance, Edam, Chèvres and Camembert.

FRESH YEAST
Many recipes for buns and fancy breads use fresh yeast. This is always to be preferred when available (health-food shops normally stock it, and so do many bakers). However, dry yeast can be used instead, followed to the letter the instructions printed on the tin, especially in calculating the proportions.

Methods

REFOGADO
Wherever there is an interest in Portuguese cuisine, a myth is created regarding the *refogado*, because so many Portuguese recipes mention it. In fact, Portuguese cookery is in essence quite simple, and nothing more so than the now famous and seemingly mysterious *refogado* which so intrigues foreigners. All it means is that the given seasonings (of which the only indispensable one is onion) are fried gently in oil.

Refogado is the first step for many stews and soups (mainly fish soups). In the same saucepan in which the dish is to be prepared, some olive oil (for preference) is taken to the heat, adding finely sliced onions. Cover and fry slowly until the onions are transparent (about 10 minutes). According to whatever this is going to be used for, sliced tomatoes, bay leaf, chopped garlic and chopped parsley may then be added, and the mixture fried again, until pulpy (8 to 10 minutes) before adding the main ingredients of the recipe.

Quantities for each *refogado* are indicated in the relevant recipes as well as the procedure. The recipe may also require that the *refogado* be fried for longer. On the other hand, the ingredients may sometimes be just added in their raw state without prior frying (as in many *caldeiradas* – fish stews, when the onions, tomatoes etc are layered with the fish and potatoes, all of them raw).

SALT COD
Salt cod should be weighed dry, to separate the amount needed for the given recipe. Then, and except where otherwise stated, it is washed and soaked in clean cold water for a minimum of

12 hours, changing the water 2 or 3 times. If the slices are thick, a 24-hour or at least an 18-hour soak is ideal. It is then ready for scaling and preparing as necessary.

Times of cooking and whether it should be flaked or not are indicated in the recipes.

Salt cod is an acquired taste, and people from outside Latin or Mediterranean countries may need a little while to become accustomed to its characteristic flavour. Once familiarized, however, its generally a taste acquired for life. See recipes starting on p.72.

SALT THE FISH

Here is another typical pre-cooking preparation used in Portugal.

It is thought that if one adds salt to the fish only when it is actually being cooked, it will not take in the flavour. Salt also makes the flesh of the fish much firmer, if applied a little while before cooking. Hence the expression 'salt the fish' in recipes.

After cleaning and washing the fish, place it on a wooden board or large plate and sprinkle with sea-salt (preferably) on both sides. Leave it for an hour or so, then wash well, dry and cut according to the recipe. The flesh should be that much easier to cut, and it is less likely to be damaged in the process.

When cooking, remember that the fish is already flavoured, so you do not need to add too much salt to the water etc. Taste the liquid before serving.

Note: Do not salt molluscs (squid, octopus, cuttlefish) in this fashion, as it would harden their flesh.

FISH STEWS

Although the flavouring ingredients for these stews are the same as for ordinary *refogado* (oil, onion, tomatoes and other seasonings), in *caldeiradas* all these items are layered between the fish (and the potatoes, if used), instead of frying them first.

WINE AND GARLIC MARINADE

'Garlic and pure wine lead to safe harbour' – Portuguese proverb.

A marinade is a kind of uncooked sauce, whose objective is to tenderize and impart flavour to meat. The basic mixture is simply wine and garlic, but bayleaves, parsley, olive oil, wine vinegar and paprika can also be added, and I have even experimented with the addition of orange juice and zest for chicken dishes – in this case omitting vinegar. One can add other herbs (in small amounts, not to overpower the sauce), according to taste. Use marinades for poultry and game, lamb, kid and pork. The basic recipe is as follows:

¼ *pint (150 ml) white dry wine*
2 *tablespoons wine vinegar (or try*
  cider vinegar)
1–2 *bay leaves*
2–3 *cloves garlic, finely chopped*
  or crushed

1 *tablespoon lemon juice*
  (optional)
1 *coffeespoon paprika (optional)*
salt and pepper

Mix well all the ingredients and steep the meat in this sauce for a few hours, prior to cooking. Some of this liquid is also used for cooking the dish, according to instructions in the recipe.

Note: Some fish dishes include their own marinade, but it is not a *vinha de alhos*, and there is no standard recipe for it. It may vary, with the use of lemon juice and wine, and each recipe will indicate the proper procedure.

BAIN-MARIE
A well-known procedure for steaming some dishes (mainly puddings and sauces) avoiding direct heat and ensuring a steady but gentle boil. The pan with the food stands inside a bigger pan containing bubbling water. This must be topped up with more boiling water when necessary and kept bubbling, until the end of cooking. The *bain-marie* can be made either on top of the stove or inside the oven.

BREAD DOUGH
In Portugal it is possible to purchase prepared bread dough, ready to bake by itself or, more likely to include in some of the various recipes for fancy breads (with the addition of meat) or even to prepare homely fried cakes (p.190) during the Christmas season. If fresh unbaked white dough cannot be bought, make up the amount needed for whatever recipe, or make more and bake the rest just as bread.

Portuguese country bread is more substantial than ordinary white bread, and I would suggest that you use strong, unbleached flour, to achieve a good texture, so different from the 'woolly' type of bread.

When preparing dough, all utensils should be kept warm, if possible, and try to ensure that the kitchen is free from draughts. All this has an influence on the finished product.

3 *lb (1.35 kg) unbleached white*
  flour
1½ *oz (45 g) fresh yeast – or the*
  equivalent dried yeast,

according to instructions on
  the tinned product
1½ *pints (900 ml) tepid water*
½ *oz (15 g) salts*

There are many procedures for preparing dough, but this one is very simple, and the results are as good as any, provided you knead it well.

Place the flour in a large warm bowl, sprinkle with the salt and make a well in the centre.

Prepare the yeast, crumbling it and mixing with a little of the lukewarm water. Add to this paste the remaining water, mix well and pour into the centre of the flour. Dust this with some of the surrounding flour and cover the bowl, leaving it in a warm place for about half an hour, in order to let it get spongy in the centre. By now the yeast has had time to rise and get airy and is ready to be mixed with the remaining flour, around it.

Knead very thoroughly, for 8–10 minutes, adding a little more tepid water if it is too dry. (This depends on the kind of flour used.) When really smooth, shape the dough into a ball, place again in the bowl, cover and set aside to rise until it doubles its volume, which will take about 1½ hours. Knead once again as before, place in a greased bowl or tin and set aside to 'prove' for another 15–20 minutes. It is then ready for baking or for using in recipes calling for plain bread dough.

Use a hot oven for the first ¼ hour (232°/450°F/Gas 8), and a less hot oven (190°C/375°F/Gas 5) for the remaining baking time, another 35–40 minutes. The bread is baked when it sounds hollow when tapped underneath.

PASTRY DOUGH FOR FRIED TURNOVERS

Portuguese cookery is much more concerned with using the top of the stove than the oven. Pasties (with savoury or sweet fillings) do not escape this, and there are many fried *pasteis* (pasties) made with a pastry dough which is suitable for frying without becoming soggy or melted in the fat. This is a good basic recipe for such pastry, equally appropriate for sweet or savoury fillings.

11 oz (310 g) plain flour   *1 tablespoon lard*
½ tablespoon butter   *water and salt*

Combine the fats with the flour with the tips of your fingers, until it resembles breadcrumbs. Make a well in the centre of this mixture and add some salt and enough cold water (approx. ¼ pint/150 ml). You may not need all the water, so add it gradually. The amount really depends on the flour. Knead the dough well and beat it until it is smooth and elastic. Form a ball with the dough and cover with a cloth. Place a damp napkin on top, to keep the dough moist. Let it rest for about 1–1¼ hours. Roll out to the required thickness and cut rounds, placing some filling in the centre. Fold in half, and press the half-moons all around. Deep fry in hot oil until golden on both sides and place in kitchen paper to absorb excess fat. Eat hot or cold.

SYRUP
Many Portuguese sweets include a syrup made with sugar and water and boiled to various consistencies according to the recipes. Generally speaking this is a very simple procedure, in which a little practice will enable one to become quite proficient and bold, dispensing with tables, thermometers and so on. But if you are not familiar with the methods, follow these hints:

Mix thoroughly the given sugar (granulated) with the water and bring to the boil over low heat, using a strong and roomy pan (to avoid overflowing when bubbling).

Try not to boil the mixture for longer than is necessary, or the syrup will get thicker and eventually turn into caramel; after that, it will burn. If the syrup becomes too thick, add a little water and simmer again to the point needed.

When talking about a light syrup, one has in mind the first stage (smooth), which is achieved very quickly, almost immediately after reaching boiling point (101°C/215°F), while a heavy or thick syrup would be at the stage known as 'the blow'. The table below shows those sugar-boiling stages likely to be met in the recipes, their approximate temperatures if you have a thermometer, and the behaviour of the syrup if you do not have one and want to test the stage you have reached.

The smooth stage (101°C/215–220°F)
 – The sugar starts boiling at this temperature. The syrup formed at this stage is thin, very liquid and leaving a spoon dipped into it shining and dripping.
The thread stage (103–106°C/225–230°F)
 – This stage is achieved when a small amount of syrup put between thumb and finger forms a fine thread, when they are separated.
The pearl stage (106–108°C/230°F)
 – This is reached immediately after the previous stage. The syrup will present pearl-like bubbles on its surface.
Caramel (141–145°C/310–350°F)
 The consistency of the syrup is very dry, resembling sand, and then turns into a golden liquid. The caramel is then boiled a little further, with great care, until the desired colour is reached.

There are many other sugar-boiling stages in between those indicated above, used for different sweets, hard and soft. However, we need not concern ourselves with them for the purpose of the recipes included in this book. Some of them describe the syrup required for their particular instance.

CARAMEL FOR PUDDINGS

For a large mould:
5 oz (140 g) granulated sugar
1½ tablespoons water

Place the sugar and water in a small saucepan and bring to the boil until a brown spot appears. This means the sugar is turning to caramel. Reduce the heat and continue boiling, stirring with a wooden spoon, until it acquires an overall dark toffee colour. Pour immediately into the mould and turn it round, covering the bottom and sides with the help of the wooden spoon if necessary. It is only too easy to burn the caramel – and thus ruin it. As soon as it reaches the desired colour, remove from the heat and use.

Equipment

Any reasonably well-equipped kitchen will cope with Portuguese cooking. Things like an electric blender, food-processor, mixer, pressure-cooker and so on are useful gadgets to facilitate and improve the cook's work. Even though the recipes may not suggest the use of one or several of these utensils, they can obviously be used whenever appropriate.

A cake-tester (a long, strong toothpick is as good as any), a good set of baking tins, pudding moulds and various ovenproof dishes, some with lid, will be necessary, as well as ordinary pots and pans. An added bonus would be some earthenware vessels, for use both in the oven and on top of the stove. They are suitable for slow cooking and simmering, and seem to improve the food prepared in them. In Portugal there are countless receptacles of all shapes and sizes made of earthenware, in which to cook and serve the food, including small ones for individual portions. At country fairs one can find cheap casseroles, pots, dishes and so on, made of local pottery. These vessels are of course brought straight from the stove to the table, saving work and keeping the food warmer.

It would be nice to have a *cataplana* (a new version is now available at some shops outside Portugal). However, traditional *cataplanas* are cooking vessels made of copper and consisting of two close-fitting concave halves, resembling a wok with handles that snap together, so all the steam and juices are sealed inside, cooking the food evenly without the need to add other liquids. They come from the Algarve, where they are used like any other pot, especially for the cockles and pork recipe (p.92). In the absence of a *cataplana*, one must use a saucepan with a well-fitting lid to keep the steam inside.

A good oven is, of course, a necessity. In some regions Portuguese cooks still use a baker's oven for certain specialities, such as the whole suckling pig and roast kid or lamb.

Spits for roast meat and charcoal grills for sardines will have to be improvised in an ordinary barbecue or grill, knowing, however, that the taste will not be exactly the same.

I indicate in the recipes the relevant alternatives, when appropriate, but I think any cook will overcome whatever difficulties present themselves, provided the ingredients are right.

Reminders Before You Start

Amounts indicated in spoonfuls mean 'level' spoons, unless otherwise stated.

Eggs will be size 2 unless the recipe mentions a different size.

Soups

In Portugal it would be unthinkable not to have soup every day, at least for dinner, if not for lunch as well. Generally speaking, soup is a must.

There is always, as the Portuguese say, room for the soup. ('What is the soup today?' is the first question to housewives from their hungry family on arriving home from work.) Some people eat their soup as a last course, instead of as a starter.

Many peasants have a thick soup for breakfast (left-overs from the previous day), before going into the fields. Indeed, a substantial soup made with beans or chickpeas and perhaps meat, *chouriço* (p.23) and a piece of bacon fat, vegetables, potatoes and rice or pasta, is a magnificent meal in itself and serves that very purpose at least in lean times.

There are countless soup recipes in Portugal, and they tend to be thick and chewy, blending only the basic thickener (potatoes, beans, chickpeas or whatever) and leaving the rest as it is (cut into small pieces, of course). Consommé-type soups are also popular, the best loved being *canja*, a broth made with pieces of chicken or just the giblets, with or without the addition of *chouriço*, for more flavour, and rice or small pasta. Fish and shellfish are also ingredients of splendid Portuguese soups. On the other hand, bread is sometimes the main ingredient of a soup (apart from being used as a garnish, as croûtons), and it is generally accepted that such soups, called *açordas*, are a relic from the Arabs, as so much else. (After all the

Arabs stayed in Portugal for five centuries.) Bread soups are included in the chapter entitled 'Bread Dishes', starting on p.56.

Green Broth/Caldo Verde

MINHO PROVINCE, BUT USED WIDELY ALL OVER THE COUNTRY

This soup, extremely simple but very tasty, is perhaps considered the most typical of Portuguese soups nowadays. It is rather appropriate that it originated in the northern province of Minho, as it reproduces the emerald colour of the countryside.

The real version of *caldo verde* includes a little garlic sausage (*chouriço*, see p.23) and, in some places a tiny amount of onion. A simpler version, with only the shredded cabbage, mashed potatoes, olive oil and perhaps a very small clove of garlic, is really all that is needed. The cabbage must be very finely shredded, which makes it look like little mounds of grass. Because of this, a misinformed British journalist wrote, a few years back, in one of Britain's leading papers, that the Portuguese people are so poor that they even make soup with grass!

Whenever a Portuguese émigré manages to get a little plot of land, he will invariably grow some of these special cabbages (called *galegas*, meaning that they came originally from Galicia, the neighbouring Spanish province), which are tall, similar to the kale and Brussels sprout plants and from which one can go on gathering leaves all the way up the stem. As this variety of cabbage is not normally available outside Portugal (unless in the private gardens of émigrés), I have experimented with other kinds and find that curly kale is remarkably similar to *galega* cabbage. Tender spring greens, when in season, can also be substituted, when nothing else is at hand, although the 'real' thing must be made with *galega* cabbage, of course.

1 lb (450 g) tender kale or spring greens, very finely shredded
4 medium floury potatoes
1 very small clove of garlic (optional)

2 tablespoons olive oil (or, if you prefer, any other good vegetable oil)
enough water and salt
½ small onion, chopped (optional)
4–8 thin slices of chouriço (p.23) or good-quality salami

Cook the potatoes and garlic, as well as the chopped onion (if used) in salt water, while you prepare the greens. For this you must gather up the clean leaves, free from the hard core, and roll them up, to be able to cut them evenly with a sharp knife. Secure the rolled leaves against a wooden board. You will probably need to make up several bunches of rolled-up leaves to facilitate the shredding. This is a very easy procedure which you will be able to follow immediately. If not, just cut the leaves as finely as you can, by any other method you prefer. Mash the potatoes with a fork, discard the garlic, return the mash to the broth, add the olive oil and the cabbage. Bring back to the boil and cook for just a few minutes.

The cabbage will take more or less time to cook according to how tender it is, but given the fact that it is so finely shredded, it normally cooks in a very short space of time. Besides, _caldo verde_ must not be served with mushy cabbage. Allow 4–5 minutes, check, correct seasoning and serve at once.

In Portugal they will give you a piece of that wonderful maize bread which is so typical of the countryside (see p.57). Otherwise you can serve the soup with a side dish of fresh wholemeal bread. Place 1 or 2 slices of _chouriço_ in each soup bowl. If you cannot find this sausage, use a very thin slice of salami. Add a side dish of small black olives, if you can.
Serves 4 to 6.

Variations
The basic potato thickener can be used for straightforward _caldo verde_ variations, all very popular with the Portuguese. Instead of kale, use watercress, turnip-tops (see Ingredients, p.27) or very tender green beans, adjusting the cooking time for these vegetables. Chinese leaves are also good for this kind of soup.

Chicken Soup/Canja

Still suspicious, he [Jacinto] tried the fragrant chicken broth and looked up at me ... His eyes shone in surprise. Another spoonful, and still another, fuller, more consistent. And he smiled, astonished: 'It's good!' And it was: divine. It had liver and gizzard. Its aroma was endearing. And thrice, with great fervour, I attacked that broth. 'I'll have some more as well,' Jacinto exclaimed, thoroughly convinced. 'I am so hungry!' he said. 'God! I haven't felt this hungry for years!' ... The rich aroma from the soup in the tureen was simply mouthwatering. On a large platter, a succulent chicken covered with moist rice and garnished with sausages had the magnificence of a meal fit for the lord of the manor.

Eça de Queiroz, _The City and the Mountains_,
(_A Cidade e as Serras_)

Apart from *caldo verde* (see p.39), *canja* is perhaps the best-known Portuguese soup. It is mentioned in the classics, ingrained in popular tradition and considered a particularly good food for the infirm. As far back as the fifteenth and sixteenth centuries, *canja* was being recommended as a food suited to those suffering from consumption. The Princess Maria medieval cookery booklets (see p.6) advised for this complaint a concentrated broth made from one chicken cooked in a minimum of water and then pounded into a purée, which was then pressed through a sieve, to extract all its goodness. This 'dose' had to be repeated daily until the person felt better. The current version is simple enough but always a winner.

1 medium chicken and giblets	*salt*
5 oz (140 g) rice	*4 small sprigs fresh mint*
2 pints (1.2 l) water	*(optional)*

Clean and prepare the chicken. Cut it into convenient-sized pieces. Bring to the boil together with the giblets and cook gently until tender. Skim the broth once or twice. When tender, drain the meats and set aside. Cook the rice in the broth, taste for salt and add more water, if needed. Serve the soup garnished with a few pieces of cooked chicken and the edible giblets, diced. Some people like to add a small sprig of fresh mint to each plate.

Use the remaining chicken for other dishes, such as chicken fricassée (p.124).
Serves 4 to 6.

Variations
1 Small pasta or noodles can be used, instead of rice. Also, for a rich tasting broth (and provided it is not intended for sick people), add a few pieces of *chouriço* (p.23) towards the end of cooking.

2 The broth can be served on its own, as a consommé, perhaps with a few cubes of toast floating in each soup bowl.

3 Again serve the broth as a consommé, enriching it with 2 egg yolks added at the last minute, without actually boiling them, to avoid curdling.

Note: *Canja* can also be prepared just with the giblets, provided these are meaty enough.

Stone Soup/Sopa de Pedra

RIBATEJO PROVINCE
There is a delightful story attached to this soup, which, in spite of its name, is very rich and wholesome.

A monk used to travel up and down the country, taking nothing with him in the way of provisions or money, so he was forced to beg for food now and then. He would knock at some door, asking for a little bowl of soup. If the people answered that they had no soup to offer him, he would suggest that they let him in to show them how to prepare a very nice soup out of a stone. The astonished hosts would then follow the monk's instructions: 'Please get a clean, biggish pan and add some water to it. Bring it to the boil and, in the meantime, wash a medium-sized stone and place it inside the pan.' 'Perhaps', he would go on to say, 'we could find a piece of bacon and some bones with meat, and maybe a few carrots. If you could also manage some cabbage and onions …' and so forth.

'Stone soup' became well known in the Portuguese countryside. Here is the recipe – although this is the kind of soup to which one can add almost any vegetable and meat that may be available.

1¾ pints (1 l) water	6 oz (175 g) red or butter beans
7–8 oz (200–225 g) boiling ham or bacon	6 oz (175 g) onions
	1 medium turnip
1 medium-sized knuckle of bacon (ham hock)	6 oz (175 g) carrots
	12 oz (350 g) potatoes
a few beef marrow bones (optional)	4–5 oz (110–140 g) cabbage
	1 small clove garlic
1 medium-sized black pudding	1 bay leaf
3 oz (90 g) chouriço (p.23)	

If wanted, instead of beans use double the amount of vegetables (except the onion) or 6 oz (175 g) of soaked chickpeas.

Bring the meat to the boil in the water and simmer together with the previously soaked beans (if used) and bones. When everything is almost tender, add the other ingredients, chopped. Skim off the soup and simmer until everything is collapsing. Correct the seasoning and the amount of liquid (the soup should be thick, like a chowder). Serve from a large tureen, whilst very hot, with crusty bread.
Serves 4 to 6.

Beef Stock Soup/Sopa de Caldo de Carne

This is a soup intended to use up any left-over beef stock or the broth which hopefully still remains after one of those big *cozido* meals (p.100).

enough stock or left-over cozido
   broth (for 4 people)
4 slices of good-quality white

bread, dried in the oven and
   crumbled roughly
4 small sprigs of mint

Bring the liquid to the boil (you can add some stock made from a good cube, if you need to resort to this) and pour over the bread. Serve with one piece of mint in each plate.
Serves 4.

Variation
Another way of using the above liquor for a good, everyday soup, is to cook some small pasta in it (1½ tablespoons of pasta per person), until tender.

Beef Soup/Sopa de Carne

1½ pints (750 ml) beef stock
2 tablespoons small pasta
1 small potato, diced very small
1 medium carrot, thinly sliced
1 small turnip, thinly sliced

¼ medium-sized cabbage (or
   equivalent amount spring
   greens), shredded
salt

Simmer all ingredients until tender (20–25 minutes). Add more stock if needed, taste for salt and serve very hot.
Serves 4.

Variation
A few slices of *chouriço* (p.23) or a little smoked bacon can be added half-way through cooking, as well as small pieces of boiled beef, for a richer flavour and texture.

Festival Soup/Sopa da Romaria

MADEIRA
The Madeira and Azores archipelagos have longstanding religious traditions, which they keep faithfully, due no doubt to their insularity. This soup will be comforting after the merrymaking of the *Romaria* (p.12).

1 lb (450 g) beef (brisket or shin,
   cut into small chunks)
1 medium tomato, peeled, seeded
   and chopped

1 large onion, chopped
2 large carrots, thickly sliced
4 medium potatoes, quartered
salt

Simmer the beef in enough water with some salt, until almost tender. At this point add all other ingredients and boil everything for about 40–50 minutes, over a low flame. The idea

is to have both the vegetables and the meat really soft and mushy, like a very thick chowder. Serve piping hot, with crusty bread.
Serves 4.

Dry Soup, Minho Fashion/Sopa Seca do Minho

The Portuguese housewife is thrifty and imaginative. Very little is thrown away in her kitchen, and it is considered almost a sin to discard good food only because it was left at the table. On the other hand, another of her traits is being a little too generous with the amount she cooks. So these are two good reasons to create different recipes out of left-overs. *Cozido* (p.100) is a dish you can count on for this, the meat being suitable for various fillings, and the vegetables and broth for soups. But if you happen to have *cozido* left over as well as some cooked chickpeas, try this substantial 'dry soup', which is a meal in itself.

Enough mixed cooked meat (for 4 people)
Some cooked cabbage (the amount depends on whether you use green beans or not) and about:

10 oz (280 g) cooked chickpeas   *2 medium onions, chopped*
7 oz (200 g) cooked green beans (if   *2 medium tomatoes (peeled,*
  in season)   *seeded and chopped)*
2 tablespoons chopped parsley   *2 tablespoons olive oil*
6–8 slices of bread

Fry the onion in the oil until transparent, add the tomatoes and parsley and fry again for 3–4 minutes. Add this to the pan with the cooked meats and some stock. Boil for 4–5 minutes. Set aside.
   Line a deep, buttered fireproof dish with half the bread. Assemble layers of cubed meat, chopped vegetables and chickpeas. Cover with more bread. Pour some of the liquor over all, to moisten, and leave in the oven (190°C/375°F/Gas 5) until golden brown and crusty on top. Serve at once.
Serves 4.

Wild Rabbit (or Hare) Soup/Sopa de Coelho
  Bravo (ou Lebre)

INLAND PROVINCES
Soups made with game are always extra-special and worth a little extra trouble. Instead of using a whole rabbit or hare, one

can of course use only part of it and the carcass, plus any trimmings especially reserved for the soup (the more the better, obviously) and the offal, if this is in good condition.

1 small wild rabbit (or part of it, see above)
3–4 oz (90–110 g) presunto (p.22) or good bacon, cubed
1 tablespoon lard
1 tablespoon butter
¼ pint (150 ml) white wine
3 tablespoons port (or dry madeira)
1 large onion, chopped
2 bayleaves
2 medium carrots, diced small
2 cloves garlic, chopped
3 stalks parsley, chopped
4–6 peppercorns
2 pints (1.2 l) chicken stock or any good meat stock without a very marked flavour, so as not to influence the overall taste
1 tablespoon cornflour, diluted in a little water
garnish – a handful of croûtons for each person

Prepare the rabbit (or equivalent amount of hare), the cubed ham or bacon and all the other ingredients (except the port and flour) and cook until everything is tender. Strain it all, keep the stock aside and discard all bones and unwanted bits. Process the meats and vegetables, add to the stock, bring to the boil and add the cornflour. Simmer for a few minutes, to thicken. Add more stock or water, if necessary, and the port or madeira. Correct seasonings and serve with the croûtons.
Serves 4 to 6.

Variation
From the same regions, another, slightly different wild rabbit soup:

1 medium-sized wild rabbit, cleaned and cut into pieces
4–5 oz (110–140 g) fatty bacon, in chunks
½ pint (300 ml) white wine
2 large carrots, halved
1 large onion, chopped
1 medium potato, halved
3 sprigs parsley, chopped
2 cloves garlic, chopped
freshly ground pepper
salt
1½ pints (900 ml) water
3 slices stale bread

Prepare a marinade with the wine, garlic, a little water, salt, some pepper and the parsley. Steep the rabbit in this and leave for 4–6 hours. Bring the remaining water to the boil with all the other ingredients, add the rabbit mixture (with the wine) and cook until the meat is tender. Drain everything in order to get hold of the rabbit pieces. Bone them. Mash the carrot and potato roughly. Return to the broth the boned meat and mashed vegetables. Add more water and salt if needed and boil again for 3–4 minutes, to blend it well. Thicken the soup with a few pieces of stale bread soaked into it.

Partridge Soup/Sopa de Perdiz

MOST INLAND PROVINCES
Any stock left when boiling partridges should be used as a basis for this lovely soup. However, any other game would be appropriate for a soup of this kind, and it can be enriched with all sorts of things, such as cream, egg yolks and port wine. Try your own experiments on a small portion first, before committing yourself to the whole stock.

1½ pints (900 ml) partridge stock
3–4 oz (90–110 g) presunto
  (p.22) or lean bacon
1 tablespoon butter
1 tablespoon lard

1 large onion, chopped
enough slices of bread for
  croûtons (toasted or fried)
seasonings to taste

Taste the stock and see whether you are satisfied with the seasoning. If not, add perhaps a few peppercorns, or just pepper. Do not add any salt until after cooking the smoked meats. Fry the onion in the fats until transparent. Add to the stock, boil with the cubed meats until tender. Pour into a tureen, add lots of croûtons and serve.
Serves 4.

Variation
Rice and shredded cabbage could be considered in addition to suggestions above, for variations using this stock.

Prawn (or Shrimp) and Mussel Chowder/Sopa de Camarão e Mexilhões

DOURO LITORAL PROVINCE
This is a very substantial soup, of the 'complete meal' kind.

1½ lb (675 g) prawns (or
  shrimps) in the shell
1½ lb (675 g) mussels (live, in the
  shell)
1 large onion, chopped
2 tablespoons butter
4 hard-boiled eggs

¼ pint (150 ml) white wine
2 tablespoons flour
3½ fluid oz (100 ml) double
  cream
1 coffeespoon paprika
3 peppercorns
salt and pepper

Prepare a pan with enough water to cover the shellfish (which must have been thoroughly cleaned) and add the wine, the

paprika, peppercorns, some pepper and salt. Bring to the boil. Cover. After 3–4 minutes remove from the heat and strain. Discard the mussels that have not opened, and remove the flesh from the others. Peel and clean the prawns (or shrimps). Keep the prepared shellfish aside. Crush the shells of the prawns to extract their juice and use the stock to wash them. Strain through a fine sieve. Now bring the stock to the boil with the onion, and boil for 8–10 minutes. Add the flour (made into a paste with water), stir well and boil, to thicken. Add more water if needed, taste for salt, add the shellfish, reheat and serve immediately, garnished with the boiled eggs, cut into small dice, and with little 'islands' of cream floating in the middle. Serve with chunks of fresh bread.
Serves 6.

Shrimp Soup/Sopa de Camarão

LISBON AREA
Shrimps impart a very distinctive and exquisite flavour to this soup, and those with a taste for hot food will no doubt find it excellent with some chillies added.

1 lb (450 g) shrimps
1 large tomato, peeled, seeded and chopped
1 large onion, chopped
1 large clove garlic, chopped
3 sprigs parsley, chopped
1 bayleaf

4 tablespoons olive oil
1 dessertspoon cornflour
2 pints (1.2 l) water
4 medium slices of stale or fried bread, cubed
salt and pepper
a few chillies (optional)

Bring some of the water to the boil, with salt. Meanwhile, wash the shrimps really well. Cook them in the boiling water for 3–4 minutes. Set aside to cool until the temperature allows you to handle the shrimps. Drain and shell them, keeping the liquor and the shells, which you then mash, using a pestle and mortar. (This will help extract all their juices and flavour.) Boil the mashed shells and the chillies, if using them, in the remaining water for 8–10 minutes. Drain, discard the shells (and chillies), keep the liquor. Meantime, fry the onion and all other ingredients (except the peeled shrimps) in the oil, over a low heat. Add the strained liquor (both lots) to the fried mixture. Bring to the boil and add the flour, mixed into a paste in a little cold water. Cook for 4–5 minutes, stirring, until it thickens. Add the shrimps. Boil again, correct the seasonings and serve over the cubes of bread.
Serves 4 to 6.

Fish Soup, Madeira Style/Sopa de Peixe da Madeira

This is a chowder-type soup, like most fish soups in Portugal. The difference in this Madeira version is the use of different herbs, which gives the soup a distinctive flavour. Scabbard fish is used in Madeira, but you can use any fish of the smooth flesh variety.

1 lb (450 g) fish, plus its head and tail
1 lb (450 g) tomatoes, peeled, seeded and chopped
6 tablespoons olive oil
1 large onion, chopped
2 large potatoes, peeled and thickly sliced

4 tablespoons white wine
10–12 oz (280–310 g) stale white bread, cut roughly
2 sprigs savory
1 coffeespoon oregano
salt and pepper

Cook the fish in enough salted water to cover, then bone it and discard all skin and bones. Pound the fish slightly and set aside. Fry the onions and tomatoes in the oil until soft (8–10 minutes), add to the fish stock with more water, the potatoes and herbs. Boil until the potatoes are tender, then add the fish pieces and the wine. Boil again for 3–4 minutes, taste for salt and correct the amount of liquid. Serve over the bread.
Serves 4 to 6.

Fish Soup, Alentejo Fashion/Sopa de Peixe

This is a rich soup with plenty of fish, which makes it a complete meal.

1¼ lb (560 g) skate or similar (white) fish
3½ fluid oz (100 ml) wine vinegar
4 tablespoons olive oil
2 cloves garlic, chopped

4 sprigs coriander, chopped
2 bayleaves
1 dessertspoon cornflour
1 coffeespoon paprika
6–7 oz (175–200 g) stale bread
salt

Make a marinade with the vinegar, bay leaves, paprika and salt. Steep the fish (thickly sliced) into this and leave for 2½ hours or so. Then sweat the coriander and garlic in the oil. Add the fish and marinade and enough boiling water to cover. Cook until the fish is tender (10–15 minutes). Remove the fish, and bone it if the slices are not perfectly presentable, otherwise leave them whole. Keep warm. Mix the cornflour with some water and add to the stock. Mix well and bring to the boil for 3–4 minutes, to thicken. Taste for seasoning and add more water if needed. Place the stale bread (cut small) in a tureen, put the fish on top

and pour the boiling soup over all, or serve directly in
individual bowls.
Serves 4.

Fish Soup, Chowder Type, Algarve Fashion/Sopa de Peixe

The objective of this soup is to make use of a fish head and
stock. Generally a sea-bass or hake is chosen and, needless to
say, the fish must be impeccably fresh.

*1 large white fish head (or 2
  smaller ones), cleaned
1 lb (450 g) potatoes, thickly
  sliced
4 tablespoons olive oil
3 sprigs parsley, chopped
1 large red pepper, seeded and
  finely sliced
1 large onion, chopped*

*5 medium tomatoes, peeled,
  seeded and coarsely chopped
4 slices of stale bread
4 poached eggs
salt
2 pints (1.2 l) fish stock, made
  with fish trimmings boiled for
  20–25 minutes, then strained*

Make a *refogado* (p.31) with the oil, onion, tomatoes and parsley.
When soft, add the fish stock and bring to the boil. Add the
potatoes, the red pepper and some salt. When half cooked
(10–15 minutes), place the fish head in the pan. Cover again
and cook for a further 15 minutes. Taste for salt. Prepare
poached eggs. Put the slices of bread in a tureen, pour the soup
over it, then the poached eggs, and crown with the fish head,
as a garnish. Serve piping hot.
Serves 4.

Cockle Soup/Sopa de Ameijoas

ALGARVE PROVINCE

Cockles are very abundant in the Algarve, and their use is
therefore very widespread. People go to the beaches to gather
them, so they could not be fresher, when cooked there. Clams
(which are much bigger) can also be used, or mussels, if cockles
are not available.

*1½–2 lb (675 g–1 kg) live cockles
2 pints (1.2 l) fish stock
3 oz (90 g) rice
6–8 tablespoons white wine
1 clove garlic, crushed
4 stalks parsley, chopped*

*2 bay leaves
2 medium onions, chopped
2 medium tomatoes, peeled and
  seeded, chopped
2 tablespoons olive oil
pinch paprika
salt and pepper*

Clean the shellfish and leave it with its shells on in salted water for a while. In the meantime bring the stock to the boil, together with all other ingredients, except the parsley. Cook for 10 minutes, then add the rinsed shellfish and boil for a further 10–12 minutes. Skim off the scum. Drain the shellfish and set aside. Cook the rice in the liquid. Meanwhile, remove the shells from the shellfish and discard. When the rice is tender, add shellfish to the soup. Taste for seasonings and add the chopped parsley. Boil for 2–3 minutes. Serve with crusty bread.
Serves 4 to 6.

Cockle Soup, Minho Fashion/Sopa de Ameijoas

Cockles are found not only in the southern coast. Minho and other coastal areas have their share as well, and Minho offers a lovely soup made with them.

2 lb (1 kg) live cockles (or   3 sprigs coriander, chopped
   mussels)   4 slices stale maize or wholemeal
4 tablespoons olive oil   bread
1 large clove garlic, chopped   salt and pepper
1 sprig parsley, chopped   water or fish stock

Prepare the shellfish, wash thoroughly and bring to the boil with a little water or fish stock, the oil and seasoning. While the shellfish open and cook for 4–5 minutes, break the slices of bread into rough small pieces and share them between the soup bowls. Remove the pan from the heat, taste for salt, add more stock if needed. Share out the shellfish between the individual bowls, using a slotted spoon. Then serve the stock, with the ladle, pouring it over the shellfish and bread. The amount of liquor you use depends on how thin you want the soup to be.
Serves 4 to 6.

Chickpea Soup/Sopa de Grão

This is a wonderfully tasty soup, a filling starter for a good lunch. It can use left-over chickpeas. Try to prepare double the quantity, to keep half for reheating in a couple of days.

12 oz (350 g) chickpeas   2 medium onions, chopped
11 oz (310 g) tender turnip-tops 1 clove garlic, chopped
  (see Ingredients, p.19) or spin- 3 tablespoons olive oil
  ach, or a bunch of watercress   salt

Soak the chickpeas overnight and cook them with the onion and garlic in 1½ pints (900 ml) boiling water until tender (it

rather depends how old the chickpeas are, but it may take over an hour, unless you use the pressure-cooker, which would finish the job in less than half the time). Liquidize, sieve (to ensure a very smooth purée) and put aside. Meanwhile cook the chosen greens in a minimum of water. Mix (with their liquor) with the purée, season and add a little more water, if necessary.
Serves 4 to 6.

Variation
Omit the greens and add 4 oz (110 g) boiled rice. Mix well.

Bean and Cabbage Soup/Sopa de Feijão

A great stand-by, one of the most common, nourishing and tasty of everyday soups in Portugal. It can be varied by adding bacon, *chouriço* (smoked sausage, p.23),smoked ham, a piece of fatty pork, or beef.

7 oz (200 g) red kidney beans,
  well soaked overnight
1 small cabbage, shredded
2 tablespoons olive oil
1 medium onion

1 clove garlic
1 bay leaf
2 pints (1.2 l) water
Salt and pepper

In a large pan put the water and beans and bring to the heat, together with the onion and seasoning (except the salt). Boil for 10 minutes and then cook over gentle heat until the beans are tender. Discard the bay leaf and sieve or liquidize, reserving a few whole beans for garnishing. Add the cabbage and salt and cook. Taste for salt, add more liquid if needed and serve, putting a few whole beans in each plate.
Serves 4.

Broad Bean Soup/Sopa de Favas

ALL NORTHERN INLAND PROVINCES
This very substantial and tasty soup can be served as a complete meal in itself and goes extremely well with maize bread or any close-textured wholemeal loaf. Alternatively, croûtons can be added.

1 lb (450 g) broad beans (after
  shelling)
3 oz (90 g) presunto (p.22), cut
  into small cubes
1 large onion, chopped

1 medium carrot, diced small
2 oz (60 g) rice
2 tablespoons olive oil
salt and pepper

Peel the shelled broad beans for a really velvety soup. Cook them in water together with all other ingredients, until tender. Blend, if you prefer a completely smooth, cream-like soup. Serve with one of the breads indicated or croûtons.
Serves 4.

Variations
1 Instead of fresh broad beans, use dried ones, after soaking them overnight. Liquidize and sieve, after cooking. Possible additions are small sprigs of cooked cauliflower and an egg yolk beaten in, just before serving, whilst the soup is still at boiling point.
2 Vegetarians can simply omit the smoked ham and add a little soya sauce, instead.

Pea Soup/Sopa de Puré de Ervilhas

This soup is made like the broad bean soup (p.51) using either fresh or dried (and previously soaked) peas. Croûtons are the classic garnish for this most delicious soup.
    The same variations also apply, or create your own.

Vegetable Purée/Sopa de Legumes

A homely soup, full of goodness, easily prepared with a blender of sieve, for a creamy texture.

6 oz (175 g) potatoes	1 small bay leaf
6 oz (175 g) turnips	2 tablespoons olive oil
6 oz (175 g) carrots	salt
4–6 oz (110–175 g) pumpkin	1 pint (600 ml) boiling water
(optional)	garnish – croûtons and a little
1 medium onion	chopped parsley
1 small clove garlic	

Cook all ingredients together for 25 minutes or until tender. Remove the bay leaf and liquidize. Add more liquid if necessary. Taste for salt and serve with the parsley and croûtons.
Serves 4.

Tomato, Egg and Bread Soup/Sopa de Tomate, com Ovo e Pão

LISBON REGION
This is a very homely dish, belonging to the thick soup kind, and is easily transformed into a light meal by itself. It is

pleasant and nutritious, and really simple to prepare. I use it very often for my family when wanting to produce something wholesome, cheap, quick, colourful and tasty.

1 pint (600 ml) water, to start with
8 oz (225 g) ripe tomatoes
6 oz (175 g) onions
10 oz (300 g) potatoes
4–6 eggs
4–6 thick slices of day-old farmhouse-type bread

2 tablespoons good olive or other vegetable oil
2 sprigs of parsley, chopped
1 small clove of garlic, peeled and crushed with some salt
bay leaf
¼ teaspoon paprika (optional)

Put the oil in a saucepan and gently fry the sliced onion until golden. Add the peeled and seeded tomatoes, cut into small pieces, and add the bay leaf, garlic, parsley and paprika, if using. Sweat all this together for about 5 minutes, then add boiling water. Add the potatoes, peeled and thickly sliced, and some salt. Cover the pan and simmer, until the potatoes are tender (about 25 minutes). Try for salt and see whether it needs any more water (it should have the consistency of a hotpot after adding the bread, which, of course, will absorb some liquid, so allow for this). Serve in soup bowls containing a slice of bread, and top with a poached egg for each person. Traditionally the eggs are poached in the soup itself, before removing from the heat and after checking the amount of liquid and seasoning.
Serves 4 to 6.

Green Bean Soup with Tomato/Sopa de Feijão-Verde com Tomate

RIBATEJO PROVINCE
When green beans are in season, the Portuguese use them very often, either as a vegetable for meat and fish dishes or in soups. Apart from a kind of *caldo verde* soup, as indicated in variations for *caldo verde* (p.39), green beans make a delicious tomato-and-onion based soup, as used in Ribatejo.

8 oz (225 g) very tender green beans
1 medium onion, cut into rings
2 tablespoons olive oil
4 oz (110 g) ripe tomatoes, peeled, seeded and chopped
2 sprigs parsley, chopped

1 small clove garlic, finely chopped
1 small bay leaf
4 medium floury potatoes
pinch of oregano (optional)
salt
enough water for 4 people

Fry the onion in the oil over gentle heat for 4–5 minutes. Add
the tomato, parsley, garlic and bay leaf and fry for another 2–3
minutes. Add about 1½ pints (900 l) boiling water and some
salt, as well as the potatoes, peeled and cut in half. Allow to boil
for 5 minutes, then add the finely cut green beans and cook
everything until tender, over a low flame. Remove and discard
the bay leaf, remove the potatoes and mash, adding the purée
to the soup again (do not worry if the potatoes have broken a
little in the soup), taste for seasoning and serve piping hot. Add
a little oregano to each plate, after serving.
Serves 4 to 6.

Variation
A richer version of this soup is obtained by adding a few pieces
of homemade bread to each plate, before pouring the soup, and
a poached egg, topping the bread. In this case do not sprinkle
with oregano.

Dried Chestnut Soup/Sopa de Castanhas Piladas

NORTHERN PROVINCES
The chestnut season is not very long, and dried chestnuts are
sometimes used. They have a chewy texture and a mild
sweetness all their own.

*3–4 oz (90–110 g) dried
    chestnuts, soaked overnight
    (keep the water afterwards)
2 oz (60 g) rice*

*3 oz (90 g) butterbeans (soaked
    overnight)
3 tablespoons olive oil
1 medium onion, sliced
salt*

Fry the onion in the oil, until soft but not coloured. Set aside.
Bring the beans and chestnuts to the boil (use the water from
soaking the chestnuts). When almost tender, add the rice and
more liquid if necessary, plus salt and the oil and onion
mixture. Cover and cook. When everything is tender, taste for
salt and correct amount of liquid. Serve very hot, on cold days.
Serves 4.

Maize Porridge/Papas de Milho

MOST INLAND PROVINCES
See Ingredients, p.19. This savoury dish can be classed as a
soup, and its thickness rather depends on personal taste.
Generally, it is served like a pap, with the consistency of a thick
custard. On cold days, it is a comforting and filling first course.
See also sweet maize porridge, p.169.

7 oz (200 g) coarse cornmeal   *2 tablespoons olive oil*
1½ pints (900 ml) water   *salt*

Bring half the water to the boil. Meanwhile mix the meal with the remaining water. Add to the pan. Combine well, over low heat and add the oil and a little salt. Cover and cook for 15–20 minutes, stirring from time to time to prevent its becoming lumpy. Add more water if you find it too thick. Taste for salt and serve piping hot. Once tried, one is sure to want *papas* occasionally.
Serves 4 to 6.

Bread Dishes

The origin of Portuguese bread dishes is credited to the Moors, but I rather imagine that the locals went mad with the idea and could not stop thinking up new exotic variations on the same theme. There are many traditional bread recipes all over the country, comprising soups, main dishes and desserts – so many, in fact, that they deserve a chapter all their own.

There are the *açordas*, which generally consist of bread boiled with a few other ingredients, forming a lumpy sort of mixture (do not be put off by the description, because even though bread dishes may not always look terribly glamorous, they are extremely attractive to the palate); the *Ensopados*, which are a kind of stew; the *Migas*, another variation on *Açorda* but with some significant differences; the 'dry soups' and *Gaspachos*; and the sweet dishes – to crown it all.

These recipes have the obvious advantage of using up stale bread lying about the house. In Portugal there is a very high bread consumption (bread is always present at every meal, serving as an accompaniment to every savoury dish, including the soup, and also eaten with fruit, as a snack), which explains why it gets to be left over in sufficient quantities to justify cooking it. There is an old Portuguese saying: 'Broth without bread only in hell.' In the countryside there is a very common snack called *Sopas de Cavalo Cansado* (Tired Horse Soup). It consists of pieces of bread soaked in red wine in a large bowl and then generously sprinkled with sugar. It is a wonderful reviver: hence the name. If it can revive a horse it can revive anyone.

Bread used in *açordas* and all other bread dishes must, nevertheless, be of good quality. In peasant homes there will perhaps be homemade bread, though now less frequently. But all over Portugal it is possible to buy the so-called peasant loaf, which is not quite white but not wholemeal either – a mixture of the two. Greek and Italian breads are similar. They are much more solid and close-textured than an ordinary white loaf. An unbleached stoneground white flour will be the nearest to the flour used for peasant bread. Although most good breads can be used for the recipes, the dish may turn out slightly different from its Portuguese original. Avoid, if possible, those excessively white, 'lifeless' breads of the 'cotton-wool' variety, which would produce a bland, less appealing pap.

Maize Bread/Broa de Milho

This heavy round loaf came originally from the northern provinces but is now common all over Portugal and is typical peasant bread at its best. *Pão de Milho* or *broa* is now available in every town supermarket, but I am sure my tastebuds do not deceive me when I compare the long-lost *broa* my grandmother used to bake when I was a child most favourably against the current commercial version.

When it is properly made, maize bread crumbles very easily and is ideal to thicken soups (*caldo verde*, for example, which is traditionally served with a slice of maize bread by the side see p.39). It is also good to eat with those delicious small black olives so typical of Portuguese tables or with cheese or, when freshly baked, just on its own, to appreciate fully its thick crust and mealy texture.

In some Portuguese provinces where white maize prevails, the *broa* is obviously made with whitish cornmeal, but ordinary yellow corn is most commonly used. The results, with either, are similar. The proportion of wheat (which is always added, as cornmeal by itself would be too heavy) varies from region to region. Recipes for maize bread are handed down from mother to daughter and followed automatically – nothing written down, just the eye and the experienced hand for measuring and calculating. I would advise beginners to start with half the amounts stated. Do not be put off by the 'boiling water method', which is an essential part of maize breadmaking.

1 lb (450 g) cornmeal (coarse
    maize flour)
6 oz (175 g) unbleached white
    bread flour

1 oz (30 g) fresh yeast (or
    equivalent dried yeast)
½ oz (15 g) salt
1 pint (600 ml) boiling water

(This is a traditional recipe for a heavy *broa*, as it should be. For a lighter loaf, use equal amounts of both flours or even a slightly higher proportion of wheat. The method will still be the same.)

Crumble the yeast and mix with a little tepid water. Add a quarter of the wheat to the flour and mix well. Set aside. Put the maize flour in a roomy bowl and pour the boiling water over it. Mix well, using a spatula, to avoid burning your hands. Cover until the temperature allows some kneading, for a couple of minutes. Add the salt, the prepared yeast and remaining wheat flour. Knead really well now, adding a little more tepid water very gradually, if you think the dough is excessively dry, but not until then. When smooth, cover with a cloth and a blanket and leave in a warm place, to rise, for an hour. Knead again for just a few minutes and divide the dough into two halves. Shape each half into a ball, rolling it in a bowl containing wheat flour, to coat it all round. This will have the effect of giving the *broa* a whitish crust, after baking, with rich yellow-brown cracks in it.

Place the shaped loaves in a greased, floured baking-tin, cover again and leave to prove in warm place for about 20 minutes. Bake in an oven preheated to 210°C/425°F/Gas 7 for 25 minutes or until it sounds hollow when you tap the underside. Do not undercook your maize bread but try not to burn it either, or it will be too dry. Remove from the tin and cool on a wire rack.

Maize bread keeps well and will still be very pleasant to eat a week later, if kept in plastic bag inside a bread bin.
Makes 2 loaves.

Açordas

Bread-Pap, Portuguese Style/*Açorda*

This is the simplest version of *açorda*, but none the worse for it. It is surprisingly tasty. Nowadays perhaps it has lost favour as a stand-by dish for feeding infants, but not long ago it was still very commonly used for this purpose – although grown-ups never turned away from it either. Like many other forms of *açorda*, it is suitable as an accompaniment to fried or grilled fish.

10 oz (300 g) stale bread, in small
    chunks
1 large clove of garlic, finely
    chopped

2 tablespoons olive oil
½ pint (300 ml) salted boiling
    water
1 large or 2 small eggs (optional)

Mix the olive oil and garlic with the boiling water, add the bread, bring to the heat. Cook gently, while stirring, until it becomes a soft pap, with the consistency of thick porridge (about 10 minutes).

You can enrich it with the beaten eggs, added just at the end of cooking. Mix thoroughly and serve at once.
Serves 4.

Salted Cod Açorda/Açorda de bacalhau

NORTHERN PROVINCES
In the very religious northern provinces of Portugal, people try to refrain from eating meat during Lent. Salted cod *açorda* is a dish especially eaten at that time of the year.

14 oz (400 g) good-quality stale
    white bread, thinly sliced
12 oz (350 g) salted cod, soaked
    for up to 24 hours, changing
    the water a couple of times
2 medium tomatoes, peeled,
    seeded and chopped
4 eggs

1 clove garlic, chopped
2 medium onions, thinly sliced
5 tablespoons olive oil
1 bay leaf
salt and pepper
1 pint (600 ml) water
a few olives for garnishing

Fry the onion in the oil for a couple of minutes, then add the tomatoes, bay leaf and garlic. While this basic *refogado* (see p.31) is cooking, rinse the cod, then skin, bone and flake it and cook in half the given water, until tender (about 15 minutes). Add the remaining water, boil, taste for salt and add pepper (if liked) and the bread. Simmer for a short while, stirring. After 8–10 minutes it should be cooked. Take off the heat and add the beaten eggs. Do not boil again. Serve immediately. The consistency will be like that of mashed potato.
Serves 4 to 6.

Variation
Instead of beating the eggs, they can be poached on top of the *açorda.*

Seafood Açorda/Açorda de marisco

ESTREMADURA, MAINLY THE LISBON AREA

This kind of *açorda* is typical of the Lisbon area and has become extremely popular in recent years, with many restaurants specializing in it. It has an absolutely glorious taste and is very filling, so do not think of adding anything else to the meal when choosing this as a main dish.

1¼ lb (560 g) mixed seafood
  (prawns, clams, cockles)
  weighed after cooking and
  cleaning, discarding the shells
10 oz (300 g) fish (with firm
  white flesh, such as monk fish)
1¼ lb (560 g) stale white bread,
  in chunks

3 tablespoons olive oil
4 eggs
2 cloves garlic, very finely
  chopped
1 pint (600 ml) liquid
2 sprigs fresh coriander, chopped
salt and pepper

If the shellfish has been prepared at home, keep the resulting liquor and strain it. Cook the fish and flake it. Keep this liquor, too, and measure the amount needed for the recipe. If there is any liquid left, keep it in case you need to add some of it towards the end, should the *açorda* become too dry. The consistency should be like that of thick porridge.

Put the liquid, garlic, salt and pepper to taste, and the oil, in a roomy pot. Add the bread and bring to the heat. Cook gently, while stirring all the time, until a pap is achieved. Add the coriander, fish and seafood, reserving a few prawns for decoration. Boil again, mixing. Taste for seasoning, and just before taking the *açorda* off the heat add the beaten eggs, stirring it all up. Put the reserved prawns on top and serve at once in the same pot. This is traditionally cooked in an earthenware pot, but any other will do. In restaurants it is served in individual earthenware pans.

Serves 4 to 6.

Variation

Prawn *açorda* is a richer version of seafood *açorda*, using only prawns (or lobster, or a mixture of the two), although in some restaurants they will also bulk it up with some firm-fleshed fish, as above. The liquid should be fish stock or, much better still, the strained liquor left after cooking the prawns or lobster, if you do cook them at home. The idea is to have a marked seafood taste in these *açordas*. This variation omits the coriander.

Coriander Bread Soup Alentejo Style/Açorda Alentejana

This is the most aromatic of bread dishes, and the Portuguese are extremely fond of it. Fortunately it is very easily made, but the use of plenty of fresh coriander is an absolute must. Should you be unable to get it, postpone preparing this *açorda* until such time as you have this delectable herb at hand.

1 lb (450 g) day-old bread (follow
* hints on the bread to use for*
* açordas on p.57)*
4 tablespoons olive oil
4 eggs, poached

3 cloves garlic
1½ pints (900 ml) boiling water
8–10 good sprigs fresh coriander
salt

Process the garlic and coriander (or crush with some salt with a pestle and mortar) and place this pulp in a large serving bowl or tureen. Add the boiling water, salt to taste, and the oil. Break the bread into small chunks and add to the water. Soak it well. Divide among 4 soup bowls and place a poached egg on each. Serve at once.

This is meant as a soup, and it should not be excessively dry. It all depends on the kind of bread used, but you may need to add a little more boiling salted water, in order to have some liquid around the bread.

This *açorda* can be served with a side dish of fried or grilled fish and olives.
Serves 4.

Açorda Madeira Style/Açorda Madeirense

The tradition of *açorda* travelled to Madeira, where a local version has been created. It is a winter supper dish (though winters are almost non-existent in Madeira). It is made more substantial by serving it with a side dish of boiled or baked sweet potatoes cooked in their skins (sweet potatoes are very abundant in Madeira).

14 oz (400 g) stale bread cut into
* 1 inch (2.5 cm) cubes*
3 cloves garlic, well crushed
1 tablespoon thyme
3 tablespoons olive oil

4–6 poached eggs
salt and pepper
3½ oz (100 g) cooked corn
* (optional)*
2 pints (1.2 l) salted boiling water

Place the bread in a large serving bowl or tureen with the corn, if used. Sprinkle with the crushed garlic and thyme. Add the oil and the boiling salt water (usually the water used for poaching

the eggs). The liquid will be almost completely absorbed by the bread. Serve at once with the side dish (sweet potatoes, or simply olives, if you do not like or do not have the potatoes).
Serves 4 to 6.

Migas

Like *açorda*, *migas* are peasant dishes full of flavour and goodness, in spite of lacking elegance.

In some places to make *migas* (*fazer migas*) really means just soaking crumbled maize or peasant bread into some liquid. Coffee *migas*, for instance, is simply bread crumbled on black coffee, sprinkled with sugar, served very hot in a small bowl, and eaten slowly with a spoon. I still remember having coffee *migas* for breakfast (followed by the most gorgeous fresh figs), when as a child, I used to spend holidays with my grandmother at her farm in the Ribatejo province. She was an early riser and, as soon as I heard her about the kitchen, on her own, I would get up and rush to have my *migas* with her. This was our little secret, because I wasn't really allowed to have coffee without milk.

The dividing line between *açorda* and *migas* is slightly blurred sometimes and may depend only on local terminology, although *migas* tend to have a different texture and to be drier, looking sometimes like omelettes (either rolled up or flat).

Migas Ribatejo Style/Migas do Ribatejo

This dish has a rich texture, being made with that glorious, heavy, moist and crumbling maize bread which is so common in peasant homes in the Ribatejo, Minho, Trás-os-Montes and Alto Douro provinces.

12 oz (350 g) maize bread (p.57) | 2 cloves garlic, chopped
– or use the heaviest kind of | ¼ pint (150 ml) olive oil
wholemeal bread, medium | enough salted boiling water to
sliced | cover the bread

Place the slices of bread in a deep, roomy frying pan and cover with enough salted boiling water to absorb it. Boil gently for 5 minutes, stirring. Mix in the olive oil and the garlic, and shape the mixture like a roll, with the help of two wooden spoons or spatulas. Cook for a further 5 minutes, shaking the pan. The bread should become quite solid, like a rolled-up omelette with a golden crust. Serve as an accompaniment for fried fish or sausages.
Serves 4 to 6.

Migas Beira Litoral Style/Migas à moda da Beira Litoral

This *migas* is made with more substantial ingredients than most of the other *migas* recipes, the resulting dish being appropriate for wintery days. The actual origin of the recipe is the Lousã mountain, in the Beira region, where winters can be bitterly cold.

14 oz (400 g) maize bread (p.57) in little chunks
1 bunch sprouted turnip tops (see Ingredients, p.27) – about 1 lb (450 g) after discarding the tough parts of the vegetable

7 oz (200 g) cooked butterbeans, with their cooking liquid
¼ pint (150 ml) olive oil
2 cloves garlic, finely chopped

Cook the greens until tender. Have the beans boiling in their cooking liquid (enough to cover them). Fry the garlic in the oil. Keep everything very hot. In a warm tureen assemble alternate layers of beans, bread and greens. The first layer must be beans, and the top one greens. Pour the oil with the garlic over the surface and serve immediately, accompanying baked Portuguese sausages (*chouriço*) or pork chops, fried in processed lard and seasoned with chopped garlic and a dusting of paprika. The bean liquor should be just enough to soak the bread through.

If you cannot get or do not want the trouble of preparing maize bread, the heavier kind (organic), wholemeal bread can be substituted.
Serves 4 to 6.

Migas Beira Baixa Style/Migas à Beira Baixa

14 oz (400 g) stale bread, thinly sliced
2 oz (60 g) presunto (p.22), thinly sliced
3 oz (90 g) chouriço (p.23) sliced
2 cloves garlic, chopped

2 sprigs parsley, chopped
4 tablespoons olive oil
4–6 eggs fried in oil
1 teaspoon paprika
¾ pint (450 ml) salted boiling water

Boil the water with the seasoning (paprika, garlic and parsley). In a separate deep container assemble layers of bread, ham and sausage. Pour the seasoned water over this and leave it for an hour or so, to get completely moist. Put half the oil in a large frying-pan, warm it up and transfer the bread mixture to this, flattening it with a wooden spatula to look like a pizza. When golden underneath, turn it over (with the help of a plate which you use as a lid and then turn upside down, sliding the *migas*

again into the pan, where you have added the remaining oil).
Fry till golden and served topped with the fried eggs.
Serves 4 to 6.

Migas Alentejo Style/Migas Alentejanas

14 oz (400 g) loin of pork
3½ oz (100 g) fatty bacon
5 oz (150 g) chouriço (p.23)
2 large cloves garlic, chopped
1 coffeespoon paprika

14 oz (400 g) stale bread, thinly
sliced (see hints on bread to use
on p.62)
½ pint (300 ml) salted boiling
water

Cut the bacon and fry slowly until all the fat has been
extracted from it. Put the cracklings aside. In this fat fry the
garlic, the sausage and the meat, cut into 1 inch (2.5 cm) cubes.
Season with salt and the paprika, and keep turning the meat
until ready (10 to 15 minutes at the most). Put the meat aside,
keep warm and reserve the fat and juices. In a separate
container scald the bread with the water, and mash it, to
resemble mashed potato. Put the mixture in the frying pan
containing the fat and juices of the fried meat, and bring to the
heat. Fry while shaping the *migas* like rolled-up omelette. Serve
after it has acquired a golden crust, surrounded by the meat.
Serves 4.

Ensopados

Bread is also one of the ingredients in *ensopados* – which means
'soaked in'. *Ensopados* consist of wet stews where the excess
liquid is absorbed by the bread, which, in this case, serves the
purpose of a thickener.

    Ensopados are popular dishes in Portuguese homes, not so
much at restaurants. They can be prepared with either meat or
fish. I give here one example of each.

Kid Ensopado/Ensopado de Cabrito

ALENTEJO PROVINCES, BUT USED COUNTRYWIDE

2 lb (1 kg) kid meat (or very
tender lean lamb)
4 tablespoons olive oil
1 tablespoon processed lard
1 large onion, chopped
1 medium tomato, cleaned and
chopped
¼ pint (150 ml) white wine
1 tablespoon wine vinegar

½ teaspoon paprika
2 cloves garlic, chopped
1 bay leaf
¾ pint (450 ml) meat stock – it
can be prepared with cubes
4 thick slices of very good day-old
bread
salt and pepper

Prepare a marinade with the wine, vinegar, garlic, bay leaf, paprika, salt and pepper. Cut the meat into medium-sized pieces and allow them to marinate for two hours. In a roomy pot fry the onion in the fat and oil. Strain the meat and fry it until browned. Add the marinade, tomato and stock. Cover the pot and cook gently until the meat is tender. Correct seasonings and serve over the slices of bread, in individual plates, adding more bread if too wet.
Serves 4 to 6.

Variation
This recipe can be made using rabbit, hare or any other game, or veal.

Fish Ensopado/Ensopado de Peixe

THE ALGARVE

2 lb (1 kg) filleted fish (for example, monk fish/sea bass/ fresh cod)	3 tablespoons butter
	1 medium onion, chopped
	2 sprigs parsley, chopped
¼ pint (150 ml) white wine	3 yolks of eggs
1 tablespoon lemon juice	4–6 large slices of toasted bread
1 tablespoon olive oil	salt and pepper

Fry the onion in the butter and oil, until transparent. Add the cleaned fillets of fish, sprinkled with salt, and the wine. Cover and simmer until tender (about 15 minutes). Drain the fish and keep warm. Beat the egg yolks with the lemon juice and add to the juices in the pan, stirring very well. Boil gently, to thicken a little. Divide the toast between the plates and place the fish fillets on top of them. Cover with the sauce, sprinkle with the parsley and serve at once, with boiled, sauté or mashed potatoes.
Serves 4 to 6.

Dry Soups

These dishes should not really be classified as soups, and neither are they dry. The name has probably been given centuries ago and nobody I asked seems to know why. A dry soup is very much like a hotpot, but with the addition of bread. Dry soups are simple, wholesome peasant meals and can be adapted to use up left-overs.

Dry Soup Minho Style/Sopa Seca do Minho

14 oz (400 g) chicken
7 oz (200 g) lean beef
3½ oz (100 g) presunto (p.22)
3½ oz (100 g) chouriço (p.23)
3½ oz (100 g) bacon

1 medium-sized white cabbage,
  cut into large chunks
10 oz (300 g) stale white bread,
  sliced
2½ pints (1.8 l) salted water
1 sprig fresh mint

Simmer all the meat in the water until almost tender (start with the beef), then add the cabbage. Simmer again. When cooked, remove the meat from the liquid in order to cut it up. Transfer the soup to an ovenproof container. Add the meat, the chopped mint leaves and finally the bread. Press a little, to get the bread soaked into the liquid. Bake in a preheated oven at 190°C/375°F/Gas 5, top shelf, until the bread is golden brown (about 15 minutes).
Serves 4 to 6.

Variation
For a more substantial *sopa seca*, Minho people add 4 or 5 potatoes, 2 carrots, a medium onion and a turnip, all thickly sliced and cooked together with the meat and cabbage. These vegetables are then layered with the meat before covering with the bread. In this case, instead of mint use chopped parsley.

Garlic Dry Soup/Sopa Seca de Alho

ALTO ALENTEJO
This is really more like *açorda*, with the difference that it is cooked partly in the oven. This recipe is the simplest of all *sopas secas* but, even so, rich tasting and filling – an excellent peasant dish.

14 oz (400 g) stale bread (see
  hints on the bread to use, p.56)
3 cloves garlic, finely chopped
4 tablespoons olive oil

1 egg
1 coffeespoon paprika
1 pint (600 ml) boiling water
salt and pepper

Fry the garlic in the oil till golden. Add the paprika and the boiling water, salt and pepper to taste. Place in an ovenproof dish. Add the bread, press it in to soak well, and cover the top with the beaten egg. Bake on the middle shelf of a preheated oven (190°C/375°F/Gas 5) till golden brown (20–25 minutes). To complement the dish, serve fried, poached or scrambled eggs or fried fish.
Serves 4.

Salted Cod Dry Soup/Sopa Seca de Bacalhau

It would be strange if salted cod did not come into the dry soups as well. This recipe is very tasty (as is everything prepared with salted cod) and a good alternative to the dry soups made with meat. This would be a way of using left-over cod and chickpeas to advantage.

*12 oz (350 g) cooked salted cod
    (see p.31)*
12 oz (350 g) cooked chickpeas
8 oz (240 g) sliced stale bread
1 large onion, chopped
4 tablespoons olive oil
2 cloves garlic, finely chopped

2 sprigs parsley, chopped
*1 pint (600 ml) liquid (if you kept
    the water in which you cooked
    the cod, use this; if not, use
    seasoned boiling water)*
salt and pepper

Fry the onion, garlic and parsley in the oil, till golden. Use this mixture between layers of flaked cod, chickpeas and bread, assembled in a deep ovenproof dish. The top and bottom layers should be bread. Pour the boiling liquid over the mixture and bring to the middle shelf of an oven preheated to 190°C/375°F/Gas 5 until golden brown, about 20 minutes.
Serves 4 to 6.

Gaspachos

Gaspacho soup has become well known to visitors to Spain, where it is served quite often during the summer months (*gazpacho*, in Spanish). The Portuguese provinces of the Alentejo and Algarve have their own versions of this soup. The main difference is that in Portugal *gaspacho* is not reduced completely to a pulp, thus keeping the crunchy texture of some of the ingredients.

   Gaspachos are refreshing soups, very welcome on the hot summer days you get in both the Alentejo and the Algarve.

Gaspacho, Alentejo Style/Gaspacho Alentejano

*7 oz (200 g) day-old bread, diced
    very small*
*1½ pints (900 ml) salted iced
    water*
*2 cloves garlic, thoroughly
    crushed with some salt (use a
    pestle and mortar for this)*
2 tablespoons olive oil

2 tablespoons wine vinegar
*2 medium-sized ripe but firm
    tomatoes (peeled and seeded)*
½ medium-sized cucumber
1 small green pepper, cleaned
½ coffeespoon dry oregano
salt

Mash one of the tomatoes into a pulp and mix with the oregano, the crushed garlic, oil and vinegar, forming a purée. Put this into a tureen or serving bowl. Dice the remaining tomato very small, and the cucumber. Cut the pepper into matchsticks. Place all these vegetables in the tureen. Add the iced water. Taste for salt. (You may also like to add a little more vinegar.) Mix in the bread and serve while it is cold.
Serves 4 to 6.

Gaspacho Algarve Style/Gaspacho do Algarve

In the Algarve the ingredients for *gaspacho* are practically the same as in the Alentejo version, but the method of preparation is slightly different.

7 oz (200 g) day-old bread
1½ pints (900 ml) iced salted
   water
2 cloves garlic
2 tablespoons olive oil
2 tablespoons wine vinegar
½ medium-sized cucumber

2 medium-sized ripe tomatoes,
   peeled and seeded
1 medium-sized green or red
   pepper
½ coffeespoon dry oregano
salt

Clean the pepper, cut into pieces and liquidize, together with half the bread, the cleaned tomatoes, the garlic and some of the iced water. Prepare a tureen by rinsing it with very cold water. Place the prepared mixture into it. Add the remaining water, vinegar, oil and oregano, mixing well. Add the rest of the bread, cut into small pieces, and garnish the top with the cucumber, very thinly sliced. Dust with a little salt and serve at once.
Serves 4 to 6.

Bread Pies/Folares or Bolas

MOST INLAND PROVINCES, BUT ESPECIALLY THE NORTHERN ONES
Folares or *bolas* can be sweet or savoury, so I will give here the savoury versions, which can be translated as 'bread pies' and leave the sweet ones to the cakes section, pp.209-11.

Folares and *bolas* are made with a kind of bread dough enriched with many lavish additions. They are made for special occasions, mainly Easter, but this does not preclude serving them at any time, and lately they have become standard 'ready meal' fare in some good bakers. The difference between *folares* and *bolas* is minimal and depends only on regional terminology. I would recommend them as picnic-basket fillers, as they make a perfect out-of-doors meal, with a salad.

At summer fairs, all over Portugal, one can find stalls selling nothing but deliciously fragrant hot rolls filled with *chouriço* (baked inside them), which are small versions of bread pies.

DOUGH
1 lb (450 g) flour
½ oz (15 g) fresh yeast
2 tablespoons butter
3 large eggs

FILLING
5 oz (140 g) chouriço (p.23)
8 oz (225 g) smoked ham
(presunto or equivalent, p.22)

Crumble the yeast, add a small amount of tepid water and a pinch of salt and mix. Add the flour and combine thoroughly, adding drops of tepid water, until smooth. Cover and allow to rest for 6–8 minutes. Beat the eggs with the melted butter and mix with the dough until well blended. Mix in a little more flour if you find the dough too runny. Beat it very well until fluffy and airy. This dough should be considerably softer than plain bread dough. Butter a square 9 inch (23 cm) baking tin (or an oblong one of the same capacity). Divide the dough into three equal parts. Place one at the bottom and sides of the tin, cover with half the filling (sliced and with the *chouriço* free from the outer skin), then assemble another third of dough, cover with the remaining filling and finally cover the pie with the last piece of dough. Leave the tin in a warm place to rise, for 45–60 minutes, covering it with a cloth. Bake at 200°C/400°F/Gas 6 for 25–30 minutes or longer, until golden. Take out of the tin, brush with butter and leave the bread in a wire rack until it cools down.
Serves 6.

Variations
1 A good recipe of bread pie with game, comes from the Entre Douro and Minho provinces.

About 2 lb (1 kg) bread dough,
  made with wheat and rye
  flours, if possible
1 lb (450 g) rabbit meat (wild or
  tame)
1 large chicken leg
1 quail (or another chicken leg, if
  quail is unavailable)

7 oz (200 g) stewing veal
6–8 oz (175–225 g) chouriço
  (p.23)
3 oz (90 g) presunto (p.22)
1 large onion
4 tablespoons olive oil
salt and pepper

To prepare the filling, fry the chopped onion in the oil until golden. Add the meat, seasoning and just a small amount of water or stock, as necessary, and cook until tender over gentle heat. Check seasonings, bone the meat and cut it into bite-sized pieces. Set aside.

Generously grease a deep baking tin 12 × 12 inches (30.5 × 30.5 cm). Spread ⅔ of the bread dough over the bottom and up the sides of the tin, leaving a little over the rim, all round. Fill the dough case with the meat and its juices (which should be reduced, if too abundant). Place the rest of the dough on top, bringing the borders over this lid, to make sure all the meat juices remain inside. Bake an hour later, in a preheated oven (210°C/425°F/Gas 7) and reduce to 190°C/375°F/Gas 5 once the pie is inside the oven. It will be ready when nicely browned (25–30 minutes). Brush the top with butter to make it shiny, when ready, and leave to cool on wire rack. It is equally good hot or cold.

Serves 6.

2 Bread pies can be varied just by ringing the changes with the fillings, providing the stew used is rich and well seasoned. The bread dough can also be varied, according to taste. A good basic dough for this purpose can be made with the following:

1 lb (450 g) flour   *1 teaspoon salt*
½ oz (15 g) fresh yeast   *3 oz (90 g) butter or margarine*

Fish, Shellfish and Seafood

Thousands of years ago fish was one of the main foods of the peoples settled along the coast of the land that would become Portugal. This is still true today, although the Portuguese fishing-fleet is in dire need of renewal just now and does not cope with demand. The small boats operating now cannot venture too far and, in spite of the great variety and abundance of fish that can be found near the coast, the amount caught is not nearly enough. Even so, there is really plenty of variety for all the dishes that are such an important and typical part of the Portuguese diet.

Salted cod plays a large role in Portuguese cookery (see p.72). Some of the cheapest fish is also some of the tastiest (such as sardines and *carapaus* – horse mackerel). Hake (a national love) is always prominent, and so is a long (more than a yard long), narrow fish called *peixe espada*, scabbard fish, which is silvery, has no scales and is beautiful when grilled or fried, especially the one caught off Sesimbra, south of Lisbon. There are many splendid varieties of sea bass and sea bream, as well as turbot, skate, dogfish, sole, dabs, conger eel, other eels, whiting, mullet, swordfish and many others.

One of the most typical sights in towns used to be the fishwives (*varinas*) selling fresh fish in the streets. One can still see a few, balancing their wares in wide, shallow baskets on their heads, stopping here and there, lowering them to the ground to attend customers, then lifting them up again and going up another street, loudly crying, '*Quem quer carapau fresco?*' ('Who wants fresh mackerel?'). To help balance the weight and to give a base to it, the basket rests on a kind of circular pad, the approximate diameter of the top of the carrier's head, either especially made or improvised with a rolled-up piece of cloth.

Much more difficult than carrying fish is the carrying, in the same fashion, of large clay containers full of water, like tall amphora, which peasant women seem to be able to hold without apparent difficulty, due to years of practice since they were children. (This was – and in remote areas still is – a very common sight in places where water is scarce or there is no plumbing.) They do more balancing acts carrying loads of wood or anything that can be tied into a bundle or put into a large basket. With their erect carriage, the women look beautifully statuesque when performing this humble and, for them, totally ordinary task.

One of the most common ways of eating fish all over Portugal is simply fried and served with tomato rice and/or a lettuce salad. Lisbon people, funnily enough, are nicknamed *alfacinhas* (much as those from Oporto are known as tripe-eaters). *Alfacinha* is a small lettuce, so one would infer that the love of lettuce, especially with fried fish, gave rise to this name.

Salted Cod Dishes

Traditional Portuguese cookery includes scores of salted cod recipes. I am going to include only a few which exemplify a range of dishes well loved by most Portuguese people, but one could, in fact, fill a whole book with only salted cod recipes. See Ingredients, p.19, for more details on this fascinating item and consult the Cooking Methods, p.31, in order to dispel any mysteries about cooking it.

Christmas Eve Cod (Cod with Everything)/
Bacalhau de Consoada (Bacalhau com Todos)

ENTRE DOURO AND MINHO PROVINCES BUT USED IN MANY OTHER REGIONS

For Christmas Eve supper, make abundant quantities of 'Cod with Everything'.

Boiled salted cod (soaked previously, as usual – see p.31), having, of course, chosen the best middle slices

Potatoes, boiled in their skins and peeled whilst still hot
Cabbage. If possible, use the so-called typical Portuguese cabbage, a
variety which is not found easily outside Portugal but which can be
substituted by any good cabbage of one's choice.
Hard-boiled eggs

All these items must be cooked at the last minute, before serving, so as to be brought to the table at their best. They are served on big platters, separately.

Oil and vinegar from the cruet-stand are the usual table seasonings for this kind of dish, together with chopped garlic salt and pepper.

For this occasion some people prepare a sauce with olive oil:

3 tablespoons olive oil per person
1 clove garlic per person
1 teaspoon wine vinegar per person

Bring the oil and garlic to the boil, remove from the heat, add the vinegar, beat well and serve in sauceboat.

Any cod, potatoes and so on left over from this meal (and, of course, this is only one of various courses on Christmas Eve!) are reheated the following day and served as a starter, before the turkey.

To reheat, use 1½ tablespoons olive oil and ½ clove garlic per person. Fry gently until the garlic is golden. Add the left-over cod (flaked and free from bones and skin), the potatoes and cabbage, all cut in small pieces, and mix with the oil. Turn carefully to reheat through. Serve at once.

Note: Although for Christmas Eve the chosen vegetable will be cabbage, 'cod with everything' is also served with sprouted turnip-tops when these are in season (see p.27)

Salt Cod Gomes de Sá Fashion/Bacalhau à Gomes de Sá

OPORTO
When there are many variations to a popular dish, the most elaborate one is generally the original. This is no exception as far as Gomes de Sá cod is concerned. It is said that a salt-cod merchant by that name, who lived in Oporto, created it first. The recipe given below is, according to the experts, the real one, having been carefully passed on by Gomes de Sá's descendants (there is still a generation of the family today). The secret of the real recipe resides in the use of milk, to soften the cod.

1 lb (450 g) salted cod, from the
  thick middle slices
1½ lb (675 g) potatoes (boiled in
  their skins, then peeled and
  sliced)
3–4 hard-boiled eggs
½ pint (300 ml) hot milk

2 medium onions, sliced
2 cloves garlic, finely chopped
4 fluid oz (120 ml) olive oil
2 sprigs parsley, chopped
salt and pepper
20 black olives, for garnishing

Soak the cod really well for 24 hours, changing the water various times. Place it in a pan with enough boiling water to cover it. Do not bring to the boil. Leave it soaking in the boiling water for 30 minutes. Put a thick cloth over the pan, to keep it hot. Then drain the cod; skin and bone it. Flake it carefully with your fingers, and put the pieces into a deep dish, pouring the hot milk over. Leave to soak for 2 hours. Put the oil, onions and garlic in a large pan and fry until golden. Add the sliced potatoes and the flaked cod (having drained off the milk). Taste for salt, and sprinkle with pepper. Heat the whole mixture in the oil, over a low flame, turning it now and then, without actually allowing it to fry. Transfer it to a fireproof dish (or an earthenware one, if possible) and bake for 15 minutes, top shelf, in a preheated oven (210°/425°F/Gas 7). Serve at once, garnished with the sliced boiled eggs, olives and chopped parsley.
Serves 4 to 6.

Salted Cod Brás Fashion/Bacalhau à Brás

ESTREMADURA PROVINCE
It is not quite known who Brás was but the dish he invented is certainly very tasty and popular in most Portuguese restaurants.

1¼ lb (560 g) potatoes
12–14 oz (350–400 g) salted cod,
  thoroughly soaked
5 eggs
2 cloves garlic

1 tablespoon chopped parsley
salt (if needed) and pepper
oil for frying (about ½ pint/300
  ml)

Prepare the cod as usual (p.31). Skin and bone and wash again (without cooking it). Pull it into small strips, using your fingers. Pat the raw cod dry with a cloth or kitchen paper. Peel the potatoes and cut them as for very small chips (like short lengths of spaghetti). In a roomy frying pan warm up the oil, fry the cloves of garlic (to transfer their taste to the oil, then discard them) and fry the potatoes slowly, turning them to cook

through but without browning. Drain and set aside. Slowly
sauté the pieces of cod in the same oil, for about 5 minutes. Add
the potatoes to the pan and mix both. Taste for salt (you may
not need any). Sprinkle with a little pepper and mix in the
beaten eggs with a large fork, so the mixture does not set like
an omelette but stays rather like scrambled eggs. When the egg
is set (try not to overcook), remove the pan from the heat at
once. Sprinkle with the parsley and serve with a side salad and
olives.
Serves 4 to 6.

Variation
Use the same recipe but add a large onion thinly sliced and
fried in the oil until transparent, mixing it with the other
ingredients before adding the eggs.

Boiled Cod and Chickpeas/Meia-Desfeita com Grão

ESTREMADURA PROVINCE
A rich, heavy and delicious luncheon dish, rightly famous all
over the Estremadura province. In Lisbon there used to be
various small restaurants specializing in this dish. They do not,
alas, seem to have survived but the dish is still available at
many places and is easy enough to prepare at home as well.

*12 oz (350 g) best salted cod, from
the middle thick slices
12 oz (350 g) chickpeas
2-3 hard-boiled eggs, sliced
1 medium onion, finely chopped*

*1 clove garlic, finely chopped
3 stalks parsley, chopped
¼ pint (150 ml) olive oil
1 tablespoon wine vinegar
salt and pepper*

Soak the cod for 24 hours or longer (assuming the slices are
thick) in cold water, changing it several times. Soak the
chickpeas separately, overnight. Start cooking the chickpeas
first (as they take 1½-2 hours if not done in the pressure
cooker, which could reduce the cooking time to 25–30 minutes)
in enough boiling water and salt. Scale and boil the cod in
enough water to cover it, until tender (20-25 minutes,
depending on thickness). Do not add salt but check at the end
whether it needs any, taking into account that you have soaked
it long enough. Prepare the garnish, mixing the onion, garlic
and parsley, all very finely chopped. In a separate bowl, mix
the oil and vinegar. For serving, place the cod at the bottom of a
deep serving dish and cover it with the cooked and drained
chickpeas. Pour the oil mixture all over this, sprinkle the

onion-garlic-parsley garnish on top and decorate with the
sliced boiled eggs.
Serves 4 to 6

Salted Cod Cakes/Pasteis de Bacalhau

'She went home to eat fishcakes. Every day, both at dinner and
supper, she would eat fishcakes, made with salted cod.'
                    Camilo Castelo Branco, *Lamego Nights (Noites de Lamego)*

Here is a great Portuguese favourite. Although their real origin
is the north, cod cakes became so popular that they were
adopted as a truly 'national speciality'. Cod cakes are ideal fare
for snacks (hot or cold) and feature at every Portuguese
function, from the most sophisticated to the humblest. If there
is anything really engrained in the Portuguese palate, loved by
everyone, this is it. Snobs may be somewhat derogatory about
cod cakes, afraid of admitting that they too love this
'poor-man's dish', but do not believe them. They will probably
eat them all the same, when nobody is looking.

Cod cakes are sold at delicatessen, patisseries, road-side
cafés, tavernas – everywhere in Portugal. If you cannot find or
do not like salted cod, they are also very nice made with fresh
cod.

10 oz (280 g) thick salted cod (soaked as usual, see p.31)	*2 tablespoons finely chopped parsley*
14 oz (400 g) floury potatoes	*3 eggs*
1 small onion, very finely chopped	*oil for frying*

Prepare the cod, soaking it and changing the water several
times (see p.31). Boil the potatoes (in their skins, for preference,
so they do not absorb water); peel them and mash well or sieve.
Meantime, simmer the cod in enough boiling water to cover it,
until tender (about 20–25 minutes, depending on thickness).
Drain, discard the skin and bones and flake it as much as you
can with your fingers, then with a fork, to reduce it to threads.
(The proper way of doing this is to place the flaked cod inside a
clean cloth, fold it and squeeze and pound the contents of the
cloth with your fists. In this way you will have mashed cod.)
Mix this mass with the mashed potatoes and add the eggs, one
by one, and the onion and parsley. Taste for salt but you may
not need to add any, as the cod itself retains enough saltiness,
in spite of being soaked and boiled. (Avoid having cod cakes
which are too salty). The mixture should be quite stiff, enabling

a spoon to stand up in it. If you find it excessively dry, add one or two tablespoons of milk. Allow this to cool completely before deep frying, as you would deep fry fish or chips. With two tablespoons, shape the fishcakes like large eggs and place in the hot oil, turning them three or four times to get nicely browned all over. As they fry, lift them with a big fork or slotted spoon and place in kitchen paper, to absorb excess fat. Go on moulding and frying until you use up the mixture. Serve hot (with cod rice, p.78, or tomato rice, p.146, and/or salad), or cold with salad, or simply on their own or with olives. Delicious.

Makes 24 to 30 fishcakes.

Salted Cod with Cheese/Bacalhau com Queijo

LISBON AREA
An everyday dish suitable for lunch.

12 oz (350 g) salted cod, soaked –	*4 oz (110 g) grated cheese,*
see p.31	*Cheddar type*
3 eggs, separated	*½ pint (300 ml) tomato sauce*
1½ lb (675 g) potatoes	*(p.135)*
3 tablespoons flour	*oil for frying*
	salt

Prepare the cod as usual and boil it with the potatoes. Do not add any salt at this stage. Remove from heat and drain. Slice the potatoes and break the cod into little pieces, discarding skin and bones. Make a batter with the flour, a little salt, 4 tablespoons water and the yolks. Beat well. In a separate bowl whip the whites and add to the batter. Divide this into two portions. In one mix the sliced potatoes and in the other the pieces of cod. Fry spoonfuls of each mixture (separately) until golden. Assemble layers of both fried cakes in a fireproof dish and cover with the tomato sauce. Sprinkle the grated cheese on top. Bake for 15 minutes (200°C/400°F/Gas 6) on top shelf, to melt the cheese and reheat the dish, or place under the grill. Serve with a crisp salad.

Serves 6.

Salted Cod Pie/Empadão de Bacalhau

LISBON AREA
This recipe is simplicity itself, and the taste is very mild, good for those who do not appreciate salted cod at its strongest. It is a useful dish for lunch when you have guests and can also be

used for the buffet party table (in which case you might want to double the quantities).

12 oz (350 g) salted cod, soaked etc (see p.31)	2 large eggs, beaten
1½ lb (675 g) potatoes	2 oz (60 g) grated cheese (Cheddar type)
1 clove garlic, finely chopped	1 tablespoon butter
1 medium-sized onion, finely chopped	

Prepare the cod as usual, and clean it of bones and skin. Boil the cod with the potatoes (without adding salt) until tender. Drain. Mash both together. Cool the mixture. Add the onion, garlic and eggs. Now taste for salt. Transfer the mixture to a fireproof greased dish. Dot with the butter and sprinkle with the cheese. Bake in preheated oven (210°C/425°F/Gas 7) on top shelf until golden (10–15 minutes). Do not overcook or it will dry too much. Serve with salad and olives.
Serves 6.

Salt Cod Rice/Arroz de Bacalhau

This is simple fare indeed, but really tasty and wholesome. It can be served on its own (maybe with a side salad and/or black olives) following a soup, for a splendid everyday lunch, or as an accompaniment to salted cod cakes (p.76). Traditional books indicate this dish as originating from the northern coastal provinces but it is really a national dish, much loved by everyone. The quantities may vary, according to whether it will be served on its own or as an accompaniment. Amounts given here will be suitable for the latter. Otherwise, they can just be doubled.

7 oz (200 g) rice	2 tablespoons olive oil
4 oz (110 g) salted cod (soaked for 6–7 hours beforehand)	2 sprigs parsley, chopped bay leaf
2 medium tomatoes, peeled, seeded and chopped	a little salt water – 2½ times the volume of rice
1 medium onion, chopped	

Put the oil in a saucepan and make a *refogado* (p.31) with the onion, tomatoes and parsley. When soft, add the cod (free from bones and skin, and flaked or made into small strips, by hand), toss around, add the water. When boiling, add the rice and the bay leaf and cover. Simmer until the rice and cod are tender (25–30 minutes). Taste for salt, add a very small amount of

pepper (optional) and serve at once. This rice should ideally be on the wet side.
Serves 4 to 6.

Sardines

Fresh sardines can be cooked in various ways, apart from the classic grilling. They can be stewed (see p.82) and fried. To fry, scale, gut and wash the sardines. Salt them (see p.32) and leave for an hour. Wash again, pat dry with a cloth or kitchen paper. Dip each sardine in flour (and shake afterwards) and deep fry as for any other fish, remembering that they do cook very quickly. When nicely golden, drain and place on kitchen paper, to absorb excess fat. Serve with salad and boiled potatoes or tomato rice (p.146). The head of the fish is left on for a better appearance.

Very small sardines, called *petingas* in Portugal, can be treated the same as whitebait and fried as above (without gutting) or using another Portuguese style: frying them in batter four or five together, until golden. These crisp, small, pancake-like sardine fritters are delicious hot or cold as a snack or with a salad as a starter dish.

Canned sardines are served in Portugal as appetizers (in either their oil or tomato version) at the *hors-d'œuvres* table. As a meal in themselves, they can be served with boiled potatoes, cooked greens or salad and olives. Mashed up with butter they make a delicious paste for spreading (p.14).

Charcoal Grilled Sardines/Sardinhas Assadas

Apart from the ubiquitous salt cod, fresh sardines are, of course, one of Portugal's national dishes *par excellence* and (in their charcoal-grilled version) what foreign palates take most readily to, when visiting Portugal. The characteristic smell of grilled sardines can be detected everywhere, during the summer months, when tonnes of them are consumed in open-air restaurants, tavernas, sea-side cafés, funfairs and, of course, private homes. It would be impossible to disguise this mouthwatering smell, which immediately conjures up a superb meal out of doors. Fortunately sardines are at their best precisely during the summer months. The quantities are tricky to calculate, because it is really easy to go on eating sardines without realizing how many one has already had. It also depends on their size. But let us say that for 4 people we need:

16–24 medium-sized fresh
   sardines
1½–2 lb (675 g–1 kg) boiled
   potatoes
8 medium tomatoes (rather firm,
   slightly under-ripe), sliced

2 medium onions, sliced
4 green peppers (optional)
seasoning for the salad (oil,
   vinegar, salt and pepper)

An essential requirement for this dish is that the sardines be impeccably fresh. They can, of course, be bought from a fishmonger who has them standing on ice, but on no account must they be soft or limp. Wash the sardines (do not scale, gut or behead them) leaving them whole, so as to keep their flesh moist whilst grilling (gutting and scaling them would have the effect of drying them too much). Sprinkle the sardines with sea salt and leave for an hour or so (see p.32) on a wooden board or in a large container. Wash them again and pat dry with a clean cloth or kitchen paper. Grill on charcoal, using a grid, barbecue style, in the open air, preferably. Failing this, use any ordinary grill, though this does not give the same results as the charcoal. While the fish is grilling (you have to do it in batches and keep warm those already done), boil the potatoes and prepare the salad. If using peppers, you must also prepare them, either raw, with the other salad ingredients, or Portuguese style – that is, grilled, the classic accompaniment for sardines, together with the salad and the potatoes.

To prepare the peppers, first wash them, pat dry with kitchen paper and place under the grill, keeping them whole. Turn them around until the skin becomes burnt and blistered, by which time they are ready. Carefully peel all burnt skin and cut the flesh into strips, discarding the centre of the peppers. Keep in a side dish.

Make a salad with the tomatoes and onions, seasoning to your taste, and serve also in a side dish. Drain the potatoes and put them in a separate container. The sardines must be served on a very large warm platter and put in the middle of the table, for the great feast.

To ensure that everything is ready at the same time and served at once, it is customary to have two people engaged in the cooking, or at least to count on a spare pair of hands at some stage. One person attends to the grilling and turning of the fish and keeps the batches flowing, giving undivided attention to this task, and the other does the peppers, salad and potatoes.

Fish Stews/Caldeiradas

Some of the tastiest and best-known Portuguese dishes come under the description of *caldeiradas* – that is, a kind of fish stew or chowder, quite wet (hence the etymology of the word, which derives from *caldo* – broth). They are traditionally served at seaside places, since the fish must ideally have just been caught. Obviously fishermen are the best cooks of *caldeiradas*, and some have established simple restaurants, which are always overflowing with people. At some of them, one must wait for the *caldeirada* to be cooked there and then, with the latest catch just brought in by a colourful small boat, handled by one or two men.

Fishing in Portugal can still be a one-man affair, but generally a few more join in the venture, to provide a living for their families. When the boats are not at sea, fishermen's wives help with mending the nets while their men repair and clean the boats, gaily decorated in vivid colours and with a large eye painted on the prow, to ward off evil.

There are famous *caldeiradas* in the north, centre and south of the country, varying according to the kind of fish and seasonings used. But basically *caldeiradas* are made in similar fashion, and all of them are magnificent, filling and not difficult to prepare. The idea with *caldeirada* is to serve more fish than potato (if potato is used at all), so don't be surprised by the seemingly imbalanced quantities in the list of ingredients.

As one might expect, salt cod can also be cooked *caldeirada* style, in which case it takes the name *bacalhau guisado* (salt cod stew). The procedure is the same as for the recipes below, with flaked cod added to the ingredients in layers and simmered for 25 minutes. Do not add salt, as the cod will have enough, in spite of having been soaked previously.

Eel Stew, Aveiro Style/Caldeirada de Enguias de Aveiro

Eels are very good and plentiful in and around the picturesque northern town of Aveiro (the Portuguese Venice, so called because of its canal). Aveiro is surrounded by saltflats, lagoons and beaches. It has good hotels and restaurants, some of them well known for their own version of *caldeirada de enguias*, followed by the local dessert, *ovos moles* (soft eggs), a very delicate, rich and sweet confection (see pp.152–3), relished by the Portuguese.

2 lb (1 kg) very fresh eels (they
   should be live ones, if you can
   bear cutting them up)
2 medium onions, sliced
1 lb (450 g) potatoes, peeled and
   cut into thin slices
1 clove garlic, finely sliced

4 fluid oz (120 ml) dry white wine
2 fluid oz (60 ml) olive oil
1 oz (30 g) lard
2 sprigs parsley, chopped
1 bay leaf
1 teaspoon powdered saffron
salt and pepper

In a large saucepan or, better still, an earthenware pot, place
the wine, the fat and oil, a little salt, the other seasonings and
then the potatoes and onions, in alternate layers. Barely cover
with boiling water and simmer for 12–15 minutes, shaking the
pot occasionally, to prevent sticking. In the meantime, prepare
the fish, cleaning it carefully and cutting into 2 inch (5 cm)
lengths. Place the fish on top of the parboiled potatoes, sprinkle
with some more salt and add some water if, at this stage, you
think it is needed, as the stew must be kept quite wet, like a
thick soup. Simmer for a further 10–12 minutes, until
everything is tender. Taste for salt. Take the pan to the table
and serve immediately, with chunks of bread.

If there is any liquid left over, strain it and use it as a fish
soup, adding some fried cubes of bread or a little boiled rice.
Serves 4 to 6

Sardine Stew/Caldeirada de Sardinhas

The same as before, substituting fresh sardines for the eels. The
sardines must be scaled, beheaded, gutted, and left whole, if
small, or cut into halves if medium or large. With the sardine
stew use one teaspoon of paprika, instead of the saffron.

Variation
Omit the wine and use three medium-ripe tomatoes (seeded,
peeled and coarsely chopped), placing them between the layers
of onion and potatoes.

Rich Fish Stew/Caldeirada Rica or Caldeirada à Fragateira

LISBON AREA
The principle is still the same as for the previous versions of
caldeirada, but in this case the fish must be of various kinds
(hence the title 'rich'), bringing a variety of flavour and texture
to this super dish. 6–8 different kinds of fish are normally used
but, if this doesn't seem practical, try to use at least three or

four, knowing, however, that the more variety, the better. Use, for example, conger eel, monk fish, sea bass, fresh sardines, ray, eels, skate, squid. Add a few prawns, if you like. The fish must be of the firm flesh kind and, this being a 'rich' stew, it contains a still higher proportion of fish than other recipes.

3 lb (1.45 kg) mixed fish (in more or less equal amounts, to add up to the given total)
1½ lb (675 g) ripe tomatoes, cleaned and chopped
4 medium onions, thinly sliced
1 lb (450 g) potatoes, peeled and very thinly sliced
2 cloves garlic, sliced
4 fluid oz (120 ml) olive oil

1 oz (30 g) lard
3 sprigs parsley, chopped
1 sprig fresh coriander, chopped
2 bay leaves
1 chilli
1 green pepper, cleaned and chopped (optional)
3 tablespoons dry white wine, or 1 tablespoon wine vinegar
salt and pepper

Start by cleaning and preparing the fish, cutting it into pieces, according to variety. Do not cut the pieces too small (1½–2 inches/3.5–5 cm will do). Have all the other ingredients prepared and at hand.

Use a roomy saucepan with a thick base, to prevent sticking. Put half the oil in first and assemble alternate layers, starting with the onions, then tomatoes, potatoes, fish, sprinklings of salt and seasonings, and so on, leaving the most fragile fish for the top layer. Sprinkle a bit more salt, add the wine and the rest of the oil, and enough water to barely cover. Bring to the boil, then reduce to simmering, to avoid burning. Do not stir but merely shake the pan now and then. Cook for 25 minutes. The potatoes must be thinly sliced, to make sure they will be tender. Serve in the same pan, after trying for salt.

You will have a good deal of delicious liquid leftover. Strain it and use as a soup, as indicated for the eel stew, or use it as a stock for your own version of fish soup.
Serves 6.

Variations
Apart from those already indicated, there are many more variations of *caldeiradas*, made just by adding or omitting parsley, fresh coriander, tomatoes, paprika, peppers and wine (or a little vinegar instead of wine), and varying the fish. Another version does not include potatoes at all: the fish stew is served over thick slices of good stale bread, which must be placed on the plate, before pouring the stew on top of it. The bread may be fried, if wanted.

Other Fish Dishes

'Hake with Everything'/Pescada com todos

LISBON AREA, BUT EATEN COUNTRYWIDE

Hake is one of the most popular fish in Portugal – and one which has gone up in price considerably in the last few years, except in its frozen form. It is a fine sea fish with white, delicate flesh, suitable for poaching, frying and filleting. It can be obtained in most countries, but fresh cod can be substituted, or haddock, large whiting or any other fish which will poach well.

'Hake with Everything' is the simplest fish dish there is, and it makes an excellent and nourishing lunch (somehow it does not seem right in the evening). All restaurants in Portugal serve it, as well as every household.

The 'everything' is made up of hard-boiled eggs, boiled potatoes and greens in season (cabbage, broccoli, cauliflower, green beans or spring greens, and add a few carrots if you like). The meal is presented in a large serving dish, with a saucer full of black olives by the side and cruet-stand containing olive oil and wine vinegar. If you prefer, you can season the dish with a little melted butter or simply serve it on its own, as I do. But it can also be enriched with a nice-looking and tasty dressing called *molho vilão*, p.136.

4 good pieces of fish	*4 small onions*
8 medium potatoes	*greens in season*
4 eggs	

Clean and salt the fish (see Methods, p.31) an hour before cooking, to allow the salt to penetrate the flesh. Wash and cook it in just slightly salted boiling water (remember the fish has already been seasoned). Use enough water to cover the fish. Cook for about 10 minutes, taking care that it is cooked but not overdone. In a separate pan boil the potatoes and the greens, and in another boil the eggs, for 10 minutes. When everything is ready, place the drained ingredients in a large serving dish and serve immediately.

You can boil the potatoes in their jackets and peel them after cooking, in which case they should be cooked on their own. *Serves 4.*

Note: In the same way as you prepare 'Hake with Everything', you can also produce 'Cod with Everything' – see p.72 for its special Christmas Version. With hake, salted cod or any other poached fish, the Portuguese will choose *grelos* (sprouted turnip-tops; see Ingredients, p.27) when they are in season.

Baked Fish/Peixe Assado

For this dish, much appreciated in Portuguese households, the fish should be on the big side and cooked whole (after gutting and cleaning but leaving the head on). One can, of course, opt for thick slices of fish instead of a whole one, if not available in the right size. Sea bream and sea bass, turbot or even fresh cod would be the best choice. Plaice, sole and any oily fish would not be suitable.

2 lb (1 kg) fish	*¼ teaspoon paprika*
6 tablespoons white wine	*1 teaspoon lemon juice*
6 tablespoons water	*3 tablespoons olive oil*
1 medium onion, chopped	*1 tablespoon melted lard*
2 sprigs parsley, chopped	*salt and pepper*
1 clove garlic, finely chopped	

Scale and gut the fish (leaving its head on, for better appearance), or use thick slices of fish. Salt in the usual way (see p.32). About an hour later wash and drain the fish and pat dry in kitchen paper. Give it a few cuts across the thickest part. Put it in an oiled fireproof dish and sprinkle it all over with the solid seasonings, finely chopped. Mix in a bowl all the liquid seasonings (and fat and oil) and pour this mixture onto the fish. Bake at 190°C/375°F/Gas 5 for 35–40 minutes, basting 2 or 3 times. If the fish is not very thick, or if you used sliced fish, about 30 minutes baking will probably be enough, or it might get too dry. Test with skewer or fork. Serve at once with boiled or mashed potatoes, with the fish juices. Or you can put some parboiled potatoes around the fish at the beginning, dotting them with butter. Turn them over when basting the fish.
Serves 4.

Variation
Some families prefer a few tomatoes, peeled and chopped over the fish, instead of using water.

Grilled Red Mullet Setúbal Fashion/
Salmonetes Grelhados

Red mullet is very common in the Setúbal fishing area (south of Lisbon), where they seem to be at their best. Perhaps the Romans who lived on the beautiful Troia peninsula, in Setúbal's estuary, knew this, for some of the many remains there (although excavations have not been extensive) reveal that they used the site as a residential area and turned it into an important fishing centre in the first to fourth centuries, producing *garum* paste – a mixture of fish, oysters, roe and crabs, which must be the precursor of our modern 'spreads'.

2 red mullet per person (or according to size)
1 tablespoon butter for each fish
1 lemon in wedges for garnishing

SAUCE:
3 oz (90 g) butter   *1 tablespoon lemon juice*
the livers of the fish   *3 sprigs parsley, chopped*
salt and pepper

Clean the fish (leaving the heads on) and salt it for an hour (see p.32). Wash and pat dry in kitchen paper. Grill under a gentle flame, brushing with the butter and turning once or twice until done (6–8 minutes each side). Prepare a sauce with the mashed livers (if available) simmered for 3–4 minutes in 6 tablespoons of water. Add the butter, the juices from the grilling pan, lemon juice, salt and pepper. Sieve, to obtain a smooth sauce, taste for seasoning, simmer again for a minute to reheat and add the parsley. Pour this sauce over the fish. If livers are not available, the sauce will consist only of the melted butter with lemon juice and parsley. Serve with boiled potatoes and garnish with lemon wedges.

Variation
The fish can be half grilled first and then finished in the oven (190°C/375°F/Gas 5) for just a few minutes, moistening it with 1–2 tablespoons of water and melted butter to prevent drying.

Cold Trout, Beira Alta Style/Trutas Abafadas

This dish is served cold and is therefore suitable for a summer menu. Trouts abound in the northern rivers and, when prepared with this kind of marinade, last for at least two days. In fact, they are better served 24 or 48 hours after cooking.

1 trout per person
2 tablespoons olive oil
1 tablespoon wine vinegar } *per trout*
2 tablespoons water
2 cloves garlic, chopped   *¼ coffeespoon nutmeg*
1 bay leaf   *salt and pepper*
3 sprigs parsley, chopped

Mix the oil, water and vinegar in a fish kettle or large pan and bring to the boil. Add all the seasonings and the fish (gutted, scaled and washed). Cover and cook until tender (10–12 minutes). Take off the heat, lift the fish carefully and set aside, in a deep serving dish. When cold, cover the fish with the strained cooking liquor and keep until the following day, at least. Serve cold, with potatoes boiled in their skins and peeled.

Tuna Steaks/Bifes de Atum

THE ALGARVE
Tuna is the one 'big' fish caught off the Algarve coast and one of the riches of that province. Apart from eating it fresh, the Algarveans have a flourishing tuna-canning industry, providing for the whole country and export. The thrills of catching tuna have led to organized tourist tuna fishing.

1½ lb (675 g) filleted fresh tuna (or halibut, if tuna is not available)
1 large onion, chopped
2 cloves garlic, chopped

4 oz (110 g) lard or a mixture of butter and lard
3 tablespoons chopped parsley
salt and pepper
lemon wedges for garnishing

Melt the fat and add the fish fillets, alternating them in layers with the onion and other seasonings. Cover and cook very gently for 15 minutes or until tender, turning the fish once, with great care. Add water only if absolutely necessary. Shake the pan now and then. Bring to the table in the same pot, garnished with lemon wedges and a side dish of boiled or fried potatoes. *Serves 4.*

Lampreys

The lamprey is a cyclostome (it is a fish with a fixed open mouth), quite abundant in the Minho river and in other northern rivers, such as the Dão. Lampreys are long, slippery (without scales) and cylindrical, not unlike eels, but larger.

Lampreys deposit their eggs in the rivers, and after spawning they die. From these eggs tiny larvae eventually emerge, choosing the mud as their habitat for a period lasting several years, until they are ready to travel down the river, all the while growing and feeding on the blood of other fish, which they suck with their specially equipped mouths. When they feel the call to the great adventure of mating, they take to the sea. Later they travel back, their destiny almost fulfilled. But man has other ideas, and many lampreys are caught before spawning, just as they have returned to the river. It is then that they are at their best, of course. But, to prolong the 'season', fishermen also catch lampreys when they are on their way down the river, before reaching the Atlantic. These lampreys are obviously smaller and less tasty than their fully grown, sea-travelled counterparts, but good enough to satisfy demand in Minho households and good restaurants in the bigger cities up and down the country. Lent is the time for eating fish, and luckily it coincides with the return of fat lampreys to the river.

Lamprey is considered a great delicacy, and in past centuries English kings and the nobility were very partial to its exquisite flesh. In fact England's King Henry I (1100–1135) is best known for having died of 'a surfeit of lampreys'.

The difficulty about this fish is that it must still be alive, when bought, just like its lesser cousin, the eel. And due to its being very viscous and slippery, it must be scraped and laboriously cleaned before further preparation. The best way to kill and clean a lamprey is to dip it, whilst still alive, in boiling water, just for a few seconds. This should kill it. Then comes the operation of scraping and washing in plenty of cold water. The next step is the gutting. The problem with this is that many recipes (indeed, most of them) call for the blood of the poor beast, and in order to collect it without getting any of the innards inside the container, which would spoil the blood, it is necessary to be very cautious. First, behead the lamprey, then proceed to slit it along its various orifices, pulling the innards in one go, without breaking them. In the meantime the blood is being collected inside a bowl containing wine, to prevent its coagulating. Wash the fish under the tap and it will be ready for cutting, according to whatever recipe you choose.

Lamprey Rice/Arroz de Lampreia

MINHO AND DOURO LITORAL PROVINCES
One of the favourite ways of serving lamprey is with rice, though this recipe could also be served with a different accompaniment.

1 medium lamprey, weighing approx. 2 lb (1 kg)
½ pint (300 ml) red wine
3 oz (90 g) medium-fat bacon, chopped
1 oz (30 g) butter
4 tablespoons olive oil

2 cloves garlic, chopped
bay leaf
1 medium onion, chopped
3 sprigs parsley, chopped
1 tablespoon lemon juice
salt and pepper

12 oz (350 g) rice or 2 thick slices of fried bread per person

Prepare the lamprey as indicated above. The blood must be kept in a container, mixed with a quarter of the wine. Discard the head and cut the fish into pieces about 2 inches (5 cm) long, placing them in a bowl containing a marinade prepared with the remaining wine, garlic, bay leaf, parsley, salt, pepper and lemon juice. Turn the fish several times, to absorb the flavours and set aside for an hour or a little longer.

In a pot fry the onion in the fat and oil, together with the chopped bacon. When golden, add the marinade and the lamprey. Cover and cook until tender (about 15 minutes, but do test first as this fish is very firm in texture). When done, transfer the lamprey and some of the liquor to another pan and keep warm. Add enough water to the remaining liquor to cook the rice (2½ times its volume), which should not be completely dry at the end of cooking. Halfway through the cooking time add the blood. Mix and continue cooking until the rice is tender. Combine the fish and sauce with the rice and serve at once.
Serves 6.

Note: If you prefer the fried bread as an accompaniment, instead of rice, add the blood to the pan whilst the lamprey is cooking.

Variation (from Beira Alta province)
Rice is again the classic accompaniment for this slightly different lamprey dish. Actually this version is, if anything, still more traditional than the previous one.

1 lamprey, prepared as above	¼ pint (150 ml) olive oil
¼ pint (150 ml) white wine	2 tablespoons butter
4 tablespoons dry white port (or more white wine if not using port)	2 cloves garlic, chopped
	2 sprigs parsley, chopped
	12 oz (350 g) rice
1 large onion, chopped	salt and pepper

When preparing the lamprey, as indicated before, keep the blood in a container with the wine, to prevent its coagulating. Bring the fats to the heat and fry the onion, garlic and parsley until soft. Add salt and pepper. Carefully combine this with the blood and wine mixture, bring to the boil and add the fish. Simmer until tender. Season to taste and add the port wine (or more white wine). Reheat. Whilst this is being done, cook the rice in plain water (add some olive oil to it if you like), drain and serve with the lamprey stew, pouring the sauce on top.
Serves 6.

Shellfish

Prawn Rissoles/Rissois de Camarão

ESTREMADURA

Here we have the most delicious kind of rissole one can dream of. They are sold at every *patisserie* in Portugal, freshly made every day, and eagerly eaten by discerning customers. This is an obligatory savoury for parties, snacks and light lunches.

One can substitute prawns for shrimps in the rissoles, which are a little troublesome to prepare at home (hence their popularity ready-made). The pastry is of the cooked choux-type and, when left to the following day, tends to harden, so the rissoles lose a lot of their appeal. Thus they should be made and eaten on the same day.

PASTRY
9 oz (250 g) flour
1 tablespoon butter
½ pint (300 ml) water
3½ fluid oz (100 ml) milk
½ teaspoon salt

COATING
2 eggs
breadcrumbs
oil for frying

FILLING
7 oz (200 g) cooked and shelled
   prawns or shrimps
½ pint (300 ml) milk
3 tablespoons flour
1 coffeespoon lemon juice
salt and pepper
dusting of nutmeg
1 coffeespoon chopped parsley

To make the pastry, first bring the water and milk to the heat, with the butter. When boiling, remove from the heat and add the flour. Beat thoroughly and bring to the heat again to cook the flour, stirring continuously until a crust has formed at the bottom of the pan and the dough comes away from the sides (about 5 minutes). Remove from the heat, beat and work the dough lightly until smooth. Allow to cool.

Meantime, prepare the filling. Make a thick white sauce with the butter, flour and milk – that is, melt the butter, add the flour to make a roux (over a very low heat), cook for a few seconds, remove from the heat and add the warm milk little by little, stirring very well; cook again until thick. Add salt, the remaining seasoning and the prepared shellfish. Mix well and set aside to cool.

Roll out the pastry to ⅛ inch (3 mm) thickness, taking care not to break it. Cut into rounds. These can be small or large, according to whether the rissoles are intended for a party or ordinary snack or meal. Small ones would be 2 inches (5 cm) across, the larger 3½ inches (9 cm). Divide the filling among all the rounds of pastry, wet the edges with beaten egg, fold in half and press well. Dip each rissole in beaten egg, then in breadcrumbs. (They will gain by being left in the refrigerator for 1–2 hours before frying.) Deep fry until golden brown, turning once. Serve on their own or (hot or cold) with a salad. Makes about 12 large rissoles or 18 to 20 smaller ones.

Variation
Cheaper rissoles can be made replacing the prawns with an equal amount of cooked fish (or half and half).

Stewed Lobster/Lagosta Suada

PENICHE, ESTREMADURA PROVINCE

1 large lobster
3 medium onions, chopped
4 medium tomatoes, skinned, seeded and chopped
2 cloves garlic, chopped
2 tablespoons butter
2 tablespoons olive oil

4 tablespoons white wine or, better still, dry port or madeira
1 bay leaf
2 sprigs parsley, chopped
½ teaspoon paprika
salt and pepper

Of course, the lobster must be impeccably fresh (there are places where they are available alive and where the fishmonger or fisherman will kill them for you). There is no such problem in Peniche and other coastal areas of Portugal where lobsters are plentiful – though always on the expensive side, nowadays. As you may know, a live lobster is rather dark in colour and turns orange only after cooking.

Have your lobster cleaned and cut into pieces. Save the liquid that escapes from the lobster whilst cutting. While you are doing this, have all other ingredients, except salt and wine, boiling gently for 4–5 minutes in a large earthenware pot, if you have one, otherwise in any roomy pan. Transfer all the lobster pieces to the pan. Do not add salt at this stage. Cover and cook gently until tender (about 15 minutes), shaking the pan now and then. Taste for seasoning and add the amount of salt you think necessary (a little at a time – do not overdo it). Add the chosen wine and boil for another couple of minutes. It is then ready to serve with white rice and a side salad, but if you can prepare it in advance and reheat it, so much the better.
Serves 3 to 4.

Cockles, Bulhão Pato Fashion/Ameijoas à Bulhão Pato

ESTREMADURA PROVINCE

Bulhão Pato (1829–1912) was a poet, writer and scholar who also translated into Portuguese various foreign works, including Shakespeare's *Hamlet* and *The Merchant of Venice*. This dish was apparently created by a cook who admired him. Cockles Bulhão Pato Fashion make an exquisite dish and are available as a starter in many Portuguese restaurants and as an appetizer for drinks in beer-houses. It is a very simple recipe which can be adapted to other shellfish.

2 lb (1 kg) live cockles	3 tablespoons olive oil
2 cloves garlic, sliced	3–4 stalks fresh coriander,
1 medium lemon in wedges plus	chopped
juice of ½ lemon	salt and pepper

Prepare the shellfish in advance, as it needs to stand in salted water for about half a day, after the first wash. Use 5–6 tablespoons salt for each 2 pints (1.2 l) of water for soaking. After soaking, wash again in plenty of cold water to remove the sand. Fry the garlic gently in the oil until golden. Add the coriander, some salt and pepper and the shellfish. Bring the flame up a little, shake the pan until the cockles open (3–5 minutes) and remove any which does not, discarding it. Squeeze the lemon juice on top, turn and serve at once, in the same pot, garnished with the lemon wedges. If you cannot find coriander, use a little parsley, but the fragrance of coriander blends much better with most shellfish dishes.
Serves 4.

Cockles in a Cataplana Pan/Ameijoas na Cataplana

THE ALGARVE

A *cataplana* is a special vessel made of copper which interlocks perfectly, permitting a complete turning (see Equipment, p.36). A good saucepan with a tight-fitting lid will have to do when a *cataplana* is not available.

2½ lb (1.25 kg) cockles	2 sprigs parsley
2 oz (60 g) smoked ham (or lean	pinch paprika
bacon)	2 small, red chillies
2 oz (60 g) chouriço (p.23)	salt
1 tablespoon olive oil	1 lemon, cut into segments
1 tablespoon lard	

Wash the cockles and leave in salted water for half a day. Then wash again. Fry the onion (in thin slices) very gently in the fat and oil in the pot, until transparent, together with the seasoning. Add the meats, in small cubes, the cockles and parsley. Cover and cook gently for 20–25 minutes. Serve adorned with the lemon.
Serves 4.

Snails, Portuguese Style/Caracois à Portuguesa

This is a delicacy, served in all regions, credited to the Romans, but probably older still.

The snails gathered in the Portuguese countryside are generally small, though a few big ones are also found. Before cooking, they are usually kept in a confined space (a wooden box, for example) to fast for 3–4 days, so their insides are as clean as possible and some of the slime is eliminated. There are places, however, where snails are fattened up (again in a confined space, so they do not go away) with herbs and all kinds of scraps from the vegetable garden, fruit peelings and water, or simply with wholemeal flour diluted in water and forming a pap, with a bowl of clean water by its side. I would, however, in view of the weight of opinion in its favour, advise you to make the snails fast, even if only briefly, to rid them of as much waste matter as is feasible.

Before cooking, wash the snails in plenty of cold running water for a while, until you are satisfied that they are clean and free from slime, as much as you can see. To cleanse them further, rinse them once again, using salted water this time, mixed with a little vinegar. Then wash again with plenty of clean water.

3 lb (1.45 kg) clean snails
1 large onion, chopped
2 bay leaves
3 cloves garlic
3 tablespoons olive oil

1 bouquet garni or 1 teaspoon of
*   mixed herbs, to taste*
2 small chillies (or a good dash of
*   hot sauce)*
salt and pepper

Place the snails in a roomy pan with enough cold water to more than cover them, and add all the seasoning. Bring to the boil over a very low heat, to force the snails to poke their heads out of their shells. Skim the surface of the liquor now and then, during cooking (45 minutes to 1 hour), adding more boiling water to the pan as necessary, to ensure the snails are covered at all times. Taste for salt. Serve hot in small plates, with a little cooking liquor. Use a long pin to prise the snails out of the shells.
Serves 8.

Seafood

Squid, octopus and cuttlefish (*lulas, polvo* and *Chocos*) abound in Portugal and are delicious, once one becomes accustomed to handling them. Squid is so plentiful that many Portuguese fishermen still use the tougher ones (cut up) as bait.

Squid and cuttlefish can be cooked in the same fashion. Logically the smaller the fish, the quicker it will cook, and you will have to bear this in mind. If small, they may take as little as half an hour, but if large you may need up to 1½–2 hours for tender squid or cuttlefish. Do not despair, because these larger and therefore tougher fish are very tasty and worth the trouble of longer cooking. Some people soak them in milk for a couple of hours before cooking, to soften their flesh. If you do this, wash the fish very thoroughly afterwards. The tentacles and protruding sides can be chopped up to form the basis for a tasty filling for stuffed squid, along with chopped onion, chopped boiled egg, cubed ham and some cooked rice for binding. Secure the stuffed fish with toothpicks and lay them over a *refogado* (see p.31) made of olive oil, onion, bay leaf, parsley and some tomato, adding fish stock or water, as needed, until tender, and salt towards the end of cooking. Serve with plain rice. The filling can be enriched with 2 tablespoons of white wine and, instead of cooked rice, white breadcrumbs and an egg yolk can be used for binding.

Stewed Cuttlefish (or Squid)/Chocos guisados (or lulas)

ALL COASTAL AREAS

2 lb (1 kg) cuttlefish or squid (can be the larger ones)
¼ pint (150 ml) fish stock (can be made with a fish cube)
4 tablespoons olive oil
1 large onion, chopped
3 sprigs parsley, chopped
6–7 oz (175–200 g) ripe tomatoes, seeded, peeled and chopped
salt and pepper

Prepare the fish, removing the ink sac (perhaps the fishmonger will be kind enough to do it for you), wash it well and cut it in small pieces. Fry the onions, tomatoes and parsley for a couple of minutes, then add the fish and some of the stock, keeping the rest for gradual additions whilst cooking. Add salt and pepper towards the end of cooking, boil again for 5 minutes and serve with potatoes or rice.

You may enrich the stew with 2 tablespoons of white wine or a teaspoon of wine vinegar diluted in a little water.
Serves 6.

Variation
Setúbal, south of Lisbon, offers a rich version for squid (or cuttlefish) stew:

1½ lb (675 g) squid
4 tablespoons olive oil
4 tablespoons white wine
½ teaspoon paprika
¼ coffeespoon cayenne pepper

1 large clove garlic, chopped
salt
garnish – 2 hard-boiled eggs,
*   sliced*

Clean the squid (or cuttlefish), remove the ink sac and cut it into small pieces, including the tentacles. Fry the garlic in the oil until golden, add the wine, seasoning and fish, cover and cook gently until tender, adding a little fish stock or water, as needed. The sauce should be rich, so add the liquid little by little, or reduce it at the end. Garnish with the sliced eggs and serve with chips.
Serves 4.

Cuttlefish with Ink/Chocos com Tinta

THE ALGARVE AND OTHER SEASIDE PROVINCES
Cuttlefish and squid are similar, but the former has a little sac full of ink inside, which, when left while cooking, provides a tasty black sauce for the dish.

2½ lb (1.2 kg) cuttlefish (the
*   small kind)*
2 cloves garlic, finely chopped
2–3 medium slices good white
*   bread (without crusts)*

½ teaspoon paprika
1 teaspoon tomato concentrate
5 tablespoons olive oil
salt and pepper

Clean the fish and wash out any sand attached to it. Leave the ink sacs on. While you are doing this, fry the chopped garlic in the oil, until golden. Add the bread, made into fine crumbs, and then remove from the heat. Mash the mixture, return it to the pan, add the fish, the paprika, salt and pepper and cook very gently, adding a drop of water if needed, until the fish is tender and the sauce reduced. Serve with boiled potatoes.
Serves 6.

Octopus with Rice/Polvo com Arroz

MINHO PROVINCE
This is one of the dishes normally included in Minho Christmas fare. The Portuguese are very partial to octopus, anyway, fresh,

half dried and fully dried. You will see it hanging in those specialized shops selling only salted and dried fish (salted cod mainly). The taste for octopus seems to have been acquired long ago, when the sailors who braved the seas, in the fifteenth and sixteenth centuries, during the 'discoveries era', packed dried food to eat during the voyages. This recipe is for fresh octopus.

1 fresh octopus, about 2 lb (1 kg)	*2 tablespoons wine vinegar*
4 tablespoons lard	*1 teaspoon chilli powder*
4 tablespoons olive oil	*14 oz (400 g) rice*
2 medium onions, chopped	*salt and pepper*
3 stalks parsley, chopped	

Ask the fishmonger to clean the octopus for you. Wash well and tie the sides of the head over it, like a hood, cutting the tentacles into pieces. Meanwhile fry the onion and parsley in the fat and oil for 3–4 minutes. Then add the fish, vinegar, chilli powder and enough boiling water almost to cover the octopus. Replace the lid and cook gently until tender (45–50 minutes or even longer), checking whether more liquid is necessary in the meantime. When tender, *and only then*, add the salt and boil again for 2–3 minutes. Lift the fish, set aside. Measure enough liquor to cook the rice (2½ times its volume). If you have too much liquor, boil it for a little while, to reduce to the proper amount. Add the rice and cook, until tender (about 25 minutes) – the rice should be on the 'wet' side. Taste again for seasoning and add the octopus, cut into pieces. Bring to the boil, to reheat through, and serve with a side dish of black olives and chunks of crusty bread.
Serves 6.

Note: Fresh octopus needs careful attention when cooking because it tends to harden if overcooked after the 'tender stage' has been reached.

Variation
The addition of rice makes this dish more substantial, but it can also be served with chunks of crusty bread or slices of fried bread.

Meat

A popular Portuguese saying declares 'Fish does not pull a cart' ('*Peixe não puxa carroça*'), meaning that fish does not give enough strength. This is a conviction still held by many people, in spite of the fact that research has proved them wrong. On the other hand, there are many others fully prepared, nowadays, to admit that meat is not the be-all and the end-all of good food. Still, meat is much used by the Portuguese. Beef, veal, kid and lamb are used, but kid and pork are especially relished and used in many varied and imaginative recipes, as are domestic rabbit, chicken and also game (mainly wild rabbit and partridge). The Portuguese are also good at creating dishes out of offal and tripe.

Note: Kid, lamb, mutton and goat can all be cooked with the same recipes, varying only the length of cooking and taking care not to allow the meat to dry up. In the same way, poultry can substitute for game when necessary, perhaps adjusting the seasonings accordingly.

Beefsteak

Fried steak is one of the most popular and sought-after quickly prepared lunches in Portugal, be it at restaurants or in the home (especially so in urban areas). The price factor may have curbed the demand somewhat, but steak used to be almost the staple diet of some people – or at least for Sunday lunches, much as the British have their joint.

Steak is called *bife* in Portugal, pronounced the same as 'beef', which clearly indicates its original inspiration. It derives from the British influence (after all the Anglo-Portuguese alliance is already into its seventh century) and, amusingly, *bife* is the name given colloquially to an Englishman. Portuguese acquaintances, in the course of conversation have said to me: 'So you are married to a *bife*?' This is not intentionally pejorative – it is just a mild slang, if you like, and it is used much less nowadays than was the case years ago. Portuguese people love to give nicknames and fond diminutives to almost anything that lends itself to it – or even if it doesn't. Referring to steak, for instance, they may say: '*Vai um bifinho*?' ('Will you have a "little" steak?') – not meaning a *small* steak but a *lovely* one, inferring that it would be a good choice.

Steak with Egg on Horseback/Bife com Ovo a Cavalo

ESTREMADURA PROVINCE

4 rump or sirloin steaks
2 tablespoons butter plus enough
  butter to fry the eggs
1 tablespoon lard
4 sprigs parsley
4 small cloves garlic
1 bay leaf
4 eggs
salt and pepper

Clean and prepare the meat as for ordinary steaks. Rub each one with its own crushed clove of garlic, sprinkle with salt and pepper and leave for 15–20 minutes. After that melt the fats in a large frying-pan, add the parsley and bay leaf and fry the steaks, turning once or twice. They are generally slightly underdone. In the meantime, fry the eggs in butter and serve an egg on top of each steak. At restaurants the steaks are cooked and served in individual earthenware pans. The classical accompaniment is thick chips (*batatas fritas*) and, if wanted, mixed pickles (in vinegar).
Serves 4.

Variations
1 A thick toast made with good white bread, well buttered, may be placed under each steak. A slice of ordinary ham, or *presunto* (see p.22) may also be served between the steak and the egg.
2 Another version omits the parsley and bayleaf, adding

more butter (2 tablespoons) and 2 tablespoons of single cream, as well as a few drops of lemon juice. The steaks (which should always be extremely tender) are sautéed briskly on both sides, in half the fat, to seal the juices. Set aside. Add the remaining butter to the pan, the lemon juice and the cream. Mix well and allow to thicken a little. Taste for salt. Add the steaks and cook for a further 3–4 minutes, turning the meat. The sauce will be thicker now. Serve at once, with chips.

Steak Marrare Fashion/Bife à Marrare

LISBON
This recipe for steak was allegedly created by a chef named Marrare who came to Lisbon from the north of Spain, or from Naples – there is a dispute over his birthplace among culinary experts; what they do agree on is the excellence of his invention. Anyway, the Marrare Café, which used to stand in the centre of Lisbon, became famous for its superb steak and was frequented by the most distinguished nobility and politicians of the nineteenth century.

4 good-sized fillet steaks
4 tablespoons single cream
4 tablespoons butter

2 cloves garlic, crushed
salt and freshly milled pepper

Rub the meat with the garlic. In a heavy pan melt half the butter. Fry each steak on both sides, over medium heat, to avoid losing the meat juices. Dust with salt and pepper as you take the steaks off the pan. Keep warm. When they are all fried, add the remaining butter to the pan and the cream. Stir well and allow to simmer, to thicken. Taste for seasoning. Add the fried steaks, to reheat. Serve immediately, with a side dish of chips (*batata fritus*).
Serves 4.

Steaks with Onion/Bifes de Cebolada

ESTREMADURA PROVINCE
This recipe produces a steak completely different from the usual, on account of the seasoning, onion and tomato.

4 rump steaks
2 cloves garlic, chopped
2 tablespoons olive oil
1 tablespoon lard
2 large onions, thinly sliced

4 medium tomatoes, peeled and
  seeded, coarsely chopped
2 bay leaves
3 sprigs parsley, chopped
salt and pepper

Use a casserole or saucepan for this. Place the fat and oil at the bottom of it and assemble layers of steak, onion, tomatoes and the seasoning. Cover the pan and cook gently for 30–35 minutes. You may need to reduce the sauce a little towards the end. Serve with mashed potatoes or plain rice. This dish is prepared very quickly and successfully using a pressure cooker (8–10 minutes).
Serves 4.

Stews

Boiled Meat and Vegetables, Portuguese Style/Cozido à Portuguesa

TRÁS-OS-MONTES PROVINCE, BUT USED COUNTRYWIDE
This is one of the most typical of Portuguese dishes, enjoying great popularity all over the country, even though it originated in the Trás-os-Montes province, where it is standard fare during the Carnival. It is widely regarded as one of the finest Portuguese specialities, notwithstanding its simplicity. This is peasant food at its best, consisting of a variety of meats and smoked sausages (the more the better) boiled with potatoes and vegetables, with a side dish of rice, cooked in the same broth. It is worth preparing more *cozido* than will be necessary, as any meat and vegetables left over can be used for other dishes or reheated and eaten as they are the following day. The broth is ideal for soups.

1 lb (450 g) leg of beef
1 lb (450 g) chicken
12 oz (350 g) spare ribs (pork) or a piece of smoked bacon or salted pork
4–5 oz (110–140 g) black pudding
5 oz (140 g) chouriço (p.23)

2 farinheiras – *flour-sausages (if you cannot obtain these, add more bacon)*
1 pig's ear (optional)
1 large cabbage (heart)
8 medium carrots
8 medium potatoes
4 medium turnips
10 oz (280 g) rice

If using salted meat, soak it first for a few hours, to desalt a little. As to the *chouriço* (p.23), I must say they are really essential for the proper *cozido* flavour. However, try some substitutes, as a last resort.

In a very roomy saucepan cook the meat in enough water to cover. Skim the surface of the liquid. Check from time to time, to remove any meat whose cooking time is less than the others, until they are all done. Keep the meat aside and in the same liquor cook all the vegetables at the same time. Cut them in big chunks and boil until tender (about 25 minutes to half an hour). Remove from the pan enough stock (you may have added a little more water, in the meantime) to boil the rice (2½ times its volume). When everything is cooked, return the meat and vegetables to the stock, to reheat thoroughly. While you are doing this, dry the rice in the oven (190°C/375°F/Gas 5) for 5–8 minutes.

To serve: make a mound of the rice in a separate dish, and surround it with the black pudding and other sausages, in thick slices. Put the meat and vegetables in a tureen or deep serving dish, with a little of the liquor, to keep them moist. Serve at once.

Serves 6 to 8.

Variations

According to availability or season, add a few very tender green beans and chickpeas (previously soaked). If using the chickpeas (7–8 oz/200–225 g), remember they take some time to cook, so put them together with the meat, at the beginning.

Beef Stew/Carne Guisada

This homely dish is often prepared without the addition of wine, but even if it is just a little, wine will improve the dish enormously.

1¼ lb (560 g) stewing beef, cubed
1½ lb (675 g) potatoes, peeled and
  cubed
1 large carrot, sliced
2 medium onions, sliced
1 large clove garlic, sliced
6 tablespoons red wine
2 medium tomatoes, peeled and
  chopped

1 bay leaf
1 small clove (optional)
3 sprigs parsley, chopped
3 tablespoons olive oil
1 tablespoon lard
salt and pepper

Prepare a marinade with the wine, bay leaf, garlic, salt, pepper and parsley. Steep the meat in this and leave overnight. The following day strain the meat and fry it in the oil and lard, together with the onion. Turn, to seal all round. Add the carrot. After a little while add the strained marinade. Cover and cook over gentle heat until the meat is almost tender. Test now and then to see if you need to add a little water or stock to the pan. Taste for salt and add the potatoes. Cover again and cook for a

further 30 minutes, when everything should be tender. Check
the liquid and seasoning. Serve at once.
Serves 4 to 6.

Goat Stew, Bairrada Style/Chanfana da Bairrada

BEIRA LITORAL PROVINCE
This festive stew used to be prepared in the baker's oven and
still is, when possible. There is no reason, however, why one
could not prepare it at home. The proper container is a large
black earthenware casserole from the same region, but you
could use any roomy, fireproof dish with a lid.

Weddings and christening feasts are whole-day affairs in the
country, with food and wine brought to the large tables at
regular intervals. This stew is but one of the succulent
celebration dishes of the Bairrada region, which rates among
the richest and most inventive in the culinary field.

Goat meat is the classic choice, but lamb can also be used.
Quantities here are given for 4 people, as in most dishes in the
book, but obviously these could be doubled or trebled, as
needed.

This stew is normally prepared a day or so in advance, and
then reheated.

2 lb (1 kg) tender goat or lamb, boned and cut into biggish pieces	3 sprigs parsley, chopped
	½ coffeespoon pepper
	1 large onion, chopped
3 oz (90 g) fatty bacon, in small cubes	1 bay leaf
	2 large cloves garlic, chopped
3 tablespoons olive oil	¾ pint (450 ml) red wine from the Bairrada region, if possible
1 oz (30 g) lard	
1 teaspoon paprika	¼ coffeespoon nutmeg
	salt

Put all the seasonings in the casserole, mix, taste for salt and
add the meat. Now pour on some of the wine, so the meat is
almost covered. Put the lid on the casserole and bring to the
oven, which must be very hot (232°C/450°F/Gas 8). Bake for an
hour at this temperature, then check the amount of liquid in
the casserole. Add the remaining wine now. Keep the oven at
the above temperature for 30 minutes longer, then reduce to
180°C/350°F/Gas 4 until the end of cooking (another 1–1½
hours). Remove from the oven, test for salt and liquid (it should
be swimming in gravy) and keep for a day or so, until needed.
Then place it in the oven again until really hot. Serve
accompanied by boiled potatoes.
Serves 4.

Bean Stew, Portuguese Style/Feijoada à Portuguesa

A marvellous stand-by of the Portuguese kitchen. Each region may have its own variations, but basically *feijoada* is a rich bean stew with pork and sausages.

1 lb (450 g) dried beans (butterbeans or red kidney)	2 cloves garlic, chopped
6 oz (175 g) chouriço (p.23)	2 medium onions, chopped
6 oz (175 g) streaky bacon (in cubes)	2 tablespoons olive oil
	2 tablespoons lard
3 oz (90 g) black pudding (optional)	3 sprigs of parsley
	1 bay leaf
1 medium tomato (peeled and seeded)	1 clove (optional)
	salt and pepper

Soak the beans in plenty of cold water, overnight. Butterbeans are smooth and soft and a good choice for this dish. Place the beans in cold water, seasoned with half the olive oil, half the lard and salt. Add one of the onions (with the clove stuck in it, to discard later). Bring to the boil and cook until tender. The cooking time depends on the type of beans. Check now and then, also for liquid, as it should not dry out. Do not overcook the beans, nevertheless. When tender, drain the beans and set aside, keeping the liquor.

Take some of this to another pan to cook the cured meat, boiling until almost tender (15–20 minutes). Meantime fry the other onion in the remaining fat and oil, together with the chopped tomato and the other ingredients, for 3–4 minutes, over low heat. Add the meat (cut into pieces), boil for a further 2–3 minutes, add the beans, boil again and of course mix in the pan any liquor still left, for a moist consistency, but do not add an excessive amount. Taste for seasoning and serve at once. If you have any left-over liquor, this can be used later for a soup.

In some northern provinces this dish is further 'reinforced' by an accompaniment of *Arroz no Forno* (p.108).
Serves 6.

Variation
The beans can also be served with slices of fried bread, which will then be soaked in the gravy. A larger amount or variety of pork meat can also be added, such as a knuckle, pig's ear, piece of belly and so on, to taste. These can be cooked with the beans.

Note for Vegetarians
Feijoada is a very good dish even without the meat. Use a little more onion and other seasonings, if desired, for a rich flavour.

Kid
Roast Kid/Cabrito Assado
BEIRA BAIXA PROVINCE

> Quite so. Horace would have dedicated an ode to that roast kid. And with the trout, and Melchior's wine, and the *cabidela* – prepared by the sublime squinting dwarf with an inspiration not of this earth – and the sweetness of that June night, showing its dark velvet mantle through the open window, I felt so comfortably lazy and contented that, as the coffee awaited us in the sitting-room, I just collapsed in one of the wicker chairs – the largest, with the best cushions – and shouted in pure delight.
>
> Eça de Queiroz, *A Cidade e as Serras* (*The City and the Mountains*)

The idea is to have extremely tender and delicate meat, so the animal should be as young as possible. In Portugal it is usually only about a month old. The skin is allowed to get nicely browned all over.

1 kid (or a small lamb) whole (if it is a small kid, otherwise use half – about 5 lb/2.5 kg)	1 bay leaf, cut into little pieces
	4 sprigs parsley, chopped
	2 oz (60 g) lean bacon, minced
5 oz (150 g) lard	8 tablespoons white wine
2 tablespoons olive oil	salt
3 cloves garlic, minced	

Open the kid, empty and clean it inside, wash thoroughly and allow to drain, preferably overnight. Wash the offal and keep it refrigerated until the following day as well.

Prepare all the seasonings, mixing them with the oil and 3 oz (90 g) lard into a paste. Brush the kid inside and out with this. Mix any remaining paste with the offal (cleaned and cut into small pieces) and stuff the kid with it. Sew up the opening. Let the meat rest for a couple of hours, then spread the extra 2 oz (60 g) lard all over it and bake in a preheated oven (190°C/375°F/Gas 5), allowing about 25 minutes per pound (450 g) meat, plus 30 minutes. Baste, and turn 2 or 3 times, to brown evenly. Serve with roast potatoes.
Serves 8.

Kid, Ribatejo Fashion/Cabrito à moda do Ribatejo

Whenever it is possible to get young kid (or a small lamb), the Portuguese love to roast them whole, just as they do the suckling pig. These are very special and prized regional dishes, served on the large kitchen table with all the family sitting around, sharing in the feast.

Whole kid or small lamb, or part
of one (about 5 lb/2.5 kg),
cleaned, but leaving the head
on
2 large onions, finely chopped
½ pint (300 ml) white wine
3 cloves garlic, finely chopped

3 sprigs parsley, chopped
1 teaspoon paprika
7 oz (200 g) chouriço *(p.23)*
2 chillies
4 oz (110 g) bacon fat
salt

Prepare a paste with the onion, garlic, parsley, paprika, chillies (finely chopped), *chouriço* (very finely chopped), bacon fat (minced or melted), some salt and half the wine. Spread this all over the animal. Place it in a large greased baking-tin and roast in an oven preheated to 180°C/350°F/Gas 4 for about 2 hours or until done, basting now and then. Add the remaining wine half way through the cooking time, to bulk up the juices. Turn the kid over at this point, to cook evenly. Serve with roast potatoes cooked at the same time, if possible, or cubed fried potatoes. *Serves 8*.

Kid Beira Alta Style/Cabrito à Moda da Beira

Kid or lamb can be used for this dish. In the mountains the free-ranging herds get a good diet of wild herbs, and their meat is deliciously aromatic. This recipe enhances that fragrance, and the result is a mouthwatering dish.

2–2½ lb (1 kg–1.225 kg) kid or
lamb, cut into convenient-sized
pieces
1 pint (600 ml) red wine
2 lb (1 kg) potatoes (after peeling)
2 medium carrots, sliced
2 medium onions, chopped

2 cloves garlic, chopped
8 tablespoons olive oil
2 tablespoons lard
1 heaped tablespoon mixed herbs
(to taste)
2 stalks parsley, chopped
salt and pepper

First half-cook the meat on top of the stove by the following method: put the oil, carrots, onions, garlic, herbs, salt, pepper and meat into a saucepan, to fry gently until golden all over (8–10 minutes). Add half the wine and 2–3 tablespoons water (or chicken stock). Cover and simmer for 20–25 minutes. Check the liquid. Meanwhile parboil the quartered potatoes in salted water, drain and set aside. Keep warm. Grease a deep oven-to-table dish (an earthenware one is used in peasant cooking) and transfer the meat, vegetables and liquor to it. Surround with the potatoes, dotted with lard. Bake for 40–45 minutes, basting now and then, until golden brown (oven 190°C/375°F/Gas 5). *Serves 4 to 6*.

Other Meat Dishes

Veal Barrosã Fashion/Vitela à Barrosã

ALTO DOURO PROVINCE

*1½ lb (675 g) very tender fillet of
   veal
3 oz (90 g) butter
1 oz (30 g) lard
1 teaspoon cornflour*

*1 large clove garlic, well crushed
   with salt
juice of ½ medium lemon
salt and pepper*

Clean the meat of all tendons etc and cut it into thickish strips.
Season with salt and pepper, the crushed garlic and lemon
juice. Leave in this marinade for 3–4 hours, turning the meat
now and then, to absorb all the flavours thoroughly. Then melt
the fats in a deep frying pan and sautée the meat over a low
heat until done (12–15 minutes). Drain the meat and keep
warm. Thicken the sauce with the cornflour, mixed into a paste
with a little water or stock. Boil for 2 minutes. Taste for salt and
pour over the veal. Serve with any suitable accompaniment,
such as mashed or sauté potatoes, plain rice or spaghetti.
Serves 4.

Spit-Roast Veal/Vitela no Espeto

NORTHERN PROVINCES

To prepare a spit-roast or barbecue-style dish, one should really
use an open fire, since the traditional recipe is always cooked
that way. Modern barbecues will suffice, provided the meat is
turned regularly.

*2 lb (1 kg) veal (tender fillet from
   the top of leg, or loin, off the
   bone)
4 tablespoons olive oil
1 tablespoon wine vinegar*

*1 bayleaf, cut in small pieces
½ teaspoon chilli powder
2 cloves garlic, minced
salt*

Clean the meat and remove any tendons, fat, skin etc. Sprinkle
with salt. Place on the spit or barbecue. Using a kitchen brush,
paint the meat all over with a paste made with all the
seasonings. The meat should be cooked in 45 minutes but
pierce it with a skewer first to test – no blood should come out.
Do not overlook basting with the seasoning and turning the
meat now and then. Serve with roast potatoes.
Serves 4 to 6.

Variation
From the same provinces a version of plain spit-roast veal.

2 lb (1 kg) boned top of leg
2 medium onions, thinly sliced
salt

Wet the meat slightly, so it holds a good sprinkling of salt, all round. Place it on the open barbecue and roast for 35–40 minutes, turning occasionally. When ready, put the meat in a covered dish for a few minutes, to make it sweat and give out some of the juices. Serve covered with the slices of raw onion and a side dish of boiled potatoes or chips.

Tripe, Oporto Style/Tripas à Moda do Porto

It may sound a bit strange to some, but in many countries tripe makes extremely succulent, tasty and nourishing meals. In Portugal the Oporto region specializes in tripe dishes, and the city itself is renowned for its classic tripe recipe.

Oporto's partiality to tripe seems to have stemmed from necessity – or at least this is the generally accepted explanation. When the Portuguese were engaged in the conquest of certain North African towns (for example, Ceuta was taken in 1415), Oporto contributed large amounts of provisions to keep the men going. From the cattle slaughtered for this purpose, only the tripe was retained, so that there was no option for the people but to eat it as best they could. Hence the name *tripeiros* (tripe-eaters) given to the people of Oporto, a name which is still used and which, incidentally, makes them proud, given the reason for it.

It may not always be easy to find tripe on sale in Britain, and it may be necessary to order it in advance. In Portugal it is sold all over the country, and it is generally scraped and bleached but barely cooked, so one has to start practically from scratch, which means longer cooking time. But even when it is bought already half-cooked, it will still need quite a lot of boiling at home to make it tender and extract all the jelly and juice still trapped inside. When properly cooked, tripe is surprisingly tender, well worth trying.

Veal tripe is generally chosen in the Oporto region, for its gelatinous quality, and various other types of meat are added, so this is not the 'poor man's recipe' the historical explanation might have us believe, but of course it is perfectly acceptable to use the tripe on its own, if so desired (or perhaps with just a spicy sausage or bacon, as an enrichment). The grand recipe set out below is used nowadays at restaurants in the ancient and historic city of Oporto.

1½ lb (675 g) white tripe (veal,   2 large onions, chopped
    for preference) – honeycomb,   2 medium carrots, sliced
    flat tripe and thick seam   1 tablespoon lard
½ medium-sized chicken   2 sprigs parsley
4 oz (110 g) streaky bacon   1 bay leaf
4 oz (110 g) chouriço (p.23)   1 lb (450 g) butter beans
4 oz (110 g) presunto (p.22)   ½ teaspoon cumin (optional)
1 calf's foot (optional)   salt
1 pig's ear (optional)   freshly ground pepper

Wash the tripe thoroughly, both outside and in and rub well with lemon and salt to clean still further. Wash again, under the tap. Boil in salted water until tender. It is difficult to predict how long it will take, because much depends on how the tripe dresser has prepared it. The best policy is to cook the tripe well in advance and test it now and then, keeping it waiting later on, if necessary, as it is essential that it is tender. In a separate pot, boil the other meat (remember that the cured meat contains salt already), together with the trotter and/or pig's ear. (You should at least use one or the other, for a richer dish.) Add to this pan the onions, carrots, chopped parsley, bay leaf and lard. When everything is cooked, set aside.

Using enough of the cooking liquor, bring the beans (soaking since the previous day) to the boil, and cook until tender. When all is done, drain the meat and vegetables, cut the tripe and all the other meat in conveniently-sized pieces and mix with the beans. Add some of the liquor to this and boil it all together for 10–15 minutes over low flame, to combine the flavours and thicken a little. Taste for seasoning, add some freshly ground pepper and serve, sprinkled with a few cumin seeds (optional) and/or some chopped parsley. The classic accompaniment for this dish is rice.
Serves 4 to 6.

Note: Do not discard the cooking liquor left over. You can transform it into a chowder with all the bits and pieces not used up and with the addition of cabbage and other vegetables, as needed.

Rice in the Oven/Arroz no Forno

MINHO AND DOURO PROVINCES
In some northern regions, especially the Minho province, rice is an obligatory part of the meal, served as an accompaniment to almost anything. But of course rice is also used there for main courses, if cooked with meat. There is no limit to the amount or variety of meat one can include, depending only on

how much one wants or what flavour must predominate. These rice dishes are finished in the oven, which gives them a more lavish flavour and appearance, with the top delectably crisp and the whole texture of the rice much improved.

1 lb (450 g) rice	*1 medium onion, chopped*
7 oz (200 g) braising beef	*1 tablespoon olive oil*
4 oz (110 g) leg of pork	*½ teaspoon saffron*
1 leg of chicken	*3 sprigs parsley, chopped*
3 oz (90 g) chouriço *(p.23)*	*salt and pepper*
4 oz (110 g) presunto *(p.22)*	

Boil the meat in enough water to cover and cook until tender. Remove from the heat, strain the meat and leave aside. Measure some of the liquor (2½ times the volume of rice) and set aside. Fry the onion in the oil until golden, add the parsley and saffron diluted in a little water, boil and add to the measured liquor. Bring to the boil, add the rice and cook for 12–15 minutes. Transfer to a buttered fireproof dish and finish cooking in the oven (180°C/350°F/Gas 4) for 15–20 minutes. Serve piping hot, with the meat reheated in a little of the liquor and served in a separate dish.
Serves 4 to 6.

Variation
A simpler version of rice in the oven uses left-over liquor or broth and/or gravy left from roast lamb.

1 lb (450 g) rice	
3 oz (90 g) cooked smoked ham or	*1 teaspoon saffron*
* lean bacon*	*salt and pepper*
3 oz (90 g) cooked chouriço	*Chicken broth/meat liquor/gravy*
* (p.23)*	* (as available – 2½ times the*
1 large onion, chopped	* volume of rice)*
3 tablespoons olive oil	

Fry the onion in the oil until golden, add the chosen liquid and cooked meat (of which the above are only examples) and bring to the boil. Strain the meat, keep warm. Add the saffron and the rice, cook and serve as before.
Serves 4 to 6.

Pork

The pig contributes in great measure to the sustenance of country people, from the northern provinces to the Alentejo.

Here, a local breed of pigs, leaner and with a more elongated body than is normal, roams freely like sheep in places where large oak trees grow, producing the tasty acorns which they feed on.

Especially pleasing to the countryman's tastebuds are the series of succulent feasts that follow the annual pig's slaughter. Relatives are invited to help with the many chores associated with it and to share the special meals when all the bits and pieces that must be consumed while fresh are transformed into gargantuan banquets. These meals more than compensate for the toil involved in the cutting, salting and separating of meat and fat, the making of sausages and preparation of cured hams – which will be eaten raw many months later, cut into thin slivers as the tastiest of snacks or used in various recipes. Long tables are laden with fried liver, roast loin and big platters of *sarrabulho* (pig meat and offal cooked with the blood of the animal, see pp.117–19), to be washed down with the help of splendid local wines, served from big earthenware jugs. No *caldo verde*, no sardines, no salted cod, on those days! These are winter months, when the comforting warmth of pork dishes is more than welcome, filling the kitchen with appetizing smells. These are special days, for it is not always possible to line up such an array of victuals!

Suckling pig is a highly recommended regional dish and extremely popular all over Portugal, although none is as good as the Bairrada style (p.111). In its province of origin it becomes almost an obsession. Generally it is considered too much trouble to prepare at home, so scores of restaurants, specializing solely in it, are spread throughout the region. Suckling pig is a mouthwatering delicacy, and those who have never tried it before surrender completely to the fine taste and succulence of its meat and to the characteristic crackling texture of the skin, after it is roasted to perfection.

The suckling pig must be really small, no more than a month old, so it does not have too much fat, and it must have been fed only on its mother's milk. It will weigh something like 6–10 lbs (3–5 kg) after cleaning. It should not be too difficult to purchase a suckling pig answering to this description, even if you are far removed from a farm. Have a word with the butcher and he may be able to oblige.

The good point about roasting a very young animal (apart from its greater tenderness) is that it should fit into any decent-sized oven without having to cut it. In the Bairrada region an old-fashioned baker's oven is used, the animal being supported by a long stick, which is turned now and then to allow even cooking. Underneath, a large tray collects the precious juices and holds potatoes, which are thus roasted at the same time. At home one has to adapt these things as best one can. Should you find it difficult to fit the whole pig inside the oven, or if the tin is not large enough to hold it lengthwise, cut the pig in half and cook the two halves side by side, or in two consecutive sessions (you can always reheat the half baked first, before serving). If you adopt this method, do not forget to join both halves when serving, disguising the cut with some garnishing.

Suckling Pig, Bairrada Style/Leitão à Bairrada

BEIRA LITORAL PROVINCE

In order to keep the skin really crisp (a must, in this recipe), the pig should not be placed directly on the bottom of the roasting tin, or it would become soggy. In the absence of a big trivet, use a few wooden sticks, to rest the side of the pig. Do not forget that you will have to turn it, so as to cook and crisp it all over.

1 really small suckling pig	3 cloves garlic
½ pint (300 ml) white wine (preferably from the same region)	2 tablespoons salt
	1 teaspoon pepper
	2 sprigs parsley
2 oz (60 g) bacon fat	1 bay leaf
2 oz (60 g) lard	

Ask the butcher to prepare the pig, leaving on the head (with the eyes, ears, tongue and teeth) and tail.

Prepare a paste with all the dry seasonings. Use a food processor, if you can. Add a little wine to moisten, if you find the paste too thick. Spread this paste all over the pig including inside, and place in the oven (see p.110) preheated to 210°/425°F/Gas 7. Keeping to this temperature for the first 20 minutes of cooking, then reduce to 190°C/375°F/Gas 5 towards the end of cooking (about 2–2¼ hours). There are a few jobs to do during this time: basting the pig, at least every 15 minutes, with its own juices and some of the wine (reserve a quarter of it for later), turning the pig half way through and protecting the parts that may have become too dry (for instance, the ears) with a little foil. Bairrada's cooks use cabbage leaves for this. Remember that the skin is meant for eating, so it should be golden brown but not burnt.

After the given time (or before, if you think it is done), take the pig out and, using a big spoon or ladle, extract the juices in its belly cavity, as well as the liquid accumulated in the tin. Add all this to the reserved wine and bring to the boil, to reduce and thicken a little. Taste for seasoning and keep warm, to serve afterwards in a sauce-boat. Before you prepare the gravy, put the pig back in the oven (without any liquid) for about 10 minutes, to enhance the crackling quality of the skin. After that put the pig on a very large platter or tray and serve, placing an orange in its mouth. Garnish with lettuce leaves and potatoes, for a most lavish meal.

The left-overs are excellent cold.

Serves 10.

Suckling Pig Blood Stew/Cabidela de Leitão

BAIRRADA, BEIRA LITORAL PROVINCE

Perhaps I shouldn't say this myself, but it is true that the *cabidela* is exceedingly good today. And Canon Dias corroborated that such a lunch might well tempt St Anthony in the desert.

Eça de Queiroz (1845–1900), *The Sin of Father Amaro (O Crime do Padre Amaro)*

From the same region as the suckling pig recipe on p.111 comes this extension of it, using the offal left over. The term *cabidela* is broadly applied to offal and giblet dishes, with or without other meat, where the blood of the animal is also used. Without it they would be simply *guisados* (stews).

1 suckling pig's offal (all edible parts – liver, heart etc) with the blood in them, cut into small pieces
1 large clove garlic, chopped
2 medium onions, chopped
3 sprigs parsley, chopped
1 bay leaf
2 oz (60 g) lard
1 tablespoon olive oil
4 tablespoons white wine
salt and pepper
gravy left over from roasted suckling pig

Melt the fat and oil and add the onion, garlic, parsley and bay leaf. Cook gently for 5 minutes. Add the meat and wine, season with salt and pepper and stew slowly until tender, adding a little water or stock if needed. Shake the pan now and then and be careful not to burn the stew. Towards the end of cooking add the gravy. Serve with plain rice or potatoes.

Serves 4 to 6.

Crisp Pork Viana Style/Rojões à Moda de Viana do Castelo

MINHO PROVINCE

This is a dish traditionally prepared during the pig-slaughtering season but it can be had at any time. *Rojões* really come from

Minho and the Douro Litoral, but you find variations in other provinces as well. It is an extremely tasty dish and easy to prepare, despite the seemingly long list of ingredients.

2 lb (1 kg) loin of pork
4 oz (110 g) lard
¼ pint (300 ml) white wine
1 tablespoon wine vinegar
3 cloves of garlic, finely chopped
1 teaspoon paprika

1 bay leaf
1 tablespoon olive oil
½ coffeespoon cumin seed
3½ oz (100 g) streaky bacon, cut
*   small*
salt and pepper

Prepare a marinade with the wine, vinegar, paprika, bay leaf, garlic, salt and pepper. Mix well and add the meat, cut into strips about 2 inches (5 cm) in length and 1 inch (2.5 cm) wide. Leave for 10–12 hours. Then melt the lard, oil and bacon, and add the cumin seeds, meat and marinade. Cook over medium heat until the meat is golden and the liquid reduced to a rich, fragrant sauce. Serve with plain boiled potatoes, with the sauce poured over them.
Serves 4 to 6.

Crisp Pork Trás-os-Montes Style/Rojões à Moda de Trás-os-Montes

This version of *rojões* has an important new item: chestnuts. These can, however, be omitted when not in season.

2 lb (1 kg) loin of pork, cut as
*   before*
½ pint (300 ml) white wine
3½ oz (100 g) lard
2 cloves of garlic, finely chopped
1 bay leaf

1 coffeespoon paprika
2 sprigs parsley
1 small clove
boiled potatoes and chestnuts
*   (boiled and peeled)*

Prepare a marinade with the wine, garlic, bay leaf, clove, salt, pepper and half the parsley. Leave the meat in this for at least a day, but preferably 2 days. Bring to simmering point until the meat is tender. Remove the meat from the liquid and place in a pan with half the lard. Fry until golden. In the meantime reduce the cooking liquor by a third, to use as a sauce. In a separate pan fry the potatoes and chestnuts (enough for 4 people) in the remaining lard. Serve the meat, potatoes and chestnuts with all the juices and sauces poured over them. Sprinkle with a little parsley.
Serves 4 to 6.

Pork, Alentejo Style/Porco à Alentejana

This dish has become widely known all over the country. The cockles and pork make an unusual but rich and exciting combination, and foreign visitors to Portugal find it extremely appetizing. The shellfish should be bought still alive, being opened in the prepared sauce. Keep the shells, as they give the dish its exotic appearance. If the cockles are bought already cooked, you miss out on this, but the recipe can still be attempted quite successfully.

1 lb (450 g) loin of pork, cut into
   1 inch (2.5 cm) cubes
1 lb (450 g) leg of pork, cut the
   same way
1 large onion, finely chopped
½ pint (300 ml) white wine
3 cloves garlic, finely chopped
2 sprigs parsley, chopped
1 teaspoon paprika

1 teaspoon concentrated tomato
   paste
4 oz (110 g) lard
2 tablespoons olive oil
1½ lb (675 g) cockles
1 clove
1 bay leaf
salt and pepper

Prepare a marinade with the wine, garlic, paprika, salt, pepper, bay leaf and clove. Stand the meat in this for 4–5 hours. Drain the meat and fry gently in the melted lard, until golden brown all over. Strain the marinade and add to the pan. Cover and boil with the meat until it is very tender and the sauce reduced by half. Meantime, make another sauce with the tomato concentrate, oil, onion, parsley, salt and pepper, simmering it all for 6–8 minutes. Place the cockles in this over low heat. The cockles should open. (Remove those which do not, and discard.) Shake the pan and transfer its contents to the top of the meat. Cover. Boil gently for 3 minutes and serve in the same pan.
Serves 4 to 6.

Note: When using previously cooked cockles add them to the onion sauce all the same, even though the shells are missing.

Liver with Them (Potatoes)/Iscas com Elas

LISBON AREA
The title of the recipe refers to the fact that this is such a traditional dish that nothing except potatoes would do.

Not long ago there used to be various Lisbon restaurants renowned for their *iscas*. At present *iscas com elas* are less prominent on Lisbon's menus, though they still enjoy great popularity. It is a wholesome, economical and truly delicious dish, provided the liver is not overcooked (which hardens it). A small portion of the animal's spleen is included as well, to thicken the gravy – you should be able to get this from the butcher.

14 oz (400 g) pig's liver, thinly
   sliced
3 oz (90 g) spleen (well scraped,
   using only the pulp)
2 cloves garlic, chopped
2 oz (60 g) lard

1 tablespoon wine vinegar
3 tablespoons white wine
1 bay leaf
salt and pepper
boiled potatoes

Make a marinade with the vinegar, wine, garlic, bay leaf, salt and pepper and immerse the liver in it for 4–5 hours. In a large frying pan melt the lard and cook the slices of liver with a little marinade. Boil on both sides over low heat until the liver darkens, but not longer than 10 minutes. Remove the liver from the pan, set aside and keep warm. Mix the spleen pulp in the juices left in the pan and add the strained remaining marinade. Cook gently for 10 minutes, to thicken. Add the liver again, simmer for 2–3 minutes, taste for seasonings and serve with the boiled potatoes.
Serves 4 to 6.

Eggs and Smoked Sausage/Ovos com Chouriço

ESTREMADURA PROVINCE, BUT USED COUNTRYWIDE

Eça de Queiroz (one of the best Portuguese writers of all time) must have been quite partial to eggs cooked with the smoked sausage so loved by the Portuguese, *chouriço*. In several of his bestsellers he mentions this popular dish as the delight of his heroes. Thus, in *The Remarkable House of Ramires*: 'Gonçalo ... started off by having a plateful of eggs with *chouriço*....' In *The Capital* we read again of this special combination: 'Rabeca ordered Mariquitas ... to prepare a lovely fry-up of eggs and *chouriço*....' And in *The City and the Mountains*: 'Jacinto had dined on eggs and *chouriço*. Really sublime.'

This is a rich-tasting but very simple omelette.

2 eggs per person
about 2 inches (5 cm) chouriço
   (p.23) per person

salt
oil (or butter) for frying

Make sure you buy *chouriço* that is the 'eating raw' kind. Put the fat in the frying pan and add the *chouriço*, finely sliced and free from the outer skin. Fry for 1–2 minutes. Add the beaten eggs and combine the lot. Make the omelette flat, turning it carefully with a spatula, or fold it, according to your preference.

Variation
Fried eggs and *chouriço* can be made also. In this case you do not beat the eggs but add them whole to the pan, frying them in pairs with their share of *chouriço* until they are all done.

Peas with Smoked Sausage/Paio com Ervilhas

'What a nuisance! I arrived from Paris with this voracious appetite and forgot to ask for a big platter of peas and *paio* for dinner!'
Eça de Queiroz, *The Maias* (*Os Maias*)

This is a quick and flavoursome dish, prepared simply with tender peas and smoked loin of pork (see p.24).

14 oz (400 g) shelled peas
10 oz (280 g) good paio, *sliced (p.24) – cooked smoked ham or bacon can be substituted*
1 tablespoon butter
3 oz (90 g) lard
1 medium onion, chopped
2 stalks parsley, chopped
4 poached eggs
salt and pepper

Fry the onion gently in the lard until transparent. Add ¼ pint (150 ml) boiling water, the peas and parsley. Cover the pan and simmer. Add more water if needed. When the peas are half cooked, add the butter and the meat. Boil until the peas finish cooking. If, however, there is too much liquid in the pan, boil over a high flame for 1–2 minutes to reduce it. Serve with a poached egg per person.
Serves 4.

Variations
This dish can be scaled down to the simpler versions which are common in most Portuguese households during the pea season. Try these:
1 Same portions as above, substituting 2 oz (60 g) *chouriço* (p.23) or smoked bacon for the more expensive *paio*.
2 For vegetarians, omit the meat altogether and add a medium tomato (skinned and seeded) to the stew, from the start and/or increase the number of poached eggs.

BLOOD STEWS/SARRABULHOS

Although *sarrabulhos* come mainly from the northern provinces, there are countless variations all over the country, and the recipes that follow are but a sample of them.

The blood mentioned in the recipes is prepared by allowing it to coagulate completely in containers and then boiling it in salted water. If all the blood of the animal is collected, it should amount to at least 6 pints (3.5 litres), enough for many black-pudding-type sausages and plenty of *sarrabulhos*. The 'cakes' of blood are crumbled by hand as needed.

In Britain fresh pig's blood is not easy to obtain because pigs are killed in licensed slaughter-houses from which the blood is difficult to procure. However, the following recipes have been included as they are so much part of traditional Portuguese cuisine that any book on the subject would be incomplete without them.

Blood Stew Beira Alta Fashion/Sarrabulho da Beira Alta

10 oz (280 g) loin of pork
1¾ pints (1 litre) water
5 oz (140 g) boiled blood, as explained above
3½ oz (100 g) pig's liver
3 oz (90 g) fresh lard
7 oz (200 g) slices of good country-style bread
1 clove garlic, chopped

1 bay leaf, cut into small pieces
2 tablespoons red wine (or use 1 tablespoon wine vinegar diluted in water)
½ teaspoon paprika
½ teaspoon cumin seeds
2 sprigs chopped parsley
salt and pepper

Bring the water to the boil, together with some salt, half the bay leaf, paprika and garlic. Simmer for 4–5 minutes. In a separate pan put the slices of bread, spreading over them the cooked blood, crumbled. Pour three-quarters of the prepared boiling water over this. Keep warm. Melt the lard in a saucepan and add the meat, cut into cubes, the cumin seeds, the remaining bay leaf, salt, pepper and wine. Cover and cook gently until tender (be careful not to overcook, as the liver tends to become harder the longer you cook it, and the loin is very tender, anyway). You may have to add a little of the prepared liquor, to moisten this stew. Put the cooked meat over the bread and blood mixture and bring to the boil, stirring, until a pap is formed. It should have the consistency of soft porridge. If the liquid has not been totally absorbed, remove the excess with a spoon or ladle, or boil rapidly for 1–2 minutes, to reduce it. If, on the other hand, it is too dry, add the remaining liquor. Garnish with a few olives just before serving. It is best eaten with a spoon.
Serves 4.

Blood Stew Bairrada Fashion/Sarrabulho da Bairrada

BEIRA LITORAL PROVINCE

6 oz (175 g) pig's liver
14 oz (400 g) fatty pork meat, in
   small pieces
3½ oz (100 g) fresh lard
4 oz (110 g) blood, as explained
   p.116

1 clove garlic, chopped
2 lb (1 kg) small potatoes boiled in
   their skins and peeled
salt and pepper

Melt the lard, fry the garlic and add the pork meat. Cook gently, adding just enough water to keep moist. When almost tender, add the liver, in small cubes, and the blood, crumbled. Cook for a few minutes, season and add the peeled potatoes. Mix, warm through and serve from the same pot, with olives and maize bread (p.57).
Serves 4.

Blood Stew Estremadura Fashion/Sarrabulho da Estremadura

14 oz (400 g) pig's liver
7 oz (200 g) spleen
3½ oz (100 g) blood, as explained
7 oz (200 g) fresh lard
2 sprigs parsley, chopped
1 clove garlic, chopped

1 small onion, chopped
¼ pint (150 ml) white wine
1 tablespoon wine vinegar
1 teaspoon paprika
salt and pepper

Render down the lard, having cut it into small pieces. When it has melted completely, separate the crisp golden cracklings and keep them aside. Fry the onion, garlic and parsley in the fat, then add the meat cut into 1 inch (2.5 cm) cubes. Fry it very quickly, then add the wine, vinegar and a little boiling water. Cover and cook gently for 8–10 minutes. Take off the heat. Mix the cracklings and the crumbled blood. Season with salt, pepper and paprika. Simmer for another 4–5 minutes and serve from the same pot. Traditionally it is accompanied by maize bread.
Serves 4.

Blood Stew Rice/Arroz de Sarrabulho

MINHO PROVINCE

3½ oz (100 g) fresh lard
10 oz (280 g) blood, boiled and
    crumbled, as explained p.116
7 oz (200 g) heart
7 oz (200 g) kidney
7 oz (200 g) liver

11 oz (310 g) rice
1 medium onion, chopped
1 sprig parsley, chopped
¼ teaspoon cumin seeds
salt and pepper

Fry the onion in melted lard. Add the meat (cubed), season with salt and pepper, and moisten with a little boiling water. Cover and simmer until the meat is almost tender. Add the remaining seasoning, the crumbled blood, the rice and enough boiling water to cook it (2½ times the amount of rice) for 15 minutes, then transfer to a fireproof dish to finish cooking in the oven (180°C/350°F/Gas 4) for about 15–20 minutes.
Serves 6.

Pig's Offal Blood Stew/Cabidela de Miúdos

VIANA DO CASTELO, MINHO PROVINCE
Pig-slaughtering season means all kinds of dishes using every bit of the animal. In this instance, the offal and blood are combined for a *cabidela* of superb flavour.

1½ lb (675 g) pig's offal
    (including some sweetbreads,
    throat, pancreas, spleen and
    the meats around these organs,
    with blood in them)
3 tablespoons white wine
2 slices day-old bread

3 cloves garlic
1 large onion
4 tablespoons olive oil
2 tablespoons lard
pinch powdered cumin
salt and pepper

In a large saucepan put the fat, oil, sliced onions and chopped garlic, fry gently for 3–4 minutes, then add all the other seasonings and the meat (with the blood in them and cut in small pieces). Stew over a low flame, adding the wine and water as necessary. Cover, shake the pan now and then, and add more water (or stock) if needed, but only very gradually, until the meat is tender. Remove from the heat, taste for salt and add the bread, crumbled. Bring to the boil to thicken a little, and serve with boiled potatoes or plain rice.
Serves 4.

PIG'S HAGGIS

Haggis is the stomach of the pig (or sheep) filled with an aromatic meat stuffing. It is typical peasant fare, and anyone who appreciates tripe will also like this rich dish.

Before you start cooking it, the stomach must be thoroughly scrubbed, inside and out (turn it over, for a complete job). Do this with a kitchen brush. Leave the stomach soaking in salted water for a few hours or until the following day. Alternatively scald it with boiling water, after scrubbing, and discard any loose skin and fat attached to it, then wash in plenty of running water.

There are many variations of haggis some of which involve smoking the stomach for a few days, at the end of cooking. This turns it into a sausage-like preparation. Usually, it is either roasted or boiled, securely sewn up to keep the stuffing inside.

Pig's Haggis/Bucho de Porco Recheado

TRÁS-OS-MONTES PROVINCE

1 pig's stomach	8 eggs, beaten
4 thick slices bread	¾ pint (450 ml) meat stock
1 lb (450 g) lean of pork, cubed	2 sprigs parsley, chopped
1 lb (450 g) meaty bacon, cubed	pinch powdered cloves
	salt and pepper

Soak the bread in the stock and mash. Mix with the meat and all other ingredients. Taste for seasoning. Pack this filling into the prepared stomach and sew it up firmly. Wrap with muslin and tie up without squeezing it. Do not worry if the stomach does not seem completely full, as the stuffing expands during cooking. Prick the haggis in various places with a thick needle. Boil it in a large pan of salted water, for about 3–3¼ hours. Strain and allow to cool before removing the muslin and cutting into slices. *Serves 6 to 8.*

Pig's Haggis Beira Baixa Style/Bucho de Porco Recheado da Beira Baixa

1 prepared pig's stomach (see above)	1 tablespoon butter
	4 beaten eggs
1¼ lb (560 g) tender pork meat with some fat	10 oz (290 g) fresh white breadcrumbs
½ pint (300 ml) white wine	8 peppercorns
3 sprigs parsley, chopped	juice ½ lemon
3 cloves garlic, chopped	1 clove
2 medium onions, chopped	salt
2 tablespoons lard	

Divide the wine, garlic and parsley into two. Use one half to marinate the stomach (already cleaned as indicated above) for a few hours, or overnight. Use the other half of the mixture, together with an onion, butter and a tablespoon of lard (seasoned with salt) to cook the meat, over low heat. When tender, mix 7 oz (200 g) of the breadcrumbs with lemon juice and eggs. Taste for seasoning. Stuff the stomach. Sew it and tie up with the muslin. Prick with the needle as before. Bring the marinade to the boil together with the remaining onion, peppercorns and clove, adding enough water to cover the stuffed haggis. Simmer for 1–1½ hours. Then unwrap and brush with the remaining lard, roll in 3 oz (90 g) dried breadcrumbs and bring to the oven (190°C/375°F/Gas 5) for 15 minutes, or until browned.
Serves 6 to 8.

Pig's Haggis Beira Litoral Style/Bucho de Porco da Beira Litoral

1 prepared pig's stomach (see above)
2 lb (1 kg) tender pork meat, cut into cubes
12 oz (350 g) rice
2 cloves garlic, chopped
½ pint (300 ml) white wine
½ teaspoon tarragon (or oregano)
4 peppercorns
1 bay leaf
2 sprigs parsley, chopped
salt and pepper
1 tablespoon melted lard for brushing

Leave the prepared pig's stomach in salted water overnight. Make a marinade with the wine, bay leaf, garlic and parsley, and immerse the meat in it. Leave overnight as well. Drain the meat and divide the marinade into two parts. Measure one half and add water to it to make up 2½ times the volume of rice. Mix this liquid with the raw rice, the meat (drained) and chosen herb, salt and pepper. Stuff the stomach with this mixture, sew it and tie up as before. Boil gently in water to which the remaining marinade has been added, with some salt and the peppercorns. Keep the haggis well covered all the time in the liquid, boiling for 1½–2 hours. Drain, remove the muslin, brush all over with melted lard and bake at 190°C/375°F/Gas 5 for 15 minutes or until browned.
Serves 6 to 8.

Poultry and Game

Stuffed Turkey for Christmas/Peru Recheado de Natal

Although the Iberian peninsula was very rich in game and

poultry in the Middle Ages, turkeys appeared on the table only in the sixteenth century, after the explorers brought them back from South America (the name *peru* gives a good clue as to their origin). After that, turkey became increasingly popular and a part of Portugal's Christmas fare, as in many countries.

1 medium-sized turkey
¼ pint (150 ml) white wine
1 large orange, very finely sliced
1 medium lemon, very finely
   sliced

2 tablespoons butter
2 tablespoons lard
1 teaspoon paprika
4 oz (110 g) fatty bacon, minced
salt and pepper

STUFFING
(for the breast-end)
14 oz (400 g) lean meat (pork and
   veal), minced
2 oz (60 g) lean bacon, minced
1 large slice white bread
1 small onion, finely chopped
1 tablespoon butter
1 tablespoon lard
2 sprigs parsley, chopped zest ½
   lemon
salt and pepper

(for the tail end)
1 medium onion, chopped
1 lb (450 g) floury potatoes
1 tablespoon butter
1 tablespoon lard
the turkey giblets
2 medium eggs
2 sprigs parsley, chopped
8–10 black olives, stoned
pinch nutmeg
salt and pepper

Turkey meat is considered a little dry and bland in taste, so in Portugal it is generally steeped in a special marinade, the day before cooking, to improve it. Prepare the turkey, then put it in a large basin with some cold water to half cover it, salt and the sliced citrus fruits. Turn the turkey around now and then. The following day take the turkey out of the marinade and put it somewhere to drain while you prepare the stuffing.

For the breast-end stuffing, fry the onion in the fats, until transparent, add to the minced meat, mix in the chopped olives and fresh breadcrumbs, and then the other ingredients. Combine this mixture, season and stuff the breast-end of the bird. Secure the skin with needle and thread, if necessary.

Now prepare the tail-end stuffing. Fry the onion in the fats and add the giblets, well cleaned and cut into quite small pieces. Add a little stock and allow to cook gently, until tender. Reduce the gravy, if too liquid. Meanwhile cook and mash the potatoes and combine with the eggs, olives and parsley. When the giblets are ready, mix them with the potato, check for seasoning and stuff the cavity, again securing the skin with thread.

Make a paste with the lard, butter, bacon, paprika and seasoning and spread all over the turkey. Bring it to the oven (163°C/325°F/Gas 3) for about 3½–3¾ hours for a 10 lb (approx. 4.5 kg) turkey, basting now and then with the wine and its own juices. After that time, see if it is done (piercing one leg with a skewer and observing if blood still comes out). Leave it for a little longer (perhaps increasing the temperature to 191°C/375°F/Gas 5) if it needs browning, but do not allow the turkey to stay too long in the oven, to avoid drying the flesh too much. Baste again and serve with any accompaniments to taste and a large side salad.

Serves 8 to 10.

Note: To prevent burning the more exposed parts of the turkey, you may like to cover them with a little foil half way through roasting.

Jugged Chicken or Chicken in a Deep Pot/Frango na Púcara

ESTREMADURA PROVINCE

This dish has been made quite popular in some restaurants of the Lisbon area. Traditionally it is prepared in a very deep earthenware pot with a tight-fitting lid. Though it will not taste exactly the same, it can, however, be made in any deep fireproof dish with a lid.

1 tender chicken (enough for 4 people)	½ tablespoon mild made-mustard
8 small onions, whole	2 tablespoons port or madeira wine
3 medium tomatoes (peeled, seeded and chopped)	2 tablespoons brandy or equivalent
2 oz (60 g) smoked ham or lean bacon in small cubes	4 tablespoons white wine
1 tablespoon butter	2 cloves garlic, finely chopped
2 tablespoons lard	1 tablespoon sultanas or raisins (without seeds)

Grease the chosen container. Place the cleaned chicken in it surrounded by the onions and pour over it a mixture of all the seasonings. Cover and bake at 200°C/400°F/Gas 6 for an hour or until the chicken is tender. Uncover the container, baste the chicken and continue baking for a short while, to allow the chicken to go golden on top. Serve at once with chips, salad and chunks of fresh bread, to dip into the gravy.

Note: Some people prepare this dish on top of the stove

When the chicken is tender, it is placed (without the lid) under the grill, to brown the top slightly.

Chicken Blood Stew/Cabidela de Galinha

TRÁS-OS-MONTES PROVINCE
This is one of the dishes usually prepared for Christmas, and the fact that it includes a little cinnamon dates it back to medieval times, when it was quite common to add cinnamon to poultry dishes. (Although chicken is named in the title, turkey can also be used.) The name *cabidela* gives away the fact that the blood of the animal is used to enrich the sauce.

1 chicken (or turkey) enough for 4
   people
6 tablespoons white or red wine
1 medium onion, chopped

4 tablespoons olive oil
2 stalks parsley, chopped
½ teaspoon cinnamon
salt and pepper

Keep the blood of the chicken (or turkey) in a cup containing the wine, mixing them very well, so that the blood does not coagulate. If the bird has been bought already slaughtered, use just the wine, for the final steps.

Fry the onion in the oil, until transparent, add the chicken (or turkey) cut into medium-sized pieces, cook for 2–3 minutes, turning, and add all remaining ingredients except the wine and blood. Mix a little water, reduce the flame to keep simmering point, cover the pan and cook until the meat is tender. Remove a little sauce and mix with the blood and wine. Beat well and add to the pan. Cook for 2–3 minutes, taste for salt and serve, with boiled potatoes.

Chicken Fricassée/Galinha de Fricassé

TRÁS-OS-MONTES AND ALTO DOURO PROVINCES
This is one of the dishes especially prepared for Christmas Eve supper, though it is also used (mainly in the Lisbon area) as an everyday dish in the home. It is delicately flavoured, quick and easy to prepare.

1 chicken enough for 4 people
1 medium onion, chopped
1 tablespoon lard
1 tablespoon butter
1 tablespoon olive oil

1 sprig parsley, chopped
3 egg yolks
1 dessertspoon lemon juice
salt and pepper

Cut up the chicken and fry in the fat and oil, with the onion, until golden all over. Add a little water, salt and pepper and simmer, until tender. Beat the egg yolks with the lemon juice, add a little of the chicken liquor and mix well. Add this mixture to the pan, over a very low heat, and boil just for a minute, to cook the yolks without curdling them. Serve at once with the chopped parsley on top. It goes very well with plain rice or mashed potato.

Chicken Rice, Portuguese Style/Arroz de Galinha à Portuguesa

1 medium-sized chicken, cleaned
  and quartered
3 oz (90 g) chouriço (p.23)
3 oz (90 g) fatty bacon
14 oz (400 g) rice

2 tablespoons olive oil
1 tablespoon wine vinegar
1 large onion, chopped
2 sprigs parsley, chopped
salt and pepper

Fry the onion with the oil until golden, then add the chopped bacon and the chicken and sautée for 5 minutes, turning. Add ¼ pint (150 ml) water, the vinegar, parsley, salt and pepper and cook gently until half done. Taste for seasoning and add the rice and enough boiling water or chicken stock to cook it (2½ times the volume of rice, roughly). About 5 minutes before the end of cooking, add the sliced *chouriço*. The rice must be slightly wet and therefore you may need to add more liquid at the end. Serve immediately.
Serves 4 to 6.

Duck with Rice/Pato com Arroz

MINHO PROVINCE
This is a dish suitable for a special meal.

1 medium duck, cleaned and cut
  into large pieces
10 oz (280 g) smoked ham, cubed
3 oz (90 g) chouriço (p.23)
  thickly sliced

1 pig's ear, cleaned and cut
14 oz (400 g) rice
2 tablespoons butter
juice of ½ lemon
salt and pepper

Cook all the meat together in enough water seasoned with a little salt. Drain off the liquid and measure enough to cook the rice (2½ times its volume). Add the lemon juice, a little pepper and salt (if needed). Bring to the boil. Add the rice. When half cooked (12–15 minutes), transfer the rice to a fireproof dish, dot it with the butter and finish cooking in the oven, for 15–20 minutes (190°C/375°F/Gas 5) until golden and crisp. Garnish with the ham and sausage, return to the oven to reheat them (5 minutes) and serve immediately.

An optional sauce can be made with the remaining liquor and a little cornflour, to thicken. Serve in sauce-boat.
Serves 4 to 6.

Duck with Rice and Orange, Braga Style/Pato com Arroz e Laranja, de Braga

1 medium duck (whole)	*2 tablespoons butter*
6–8 oz (175–225 g) smoked ham	*1 clove*
2 oz (60 g) bacon	*salt and pepper*
3 oz (90 g) chouriço (p.23)	*1 lb (450 g) rice*
juice of ½ lemon	*1 large or 2 medium oranges,*
3 sprigs parsley	* sliced*

Place the whole duck and the other meat in a roomy pot with enough boiling water to cover. Add the spices and seasoning. Cook until tender, skimming the top now and then. Take care not to overcook the duck. When done, drain the meat and allow the stock to cool down. At this point the fat will have gathered on top, and it will be easy to discard some of it, with a spoon. Cook the rice in stock (2½ times its volume) as for the previous recipe putting a tablespoon of butter on it when you put it in the oven. When the rice is done, put the duck on top of it and brush the bird with the remaining butter. Bring to the oven again or put under the grill, to crisp up the skin of the duck. Reheat the other meat in the left-over liquid and serve them together with the duck and the rice. Garnish with the orange slices.
Serves 4 to 6.

Rabbit with Wine/Coelho em Vinho à moda do Alentejo

Rabbit meat (wild or tame) is especially suited to cook with wine. This really improves the meat enormously – the same applies, of course, to chicken and to other game, all of which can be cooked following the recipe below:

1 medium rabbit, cleaned and	*2 tablespoons olive oil*
* quartered*	*1 tablespoon lard*
¼ pint (150 ml) white wine	*1 tablespoon butter*
1 tablespoon port or madeira – if	*2 large cloves garlic, minced*
* available, otherwise use 1*	*salt and pepper*
* tablespoon more white wine*	*4 thin slices of fried bread*
2 medium onions, chopped	

Grease a fireproof dish with lid. Place the fried slices of bread on the bottom. Add the pieces of rabbit, sprinkle with salt and pepper and distribute over it the fat, oil and seasoning. Bring to the oven (190°C/375°F/Gas 5) for about an hour until the meat is almost done. Remove the lid, add the wines and continue baking until golden (another 15 minutes). Serve with rice or potatoes, plain or mashed.
Serves 4.

Hunter's Rabbit/Coelho à Caçadora

ESTREMADURA REGION
A tempting rabbit stew, very easy to prepare. Experiment substituting with chicken.

1 rabbit (enough for 4 people) cleaned and quartered	2 large cloves garlic, finely chopped
4 oz (110 g) bacon (medium fat) chopped	2 medium onions, chopped
2 tablespoons lard	2 stalks parsley, chopped
4 medium tomatoes, peeled, seeded and chopped	8 tablespoons red wine
	1 tablespoon wine vinegar
	1 bay leaf
	salt and pepper

If the rabbit is killed at home, keep its blood in a cup, mixed with the vinegar (which will prevent coagulation). Place half the melted lard in a large earthenware pot (if you have one, otherwise use any good saucepan) and layer all the ingredients, starting with the onions and finishing with the bay leaf, parsley and remaining melted lard. Sprinkle a little salt between layers. Pour the wine on top, cover and simmer over the stove until tender (about an hour). Add the blood mixture, if you kept it, and boil for 4–5 minutes. Serve at once with boiled potatoes (or mash) or plain rice.

Grilled Hare (or rabbit)/Lebre Grelhada

MOST INLAND PROVINCES

4 good portions of hare (or rabbit)	juice of 1 medium lemon
3 tablespoons wine vinegar diluted in 5 tablespoons water	2 oz (60 g) butter
3 large cloves garlic, chopped	2 slices fatty bacon
1 large bay leaf	salt and pepper

Clean the meat and marinate overnight in the vinegar, water, garlic, bay leaf, salt and pepper. Drain and lard the meat here and there with strips of bacon. Place under a medium grill, turning it to cook evenly. While the meat is grilling, brush it with a mixture made with the melted butter and lemon juice. Save the meat juices and mix them with the remaining brushing liquid and half the marinade. Simmer for about 5 minutes to make a gravy to serve over the hare. Plain rice, thick chips or mashed potatoes and a side salad are suitable accompaniments.
Serves 4.

Giblets and Blood Rice/Arroz de Cabidela

This is a useful dish to use up the offal of a rabbit or bird. In order to have a *cabidela* stew, the blood must be included, but this is possible only when the animal is killed at home. If not, there is no possibility of collecting the blood. Nevertheless, the recipe can still be followed, using the wine and vinegar, all the same, although the end result will not be exactly a *cabidela*.

giblets from any bird, or rabbit   *1 small clove garlic, chopped*
12 oz (350 g) rice   *1 medium onion, chopped*
1 tablespoon red wine   *2 sprigs parsley, chopped*
1 teaspoon wine vinegar   *1 clove*
2 tablespoons lard   *salt and pepper*

If the animal is to be killed at home, prepare a small bowl with the wine and vinegar and allow the blood to drain into it, mixing well to prevent the blood's coagulating. Set aside. Clean the giblets well and cook them (except the liver) in enough seasoned water (or chicken stock) to cover, until almost tender. Set aside. Sweat the onion, garlic and parsley in the lard, until soft but not coloured. Add the blood mixture (or just the wine and vinegar), stir and add enough cooking liquor from the giblets to cook the rice (2½ times its volume – topping it up with stock, if needed). Bring to the boil, add the rice and the clove, and then all the meat you can extract from the giblets (discarding the bones and gristle). Add the liver, in small pieces. Simmer it all, undisturbed, for about 25 minutes, until the rice is tender. Check seasoning. Remove the clove. Serve piping hot.
Serves 4.

Partridge in Vinegar Sauce (to serve cold)/Perdiz de Escabeche

INLAND PROVINCES

> On the table the supper was laid – consisting of cheese, apples, walnuts, chestnuts, two tureens full of *escabeche*, his speciality, and a bottle of port wine with a promising topaz colour.
>
> Júlio Diniz (1839–71), *The Lady of the Reeds*
> (*A Morgadinha dos Canaviais*)

4 small partridges (1 per
* person) or 2 bigger ones*
2 medium onions, thinly sliced
7 tablespoons olive oil
5 tablespoons wine vinegar
4 cloves

2 bay leaves
4 cloves garlic, thinly sliced
8 peppercorns
4 sprigs parsley, chopped
salt

Prepare the partridges, tie them with string, to keep their shape, and parboil in enough water to cover them. Season with salt. Remove the partridges (keeping the stock for later) and fry them in a roomy pan, using the olive oil. Turn the birds until golden. Then add all the seasonings and enough cooking liquor to cover them. (Reserve any left-over liquor for a game soup.) Bring to simmering point, cover and cook until tender, adding a little more liquid if needed and turning the birds once or twice for even cooking. Leave in the same pot with the liquor until the following day. Serve cold, with chips.

The dish will keep for several days.

Partridge with Villain Sauce/Perdiz com Molho de Vilão

TRÁS-OS-MONTES AND ALTO DOURO PROVINCES

4 small partridges (1 per person)
* or 2 bigger ones*
1 oz (110 g) smoked ham or lean
* bacon*
Salt

FOR THE SAUCE
2 medium onions finely chopped
¼ pint (150 ml) wine vinegar
2 tablespoons white wine
¼ pint (150 ml) olive oil
2 stalks parsley, finely chopped
salt and pepper.

Boil the partridges and ham or bacon in salted boiling water. Allow the meat to become tender but do not overcook. Strain and quarter the partridges and cube the ham. Put the meat in a fireproof dish under the grill for 4–5 minutes, until golden. Cool and cover with the sauce.

Prepare a couple of days before it is eaten – it will keep for about a week. It is generally served with boiled potatoes.

To make the sauce: beat the vinegar, wine and oil with some salt, then add the chopped onion and parsley. Add some pepper to taste. Check for seasoning.

Note: Keep the liquor in which the meat was cooked, for a magnificent game soup (p.44).

Cold Partridge/Perdiz Fria

COIMBRA REGION
Although the name implies that this is a cold dish, it can be eaten whilst it is hot. It is very succulent either way. Partridge may not be as plentiful as it used to be, but it remains one of the most popular game birds in Portugal.

4 partridges (allow 1 small bird per person)	3 medium onions, thinly sliced
	2 cloves garlic, thinly sliced
8 tablespoons olive oil	2 cloves
8 tablespoons white wine	8 peppercorns
2 tablespoons wine vinegar	salt

Clean the birds and tie them with string, to keep the shape. Marinate them for a few hours in the wine, vinegar, salt and oil, turning now and then, to tenderize the meat. Put the partridges, marinade and all other ingredients in a roomy pot with a tight lid, and bring to the boil. Reduce to simmering point, cover and cook until tender, adding some water (or chicken stock) as necessary. Remove the partridges to a deep serving dish, pour the strained liquor over them and serve hot or cold with crisps and salad.

Chicken Pies Alentejo Style/Empadas de Galinha

These are small, individual pies, made in patty tins, which over the years have become exceedingly popular and which are now sold in pastry-shops all over the country but especially in Lisbon. They are much favoured for light lunches and snacks, during office breaks, for picnics and parties. They are eaten cold, but should ideally be baked on the same day.

PASTRY
12 oz (350 g) flour
5 oz (140 g) butter (soft but not melted)
1 teaspoon salt
4 egg yolks

FILLING (to be prepared beforehand)
1 lb (450 g) chicken meat, without skin or bones
1 medium onion, chopped
2 oz (60 g) lard
1 tablespoon wine vinegar
2 tablespoons white wine
3 sprigs parsley, chopped
1 clove
2 oz (60 g) lean bacon, cut into small pieces
dusting of nutmeg
salt

Cut the chicken into small pieces and fry in the lard, together with the bacon. When golden, add all the seasonings, including the wine and some water almost to cover it. Cook gently until very tender. Reduce the liquid but leave the mixture moist. Taste for seasoning. Set aside, to cool completely.

To start the dough, mix all the ingredients in a bowl, adding just enough water to make it pliable. Knead it very lightly. It should not be sticky. If it is, add a dusting of flour, to remedy this. Roll out to ⅛ inch (3 mm) and cut out rounds slightly larger than the patty tins. Set aside half the rounds, to use as lids. Line the tins, pressing the pastry against the sides, and fill them to three-quarters with the chicken stew, which will be almost solid by then and therefore easy to divide. Moisten the edges of the pastry with water and place the lids on top, pressing the edges together and turning them upwards. Brush with milk or a mixture of milk and egg yolk. Bake in an oven preheated to 200°C/400°F/Gas 6 for about 20 minutes or until the pies are a rich golden colour.
Makes about 12 pies.

Note: The chicken pies sold at patisseries do vary a little in that the pastry used is generally puff pastry or similar, while this recipe is the original one, from the Alentejo.

Veal Pies Castelo Branco Fashion/Empadas de Vitela de Castelo Branco

BEIRA BAIXA PROVINCE
These veal pies are a splendid speciality, which, like chicken pies (p.130) have transcended the limits of their place of origin to become very popular all over the country.

PASTRY
8 oz (225 g) flour
1 egg
2 tablespoons olive oil, slightly
warm
scant 1 oz (25 g) lard, melted
salt
egg for brushing

FILLING
11 oz (310 g) boned cooked veal
2 tablespoons white wine
1 medium onion, chopped
2 tablespoons olive oil
1 clove garlic, chopped
1 bay leaf
½ teaspoon marjoram
sprinkling nutmeg
salt and pepper

Prepare the pastry first. Mix the flour, oil, lard, egg, salt and some tepid water, to make a medium-soft dough. Knead for a moment, cover with a cloth and put aside for an hour.

Meanwhile, put all the ingredients for the filling (except the meat) in a pot and cook gently until the onion is soft. Add the meat cut into small pieces. Cover and simmer for a few minutes, adding a little stock if necessary. Taste for seasonings and leave to cool.

Roll out the pastry to ⅛ inch (3 mm) thickness and cut rounds somewhat larger than the diameter of your patty tins (which must be well greased). Cut out another lot of rounds for the lids. Line the tins, fill with the cold meat mixture, place the pastry lids on top, fold up the edges while pressing them, to seal (moisten with a little water, to make it easier) and twist a bit to form a kind of crown. Brush with the beaten egg. Bake at 200°C/400°F/Gas 6 for 20–25 minutes or until the pies are a golden brown.
Makes about 10 pies.

Variation
A mixture of veal and pork can be used, instead of veal alone.

Celebration Chicken Pasties/Fogaças

> 'Many women bring olive oil for the convent's oil-lamps, offerings of bread and chicken *fogaças* [pasties].'
> Fialho de Almeida, *Os Contos* (Short Stories)

Fogaças are like pasties, tasty and decorative, equally good hot or cold and ideal for picnics. In Portugal they are made especially for religious festivities, as part of traditional offerings to the Church (to be distributed afterwards among the needy, together with bread). But the word *fogaças* also came to be applied to the ornamental tall frames, looking rather like elongated crowns, that hold these offerings, which are carried solemnly on girls' heads. These contraptions are gaily ornamented with paper flowers and ears of wheat, while the bread and the pastics (and any other offerings) are skilfully displayed all the way up the frames, which are almost as tall as the girls who carry them. The girls bear these *fogaças* with great dignity and poise, balancing them perfectly with the help of one hand only, while the other hand rest on the waist.

Fogaças are also called *tabuleiros* in some places, hence the Tabuleiros Festival in Tomar (Ribatejo province), which is renowned throughout the country and considered one of the best of these magnificent country celebrations. Such festivities are carefully prepared, with the involvement of the entire community, and afford a very good excuse to interrupt the hard routine of peasant life.

Fogaças can be savoury, like these, or sweet (p.199).

DOUGH
14 oz (400 g) flour
½ oz (15 g) fresh yeast
2 oz (60 g) lard
1 tablespoons olive oil
3 large eggs, at room temperature
about 5 tablespoons tepid water
salt

FILLING
1 lb (450 g) boiled chicken
3 oz (90 g) smoked ham (or lean
  bacon)
1 medium onion, chopped
4 tablespoons white wine
6 tablespoons chicken broth
1 oz (30 g) lard
1 bay leaf
3 sprigs parsley, chopped
salt and pepper

For the filling, fry the onion in the lard until soft, add the parsley, bay leaf, salt and pepper, ham or bacon (cut into small cubes), broth, wine and chicken (boned, skinned and cut into very small pieces). Cook gently for a little while until it is all mixed and the liquid reduced to almost nothing. Taste for salt. Set aside to cool. Discard the bay leaf.

While the filling is resting, prepare a dough, mixing the flour, salt and yeast (crumbling this first). Make a well in the centre and add the warm water, 2 of the eggs and the melted fat and oil (still warm but not boiling). Mix well and knead as for a bread dough. Cover and leave to rise in a warm place for about an hour. Roll out the dough (to ⅛ inch/3 mm) on a floured board and cut half of it into 4 inch (10 cm) squares and the other half into rounds 3 inches (7.5 cm) in diameter. Divide the cold filling between the squares, placing it well in the centre and covering with the round lids. Fold up the corners of the squares over the round lids. Place the *fogaças* in greased baking trays and leave to rest in a warm place for about 30 minutes.

Preheat the oven to 190°C/375°F/Gas 5 and brush the pasties liberally with the remaining egg, well beaten. Bake for 25–30 minutes or until golden.
Makes about 10 *fogaças*.

Note: Try this appetizing filling for vol-au-vents or pies.

Sauces

Tomato Sauce, Portuguese Style/Molho de Tomate à Portuguesa – or Tomatada

Whenever you see a menu indicating a dish 'Portuguese Style', it usually means that there is a tomato sauce or some kind of tomato mixture in it. Tomatoes are widely used in Portuguese cookery, so dishes deserve that label.

Tomatoes did not appear in Europe until the Portuguese and Spanish explorers brought them in the sixteenth century from South America, where they were considered solely as a decorative plant with poisonous fruits (belonging, so it was said, to the 'nightshade' family). It was only later that the fruits tempted some people – who probably did not realize they might be poisonous, and having found out that they tasted good and did not do any harm, they started cultivating them as food. In nineteenth-century Britain they were still regarded as poisonous. Known as 'love-apples', they were hawked by itinerant pedlars as curiosities.

Tomato sauce 'Portuguese Style' is one in which onion is also quite prominent.

1 lb (450 g) fleshy ripe tomatoes, peeled, seeded and chopped
8 oz (225 g) onions, finely chopped
1 bay leaf
2 sprigs parsley, finely chopped

1 small clove garlic, finely chopped
4 tablespoons olive oil
1 tablespoon lard
salt and pepper

Cook everything together until tender, reduce any excess liquid, taste for seasoning and use for fish, meat or vegetable dishes. If you prefer a smooth sauce, blend or sieve it, discarding the bay leaf first.
Makes about 1 pint (600 ml).

Villain Sauce/Molho Vilão

To liven up 'Hake with Everything' (p.84) some people serve it with this sauce – although mainly that dish is served with just olive oil and a little vinegar. Villain Sauce is also used with other dishes, such as partridge and poached fish apart from the hake. It is especially good with poached mackerel (*cavala*), as prepared in Madeira.

¼ pint (150 ml) olive oil
1 small onion, finely chopped or
    grated
2 tablespoons wine vinegar
1 large egg, hard-boiled

1 medium clove of garlic, very
    finely chopped
2 sprigs parsley, chopped
1 sprig fresh coriander, chopped
    (optional)
salt and pepper

Chop up and sieve the hard-boiled egg. Mix the resulting paste with the grated onion, garlic, parsley and coriander (the latter gives a fresh, aromatic taste to the sauce and it is a good idea to include it). Beat the mixture with the liquid ingredients, taste for salt, dust with pepper and serve in a sauce-boat. If a completely smooth sauce is preferred, liquidize it. It should then look like a mayonnaise-type sauce.
Makes about ½ pint (300 ml).

Vinegar Sauce from the Algarve/Molho de Escabeche

This sauce, poured over fried fish, is made with the oil in which the fish was fried. Nice as an appetizer or first course.

¼ pint oil (kept from the frying
    pan)
1 large tomato, peeled and seeded
2 sprigs parsley, chopped
1 medium onion, chopped

3 tablespoons wine vinegar
1 small clove garlic, chopped
½ small green pimento (pepper),
    chopped (optional)
salt and pepper

Cook everything except the vinegar over a low heat until soft. Remove from heat, add the vinegar, bring to the boil again, taste for seasoning and then allow to cool. Serve cold, poured

over cold left-over fried fish. This sauce preserves the fish, which can be kept in it for a few days – if the weather is not too hot. Really nice, once you become accustomed to the highly seasoned taste.
Makes ½ pint (300 ml).

Vinegar Sauce/Escabeche

This *escabeche* (vinegar) sauce differs from the Algarve version in that it is used for game (especially partridge) and boiled beef, in addition to being good with cold fried fish.

¼ pint (150 ml) olive oil
2 tablespoons wine vinegar
2 tablespoons white wine
1 medium onion, finely chopped
1 clove garlic, finely chopped

1 coffeespoon paprika
2 sprigs parsley, chopped
1 bay leaf
1 clove
salt and pepper

Mix all ingredients except wine, vinegar and paprika, and simmer until soft. Remove from heat, discard bay leaf and clove and allow to cool. Then stir in the paprika, vinegar and wine, and taste for seasoning.
Makes about ½ pint (300 ml).

Port Wine Sauce

For this delicious sauce one can use either port or madeira (in their dry version). This is a rich, thick sauce, ideal for special occasions. Use it for livening up cooked meat.

½ pint (300 ml) meat or chicken
    stock (can be made with a good
    cube)
1 small onion, chopped
1 medium carrot, chopped
2 sprigs parsley, chopped
1 bay leaf

1 oz (30 g) butter
1 tablespoon flour
1 tablespoon tomato concentrate
3 tablespoons white wine
4 tablespoons port or madeira
    (dry)
salt and pepper

Sweat the onion, parsley and carrot in the butter for 5 minutes. Stir in the flour and add the white wine and bay leaf. Mix well and bring to simmering point again. Gradually mix in the stock and tomato concentrate. Allow to cook gently for 30–35 minutes. Sieve and taste for seasoning. Bring to the boil again and add the port or madeira. Serve hot. If the sauce is too thick, add a little more stock, before mixing in the port or madeira.
Makes ½ pint (300 ml).

Homemade Mayonnaise

This homemade sauce is much nicer than the bought variety, and it is not as difficult to make as most people think.

For each egg yolk use ¼ pint (150 ml) very good olive oil and ½ teaspoon wine vinegar, seasoning with a little salt and ½ teaspoon/made-mustard (the mild French type). In a deep bowl beat the egg yolk with the vinegar, then add the oil very gradually with one hand, whilst with the other you go on beating the sauce, always in the same clockwise movement. When thick, add a little salt and mustard and taste for seasoning. It can be kept in the refrigerator for several days.

Note: You may like to add a little more vinegar and/or mustard, but do this only after tasting and then add just small amounts at a time, until it tastes right.

Beirão Style Sauce/Molho Beirão

BEIRA ALTA PROVINCE

This sauce can be used in place of mayonnaise.

½ pint (300 ml) olive oil
3 hard-boiled eggs, very finely chopped
3 tablespoons wine vinegar
1 medium onion, finely chopped
3 sprigs parsley, finely chopped
salt and pepper

Combine all hard ingredients and stir in the oil. Beat well. Add the vinegar and beat again. Season and beat again. Serve cold. You can liquidize the sauce, if a completely smooth texture is preferred.
Makes about ¾ pint (450 ml).

Vegetables and Accompaniments

Little Fish from the Kitchen Garden/Peixinhos da Horta

FROM THE CENTRE OF PORTUGAL BUT USED COUNTRYWIDE

This is a curious name for a humble but nonetheless very tasty accompaniment for a meat dish as it does not, in fact, contain any fish. It is prepared with green beans in a batter, and so resembles small fish. *Peixinhos da Horta* are common fare in Portugal, while beans are in season, being served mainly at home, although some restaurants also have them.

14 oz (400 g) tender green beans,
cooked and cut into equal
lengths

FOR THE BATTER
4 oz (120 g) white plain flour
water
2 eggs

salt
oil for frying

In a deep plate or roomy bowl mix the flour with enough water to make a paste with the consistency of thick cream. When the flour is well mixed and free from lumps, add the beaten eggs and a little salt, and beat well. Use this batter for coating the green beans, frying them (in twos or threes) over medium heat until golden. Absorb excess fat on kitchen paper as you take the 'fishes' out of the frying pan.

They are good hot or cold. Although they are generally intended to go with any meat dish, you can serve them alone, with a tomato sauce or perhaps with a salad for a self-contained starter dish.
Serves 4.

Some people use milk instead of water for the batter, in which case they do not use eggs. White wine can also be substituted for the water.

Black-eyed Beans Salad/Salada de Feijão Frade

Black-eyed beans are quite popular in Portugal. They are much quicker to cook than ordinary beans, and their characteristic flavour makes them suitable for tasty hot or cold salads or as a starter dish. If served hot, they will be good with poached salt cod and hard-boiled eggs. If cold, they go well with canned sardines (in tomato or oil), canned tuna-fish or the well-loved salt cod cakes (*pasteis de bacalhau*, p.76). They are also very good on their own or with slices of hard-boiled egg, but either way black-eyed beans (hot or cold) must always be laced with some oil and a little vinegar, grated or finely cut raw onion and a good sprinkling of fresh parsley, to bring out their flavour.

8 oz (about 225 g) black-eyed beans	3 tablespoons olive oil
1 small onion, very finely chopped	1 teaspoon wine vinegar
	2 sprigs of parsley, chopped

Wash the beans, and sort out any debris. Soak overnight or at least for half a day. Cook in twice their depth of water. Add some salt towards the end of cooking. These beans get tender surprisingly quickly, but do not leave them undercooked. After simmering for about 35–40 minutes, they should be ready, but test them before taking the pan off the flame and allow the beans to boil a little longer, if needed. When tender, drain and discard the water, and use the beans as required, following either of the suggestions above, after seasoning them with the onion, oil and vinegar, well mixed. Sprinkle with plenty of chopped parsley.
Serves 4.

Variation
A very good lunch dish is a mixture of cooked black-eyed

beans, as above, with the addition of canned tuna and boiled eggs (with raw onion and parsley seasoning).

Stewed Green Beans, Portuguese Style/Feijão Verde Guisado à Portuguesa

As mentioned before, in any recipe named 'Portuguese style', you may expect to have some tomatoes among the ingredients. Stewed green-beans make a good accompaniment for eggs and fried food. Choose very tender beans for a perfect result.

1 lb (450 g) tender green beans
2 medium tomatoes, peeled,
  seeded and chopped
1 medium onion, chopped
1 tablespoon olive oil

1 tablespoon lard
1 small clove garlic, chopped
1 bay leaf
1 sprig parsley, chopped
salt and pepper

Wash and cut the green beans lengthwise and then again in 2 inch (5 cm) lengths. Melt the fat and oil, add the onion, tomatoes and seasonings and cook as a *refogado* (p.31) for 5–6 minutes, over a low flame. Add just a little boiling water and the green beans. Cook gently until tender, adding more water if it becomes dry. Taste for salt and serve very hot.
Serves 4 to 6.

Green Mousse/Esparregado

This vegetable accompaniment is very common in Portugal. It can be prepared either with tender turnip-tops or with spinach. It is good with meat or fish.

1 lb (450 g) cleaned turnip-tops or
  spinach (only leaves) – see
  Ingredients, p.19
2 tablespoons olive oil
1 tablespoon flour

few drops lemon juice or scant
  teaspoon wine vinegar
1 clove garlic (whole)
salt

Cook the greens until tender. Drain and cut them to a pulp or liquidize. Fry the garlic in the oil over a low flame, until the garlic is golden, then discard it (the objective is to flavour the oil). Add the flour, mix to a paste, combine the green pulp and boil gently for a couple of minutes, to cook the flour and thicken the mousse. Season with a few drops of lemon juice and more salt if needed.
Serves 4 to 6.

Variation
A less 'rural' *esparregado* can be prepared substituting the olive oil for butter, omitting the lemon juice or vinegar and adding a little milk to the flour-and-butter paste, to form a thick white sauce.

Stewed Wild Mushrooms/Cogumelos Guisados

TRÁS-OS-MONTES PROVINCE
Peasants in the northern inland provinces immensely value the wild mushrooms that grow in the region, for their protein content, and use them in tasty recipes when in season. Wild mushrooms have a much richer flavour than the rather bland cultivated ones. The amounts given here are for a main-course dish. If used only as an accompaniment, the quantities can be reduced.

2 lb (1 kg) wild mushrooms (or
    cultivated ones)
3–4 oz (90–110 g) smoked ham or
    lean bacon (in small cubes)
4 medium slices of bread

1 clove garlic, finely chopped
4 tablespoons olive oil
1 medium onion, finely chopped
salt

Wash the mushrooms or merely wipe them and cut off the end bit of the stalks. Cut the mushrooms into small pieces, or slice them to your taste. Set aside. Cook the bacon and the onion very gently in the oil. Add the mushrooms, shake the pan and season with the other ingredients. Cover and cook over low heat for 8–10 minutes. Do not add water, as the mushrooms create their own juices. Serve on top of slices of bread, which can be toasted or fried.
Serves 4 to 6.

Variation
The same recipe can be prepared omitting the bacon and adding a little nutmeg.

BROAD BEANS

He [Jacinto] cautiously tried a mouthful – and again his eyes, clouded by his chronic pessimism, lit up and caught mine. Another mouthful, deliberately slow, followed, like a friar savouring his food with delight. And finally the unrestrained exclamation: 'Marvellous! These broad beans are different! What broad beans! What a wondrous thing!'
    Eça de Queiroz, *The City and the Mountains* (*A Cidade e as Serras*)

Broad beans are extremely popular in Portugal, when in season. An old morning cry in Lisbon used to be *'Fava rica!'* (*'Rich broad beans'*). Women carrying the prepared dish, in large quantities, on their heads, would stop and sell a portion to the housewives who had come to their doors. This cry is now part of the past (not a very distant one, though), but broad beans are still consumed in great amounts all over the country, in a wide variety of splendid regional dishes, of which I include some of the best-known recipes.

There is an old saying referring to broad beans: *'Vai à fava!'* (*'Go to broad beans!'* literally, but meaning 'Go to Hell!') which is really an insult, though not a very strong one and used sometimes in a jocular way. As dried broad beans are commonly fed to donkeys in Portugal it is also the same as calling someone an ass.

Rich Broad Beans/Fava Rica

LISBON

Being made with dried broad beans, this dish used to be prepared all the year round and was a most popular dish, sold in the streets of Lisbon. Alas, it has disappeared in modern times, but *fava rica* is easy enough to prepare at home.

1 lb (450 g) dried broad beans	*1 coffeespoon wine vinegar*
3 cloves garlic, chopped	*salt and pepper*
4 tablespoons olive oil	

Soak the broad beans for 12–15 hours at least, in plenty of cold water. Drain and cook in fresh salted water until really tender. Drain and keep warm. Cook the garlic slowly in the oil, until golden. Toss the broad beans in the flavoured oil, add the vinegar, taste for seasoning and mash a few broad beans to thicken the sauce. Boil again for 2–3 minutes and serve piping hot.
Serves 4.

Broad Beans Lisbon Fashion/Favas à Moda de Lisboa

3 lb (1.5 kg) broad beans (unshelled)	*1 tablespoon lard*
	1 tablespoon butter
4 oz (110 g) fatty bacon, in cubes	*3 large sprigs coriander, chopped*
4 oz (110 g) chouriço (p.23), thickly sliced	*1 large onion, chopped*
	salt and pepper

Cook the meats with the seasonings (do not add much salt in the beginning) for 4–5 minutes, until golden. Add the shelled broad beans, toss, cover and cook gently for 20–30 minutes or until the beans are tender. Add enough water to prevent sticking and keep moist at all times. Shake the pan occasionally. Taste for seasoning and serve with lettuce salad.

An earthenware pot is ideal for cooking this dish.

Serves 4.

Broad Beans Ribatejo Fashion/Favas à Moda do Ribatejo

3 lb (1.5 kg approx.) tender broad beans (unshelled)
10 oz (280 g) lean pork, cut into small pieces
5 oz (140 g) lean bacon, cut into small cubes
5 oz (140 g) chouriço (p.23) thickly sliced
5 oz (140 g) black pudding, whole (p.24)
2 tablespoons olive oil
2 tablespoons lard
1 clove garlic, chopped
2–3 spring onions, chopped
4–6 sprigs coriander, chopped
salt and pepper
pinch of sugar

Shell the broad beans, wash and set aside. Fry the pork in the fat and oil over low heat, until golden. Add the other meat. Fry again. Mix the garlic, coriander, spring onions, pinch of sugar and broad beans. Toss around then reduce the heat and cover. The idea is to cook the broad beans with the steam generated inside the pan, but you will also need to add small amounts of water, gradually. Shake the pan now and then. Taste for salt (do not add the salt at the beginning, as some of the meat contains a certain amount of salt). Serve with lettuce salad, the classic accompaniment for most broad bean dishes.

Serves 4 to 6.

Broad Beans with Coriander/Favas com Coentros

THE ALENTEJO

Coriander is a herb very widely used in Portugal, especially in the Alentejo provinces (perhaps because of the Arab influence). Broad beans acquire a beautiful fragrance when cooked with it, as in this regional dish, meant as an accompaniment to local pork dishes but also apt to be served on its own (in which case the amounts should be doubled).

2½ lb (1.2 kg) broad beans
   (unshelled)
2 spring onions, chopped
6 sprigs coriander, chopped
3 sprigs parsley, chopped

1 tablespoon wine vinegar
4 tablespoons olive oil
2 large cloves garlic, finely
   chopped

Shell the broad beans and cook until tender in salted boiling water, adding just a third of the coriander and a spring onion. Drain and season with all other ingredients (raw), the oil and vinegar. Toss and serve.
Serves 4 to 6.

Broad Beans with Yellow Sauce, Bairrada Style/Favas com Molho Amarelo

BEIRA LITORAL PROVINCE

A very traditional recipe of the Bairrada region, prepared as an accompaniment to meat dishes but excellent for vegetarians if served with a salad instead of meat. Its special aroma is imparted by the use of savory.

2½ lb (1.2 kg) broad beans
   (unshelled)
2 sprigs parsley, chopped
2 sprigs savory, chopped

2 tablespoons butter
2 egg yolks
2 tablespoons flour
salt and pepper

Shell the broad beans and boil with a sprig of savory in salted water until tender (20–25 minutes). Drain and set aside but keep some of the liquor. Make a thick sauce with the butter, flour and part of the cooking-liquor. Add the chopped parsley and remaining chopped savory and boil again. Taste for seasoning and add the egg yolks. Beat well over a very low heat, add the cooked broad beans, reheat and serve at once.
Serves 4 to 6.

Broad Beans with Olive Oil/Favas com Azeite

RIBATEJO PROVINCE

3 lb (1.5 kg approx.) broad beans
   (unshelled)
2 spring onions, chopped
1 large clove garlic, chopped

4 tablespoons olive oil
salt
4 thin slices maize bread (p.57) or
   wholemeal bread

Shell and wash the broad beans and add to a pan containing oil and seasoning already sweated. Toss it all together, cover and

cook over a low heat, shaking now and then and adding a drop
of water if needed, to prevent sticking and to create a thickish
sauce. Serve immediately in individual plates, over the maize
bread. Have the classic lettuce salad as a side dish.
Serves 4.

Tomato Rice/Arroz de Tomate

This is especially good with fried fish, salted cod cakes and
omelettes.

*8 oz (225 g) long-grain rice
1 medium onion, finely chopped
2 medium tomatoes, peeled,
    seeded and chopped
2 tablespoons olive oil*

*water – 2½ times the volume of
    rice
1 sprig parsley, chopped
salt*

Fry the onion in the oil, for a good *refogado* (p.31), then add the
tomatoes and parsley and cook again for 5 minutes. Add the
water, bring to the boil and then add the rice and some salt.
Simmer until tender (about 25 minutes) and taste for salt before
serving. This rice should not be too dry. When left more on the
wet side, rice is sometimes called *malandrinho* (naughty). This
suggests just how succulent and tasty it is when made in this
fashion, either in its simple version with tomato and onion, or
made with fish, salt cod, seafood or meat. A risotto-type rice is
a good choice to make a wet rice.
Serves 4.

Variations
1 Pea Rice/*Arroz de Ervilhas* is another countrywide
accompaniment worth trying. Use only half the tomatoes and
add a handful of peas, which will cook with the rice. If the peas
are very tender, add them only later. Good with meat dishes.
  2 Chickpea Rice/*Arroz de Grão* is countrywide also. Omit
the tomatoes and add a handful of cooked chickpeas. Nice with
any kind of fried food.
  3 Bean and Coriander Rice/*Arroz Malandrinho* is an
accompaniment served in Lisbon restaurants. A generous
handful of cooked butter or kidney beans together with a
tablespoon of chopped fresh coriander is added five minutes
before the end of cooking to the rice. It is delicious with fried
food.

Vegetarians would, of course, enjoy these recipes with salads
and vegetable protein rissoles or pasties.

Sweet Things

The sweet-toothed Portuguese cannot face the day without cakes and desserts. Each town or village seems to have its own specialities, and so the variety and richness of sweets, all over the country, is quite impressive. The liking for very sweet things is probably a result of the Arab influence in Portugal. The marzipan cakes, moulded into fruit shapes and filled with sugary egg yolks found in the Algarve (Al-Gharb in Arabic) are very similar to sweets found in various North African countries and wherever there are Arabs.

To facilitate browsing through the recipes, I have grouped them (cakes, desserts, sweets and so on), hoping that in this way you will not be lost in the maze of the different kinds of 'sweet things'.

Puddings

Rice Pudding/Arroz Doce

FROM THE MINHO PROVINCE, BUT ADOPTED COUNTRYWIDE

> Vicencia brought in the rice pudding, and we said grace.
> Eça de Queiroz, *A Relíquia* (*The Relic*)

This is an absolute must at the Portuguese table for any celebration, be it Christmas, birthdays, weddings, parties, special days of all kinds. It is so widely appreciated that any day, in fact, is 'rice-pudding day', and restaurants, snackbars and other eating-places always have it at hand.

Rice pudding Portuguese style is made on top of the stove and is meant to be creamy but not very wet (it can in fact be taken out of the mould when cold). Whether served in individual dishes or on a large platter, Portuguese rice pudding must always be adorned with embroidery-like motifs made with cinnamon: heart shapes, initials (if it is intended for someone's birthday), flowers, lattice designs. This is done by pinching a little cinnamon between one's thumb and the first finger and skilfully letting it drop over the rice. The operation may take a little while, depending on the amount of decoration needed and on the dexterity of the decorator! The children of the house soon get interested and quite adept at this pleasant occupation and normally share it among themselves, comparing results afterwards – and, more often than not, boasting if they think their work was the best!

It is worth making more rice pudding than the amount needed for one sitting, because it keeps well from one day to another (or even for a couple of days), and although it dries out, it will certainly be very good to the end.

1 lb (450 g) short-grain rice   *½ coffeespoon salt*
10 oz (280 g) granulated sugar   *piece of lemon rind*
2 pints (1.2 l) full-cream milk   *cinnamon*
3 egg yolks

Wash the rice and cook it for 25 minutes (until tender) in 2½ times its volume of boiling water, with the salt and lemon rind. When cooked, remove the lemon rind and add the boiling milk, mixing well with a wooden spoon. Simmer until the liquid is reduced and the rice is really soft and creamy (20–30 minutes). Stir now and then. Add the sugar and boil again for 3–4 minutes. Remove from the heat and mix in the egg yolks. Bring to the boil (without allowing further boiling) just to cook the yolks. Taste for sugar (remember that it tastes sweeter when hot than after it has cooled down) and add a little more if liked. Pour into individual bowls or onto a large platter. Decorate, Portuguese style, as indicated above.

Do not be alarmed if some rice sticks to the bottom of the pan. This always happens, and care has to be taken not to allow it to burn, by stirring with the wooden spoon but without attempting to bring up the stuck layer, which would ruin the appearance of the rice. That layer can be scraped at the end and eaten by the cook as a special reward (it is the best part).
Serves 8 to 10.

Variations

1 Some short-cuts are allowed, especially when the *arroz doce* is to be eaten at an ordinary meal, with no one around likely to criticize it. Instead of using 3 egg yolks, use just one, and add a level teaspoon of custard powder made into a paste with a little milk, 3–4 minutes before the end of cooking. This will give the colour and thickness needed. Decorate with cinnamon as for the previous recipe.

2 Another idea that I have tried many times is to use sweetened condensed milk instead of sugar. This also enables a reduction of half the amount of fresh milk, which cuts the cooking time in half, after the milk is added. Mix in sufficient condensed milk to sweeten just 2 minutes before the end of cooking. I find that half an ordinary full-cream can (equivalent to 7 oz/200 g condensed milk) is generally enough. Use an egg yolk and the custard powder, or 2 or 3 egg yolks, depending on how rich you want the *arroz doce*, following the procedure above. Decorate with cinnamon as for the main recipe.

Egg Custard/Leite-Creme

BEIRA PROVINCES, BUT USED COUNTRYWIDE

Egg custard, with more or fewer egg yolks, according to how rich one wants it, is a delectable and wholesome pudding with which to finish a meal, and although it may now be considered old-fashioned, it continues to be a good stand-by, always appreciated in Portugal. Indeed, a good *leite-creme* is the pride of many a housewife.

This custard is not baked but simply made on top of the stove and eaten when cold.

1 pint (600 ml) milk
3–4 egg yolks (depending on size of the eggs)
1 tablespoon plain white flour
5 oz (140 g) granulated sugar

1 piece lemon peel or vanilla pod
cinnamon for sprinkling or a little sugar, if a burnt top is preferred

Take 3 tablespoons of the milk to mix with the flour until it is smooth. Keep 2 tablespoons of milk aside to mix with the egg yolks. Warm up the remainder of the milk over low heat, together with the sugar and lemon peel or vanilla pod. Before it starts boiling, mix in the flour paste carefully, with a wooden spoon, and bring gently to the boil, stirring all the time. Let it cook for about 4 minutes. Remove from the heat and very gradually add the egg-yolk mixture. Bring back to the heat, always stirring, to cook the yolks (for about a minute). Remove

the vanilla pod or lemon peel and pour the cream into a pyrex dish, sprinkle with some sugar and place under the grill for a very short while, until the sugar caramelizes on top. Alternatively, sprinkle the surface of the pudding with a little cinnamon. It can also be served in individual glass bowls. It gets thicker after cooling, so do not worry if it looks a little thin when pouring.
Serves 4 to 6.

Variations
1 A richer version of egg custard can be made with 6 egg yolks instead of the 3–4 indicated above.

2 Another method of preparing this pudding is to mix the yolks with the sugar until really smooth and almost white in colour. Then add 2 tablespoons of milk to make the mixture more fluid and combine with the flour, beating very thoroughly again. Pour this into the remaining milk, beating well and bring to the heat, stirring, allowing it to simmer for a few minutes as above, until creamy. It thickens further after cooling down.

3 A more homely version is the following:

¾ pint (450 ml) milk   *1 heaped teaspoon cornflour*
3 oz (90 g) granulated sugar   *flavouring, as above*
2 egg yolks

Mix the flour with a little milk and then add the sugar and egg yolks. Beat well. In the meantime have the milk heated to boiling point. Pour it over the prepared mixture, beat thoroughly and bring back to the heat. Keep stirring. Once it reaches boiling point, remove the pan from the heat, then bring it back again. Do this several times, until the custard is creamy.

4 From the Beira Litoral province comes this luscious egg custard:

¾ pint (450 ml) milk   *1½ tablespoons flour*
9 oz (250 g) granulated sugar   *flavourings – as above*
5 egg yolks

Beat the yolks with the sugar, until smooth and almost white. Add the flour and a little milk. Beat again. Combine gradually the remaining milk. Bring slowly to the boil and then simmer, stirring all the time. Allow it to thicken (about 8 minutes). Pour into a serving dish, sprinkle with sugar and place under the grill, to form a golden-brown crust.

Note: The real secret of these variations is to keep stirring the sweet while cooking.

Crème Caramel/Pudim Flan

ESTREMADURA PROVINCE

A popular pudding, anywhere. At restaurants, little puddings
are served, but they are troublesome to prepare at home, where
it is much more practical to use a large mould.

¾ pint (450 ml) milk　　　　　*7 oz (200 g) granulated sugar*
4 large eggs, well beaten

Prepare the caramel first: bring 4 oz (110 g) of the sugar to the
boil with 2 tablespoons of water, in a saucepan. Allow it to turn
into a liquid caramel and pour immediately into the mould,
turning it around, to coat evenly. A spoon may be helpful, to
cover the interior of the mould. This operation must be done at
great speed, as the caramel dries very quickly. Any lumps left
around the mould will melt later, so do not worry much about
them. Leave the mould aside. Warm up the milk to blood
temperature and beat in the eggs and the rest of the sugar.
Combine really well and pour into the prepared mould, 6–7
inches 15–18 cm in diameter. Bake in a bain-marie (placing the
mould inside a tin containing boiling water) in the oven
(180°C/350°F/Gas 4) until set (35–40 minutes).
Serves 6.

Note: I save a lot of time and trouble by cooking this pudding
in the pressure-cooker, using the trivet. 10–12 minutes are
enough for the cooking under pressure. Be sure to cover the
mould with a tight lid or foil, to avoid water coming into the
pudding. Take out of the mould when cold.

Chocolate Mousse/Mousse de Chocolate

The Portuguese are terribly fond of chocolate mousse, which
appears on menus everywhere, and housewives like to boast
about their particular mousse. To make a good mousse, one
must use excellent chocolate and several eggs. This is a superb
pudding, and one might as well be generous with the
ingredients.

7 oz (200 g) plain or bitter　　*2 tablespoons butter*
　chocolate　　　　　　　　*a little dusting of powdered*
4 large eggs, separated　　　　*vanilla*
6 tablespoons caster sugar (or
　more if you prefer the mousse
　sweeter)

Beat the egg whites until really hard. Set aside. Break the

chocolate into small pieces and put it in a pan inside a bigger one containing boiling water, to melt. Mix in the sugar, vanilla, butter and beaten egg yolks. Keep the mixture in the bain-marie (p.151), all the while stirring it carefully. When you have a perfectly homogenous paste, remove the pan from the heat and add the stiffly beaten egg whites. Fold them over and over until well mixed. Note that all this must be done without delay, or the chocolate mixture will harden too much and it will be impossible to mix it evenly with the egg whites. Put the prepared mousse in a serving bowl and leave in the refrigerator until needed. It should be slightly cool but not iced. Serve it without any additions, which might detract from the wonderful taste and texture. The mousse can also be used as a filling or topping for cakes.
Serves 4 to 6.

Soft Eggs/Ovos Moles

AVEIRO, BEIRA LITORAL PROVINCE
This is one of the best-loved and most renowned Portuguese puddings, and in Aveiro it is sold in little wooden barrels, gaily decorated, to be eaten by the spoonful, or as a filling for white shell-like cases (made commercially in Aveiro and sold all over the country). *Ovos moles* are used for all kinds of confectionery: as a topping and/or filling for sponge cakes and tarts, as a thick sauce for puddings, as a decoration for small cakes, and so on. *Ovos moles* are also served as a dessert, combined with a handful of walnuts or roast almonds, roughly ground, sprinkled with just a dusting of cinnamon, or simply on their own.

Ovos moles are easy to make and, although expensive, due to the use of many egg yolks, they can be 'stretched' by adding rice flour or mashed boiled rice. Variations like these are fine to use as fillings, but the basic recipe is much richer, obviously, when intended to be eaten by the spoonful.

9 oz (250 g) granulated sugar   *¼ pint (150 ml) water*
8 egg yolks

Bring the water and sugar to the boil over a low flame, until it reaches the 'pearl stage' (p.35). Allow to cool a little and mix with the beaten yolks, dropping the sugar syrup over them slowly and beating vigorously all the time. Bring to a gentle boil again, stirring, until it resembles a thick custard. Divide the sweet between small glass serving bowls or pour into a larger bowl.
Serves 4.

Variations
1 With boiled rice. Same amounts as before, regarding sugar
and water, plus 6 egg yolks (instead of 8) and 2 oz (60 g)
pudding-type rice, boiled until very soft and made into a pap
with fork or liquidizer. Make the syrup, add the rice purée,
simmer for 2 minutes while stirring, and then add to the yolks,
beating the whole mixture very well. Bring to the heat, stirring,
to cook the yolks and thicken. Suitable for fillings and
toppings.
    2 With rice flour. Same amount of sugar and water, and only
4 yolks. Add 4 level tablespoons of rice flour, made into a paste
with a minimum of water, to the sugar syrup. Boil a little,
stirring, to cook the flour. Cool slightly and add to the beaten
yolks, boiling gently for a short time, while stirring. This
simpler variation is especially suitable for fillings or to
sandwich sponge cakes. It gets really thick when cold.
    Note: The pumpkin jam on p.215 can also be used as a cheap
version of *ovos moles*, if 2–3 egg yolks are added to about 6–7 oz
(175–200 g) of jam. This will produce a very good filling for
cakes. Just boil the jam very gently with the beaten yolks for a
minute or so, to cook them, allow to cool and use.

Bacon from Heaven/Toucinho do Céu

ODIVELAS, LISBON AREA BUT FOUND COUNTRYWIDE
Although many other places have their own 'Bacon from
Heaven' and claim the original recipe, this pudding is said to
come traditionally from Odivelas, a Lisbon suburb which was
of some importance as far back as the thirteenth century when
kings found it convenient for discreet 'love nests' near the
capital. Philippa of Lancaster (born in London in 1350), the
daughter of John of Gaunt, Duke of Lancaster, who became
Queen of Portugal through her marriage to King João I, also
liked the place and died (of the plague) in the convent at
Odivelas in 1415.
    The old convent used to be famous for its poetry sessions (at
which well-known poets would be invited to recite their work),
followed by drinks accompanied by glacé pumpkin and lemon
peel, meringues and little quince-cheese squares, also an
Odivelas creation (still available at every good grocer in
Portugal). But the most tempting of all the convent's
confectionery was the 'Bacon from Heaven', a cross between a
cake and a pudding, nowadays eaten as a dessert or with tea.
The original convent recipe was extraordinarily rich, with
many more eggs and possibly the inclusion of bacon – hence
the title – and simpler versions, like the one below, have since

evolved. These versions are themselves rich – otherwise there would be no point in saying that it is a sweet from Heaven!

9 oz (250 g) ground almonds	*2 tablespoons flour*
11 oz (310 g) granulated sugar	*½ teaspoon cinnamon*
7 eggs	

Beat the sugar, cinnamon and eggs until very fluffy. Add the flour and ground almonds. Beat well again. Bake in a buttered and floured round cake tin 7–8 inches (18–20 cm) in diameter, at 163°C/325°F/Gas 3, for 25 minutes or until set and golden on top. Take out of the mould after cooling a little, and scrape off the flour from the sides. Sprinkle thickly with caster sugar.
Makes about 8 slices.

Variations
1 There are several regional variations to this pudding. One of the simplest is another convent creation, from Beja (Alentejo province) and, although not strictly a 'Bacon from Heaven', this version has the virtue of being cheaper while still a very good pudding in itself.

7 oz (200 g) caster sugar	*5 oz (140 g) ground almonds*
3 oz (90 g) flour	*3 eggs, separated, plus 2 egg yolks*
2 tablespoons milk	

Beat the sugar with the egg yolks until foamy. Add the milk and beat well. Mix in the almonds and flour. Beat again. Fold in the stiffly whipped whites. Bake in a buttered round cake tin 7–8 inches (18-20 cm) in diameter in an oven preheated to 180°C/350°F/Gas 4 for 25–30 minutes or until golden and well set. Take out of the tin when lukewarm. Sprinkle with caster sugar and cinnamon or soak with a light syrup made with 5–6 tablespoons granulated sugar and enough water to melt it, boiled for 2–3 minutes over gentle heat.

2 This is a rich version, from Murça (Trás-os-Montes and Alto Douro province) and must be mentioned here as it is considered one of the best and most authoritative recipes for 'Bacon from Heaven'.

7 oz (200 g) granulated sugar	*4 whole eggs plus 6 yolks, all*
3 oz (90 g) ground almonds	*beaten together*
	1 coffeespoon cinnamon

Make a syrup with the sugar and a little water (just enough to melt it), by boiling it until thick (2–3 minutes) – see p.35 for the 'pearl stage'. Add the almonds and simmer for a couple of minutes, stirring. Remove from the heat. Beat in the cinnamon and eggs. Simmer again, to thicken. Pour into a 7 inch (18 cm) round cake tin, well buttered, and bake at 190°C/375°F/Gas 5 until set (about 15 minutes). Do not overcook, to avoid its drying too much. Take out of the tin after cooling a little and sprinkle with caster sugar.

Orange Roll/Torta de Laranja

A lavish pudding, very popular and almost always available at Portuguese restaurants, though this homemade version may be better still.

¼ pint (150 ml) pure orange juice   *7 oz (200 g) caster sugar*
5 large eggs   *grated rind of 1 orange*
1 tablespoon cornflour

Dissolve the flour in the juice and mix in the sugar, grated rind and beaten eggs. Combine well, without whisking too hard. Prepare a baking tray suitable for Swiss roll, 8 × 12 inches (20.5 ×30.5 cm) well greased and lined. The lining paper must also be greased and sprinkled with sugar. Pour the mixture onto this and bake at 180°C/350°F/Gas 4 for 15–20 minutes, until firm and with a rich orange colour. Turn into a slightly damp cloth, sprinkled with sugar. Trim the edges and roll up carefully, with the help of the cloth. Place in a sugared serving dish and again sprinkle with sugar, when cold. Cut into thick slices, which are served on their own, as a pudding.
Serves 4 to 6.

Nun's Belly/Barriga de Freira

BEIRA LITORAL PROVINCE
During the sixteenth and seventeenth centuries, it became a custom in convents to celebrate the election of a new superior with a music-and-poetry evening, to which artists would be invited and later offered delicious sweets and wine by the nuns. Almeida Garrett (1799–1854), in *The Lyrics of João Mínimo* (*A lírica de João Mínimo*) describes it thus: '... music and more sonnets and verses of all kinds, with many delicious sweets offered to us by the nuns. As far as I am concerned, this was not by any means the least pleasing of the events of the evening.' One can imagine that 'nun's belly' would be one of the sweets offered to special guests. Such a title, though – and that of so many other sweets of convent origin, makes one think that medieval nuns considered themselves great temptresses. Anyway, all those sweets are somewhat similar, because they are based mainly on eggs and sugar.

10 oz (280 g) granulated sugar
2 small slices white bread (no
  crust) crumbled
5 egg yolks

small piece of lemon rind
1 oz (30 g) butter
1 teaspoon cinnamon

Make a light syrup (see p.35 for the 'smooth stage') with the sugar and enough water to melt it, adding the lemon rind. Remove the rind, then add the breadcrumbs, the butter and finally the lightly beaten yolks. Boil very gently, stirring all the time, for 2–3 minutes, to thicken. Pour into a serving dish and sprinkle with the cinnamon.
Serves 4 to 6.

Slices, Tomar Style/Fatias de Tomar

RIBATEJO PROVINCE

Near Tomar there are interesting Roman remains (the towns of Sallium and Nabancia), but the town itself was founded during the twelfth century, when a castle was built on the margins of the Nabão river. This was to be the Templars' headquarters in Portugal. In 1312 this powerful and rich Order became extinct, and it was replaced in 1321 by the Order of Christ, destined for a special role during the voyages of discovery. Prince Henry 'the Navigator' was nominated its governor, in 1416, and this position enabled him to use some of the Order's resources to finance the voyages (together with his own fortune). In return, the Order acquired the privilege of overseeing the spiritual welfare of the lands discovered.

Tomar has never quite lost its medieval flavour, and many questions still await an answer from those times when the mysterious Templars first dominated it. For example, what is the meaning of the *signum solomonis* on the façade of the main temple, and its orientation in relation to the towers – which, according to old tales, are connected to the castle by a secret tunnel? There is an undeciphered symbolism in the main window, and even in the plan of the old town, with four main streets crossing each other and orientated to the cardinal points. Only those secretive 'soldier-monks' would be able to lift the veil.

Today Tomar is an important market centre for neighbouring farms, and it has many festivities, processions and old traditions regarding food, such as these lovely slices.

12 oz (350 g) granulated sugar
10 egg yolks

In Tomar there is a special deep oval mould for this glamorous sweet, but it can be baked in any ordinary pudding mould, providing it has a lid.

Beat the egg yolks on their own for a long time, until very light and foamy. The idea is to introduce as much air into the mixture as possible. An electric mixer will do the job in 8–10 minutes, otherwise you need a strong arm to beat it for the best part of half an hour. Pour the beaten yolks into a liberally greased and deep mould (about 6 inches/15 cm in diameter) and place it in a pan containing boiling water, therefore baking it bain-marie style (p.151). You can do this either in the oven or on top of the stove. Do not forget to cover the mould with its lid, or with foil, failing this. Keep the surrounding water boiling (topping it up, as necessary) until the eggs are well set (about 30 minutes). Take it out of the mould very carefully after cooling. When quite cold, cut the pudding evenly with a very sharp knife into ¾ inch (1.5 cm) slices and boil them, one by one, for a minute, in a light syrup (see the 'smooth stage', p.35) made with the sugar and a bit more than enough water to melt it – about ½ pint (300 ml). Keep the syrup simmering throughout, but add a little water now and then, when it becomes too thick. When all the slices are ready, cover them with any remaining syrup. Serve cold on a glass platter.
Makes about 8 slices.

Christmas Golden Soup/Sopa Dourada

VIANA DO CASTELO, MINHO PROVINCE
In *The City and the Mountains*, Eça de Queiroz recalls his leaving Paris to return to his native village – for family reasons. What a nuisance. But then he realized that there might be compensations awaiting him: 'I thought how good Aunt Vicencia's golden soup would be. I hadn't savoured it for years, nor the roast suckling pig, nor the rice, made at our home!' He confided afterwards: 'I ate with delight Aunt Vicencia's golden soup ...'

Golden soup is a dessert served usually during the Christmas season in the Minho province and more specifically in Viana do Castelo.

6 oz (175 g) sponge cake (it can be stale cake) in thin slices	7 egg yolks
12 oz (350 g) granulated sugar	¼ pint (150 ml) water
	cinnamon

Mix the sugar with the water and bring to the boil to make a thick syrup (see p.35 or the 'thread stage'). Remove from the heat. Using a slotted spoon, dip each slice of cake into the syrup, and place them in a large serving dish. When they are all soaked in the syrup, beat the egg yolks and mix them with the remaining syrup. Bring to the heat for one moment and stir, to thicken, without allowing the yolks to curdle. Pour this custard over the slices, sprinkle with cinnamon and serve when cold. *Serves 6*.

Variation
In Fafe, also in Minho province, there is another, still richer version of this recipe:

½ pint (300 ml) ovos moles (see   8 medium slices very slightly
   p.152 and choose one of the   stale sponge cake (pão-de-lo,
   richer variations)   p.203)
                                   1 oz (30 g) candied fruit to taste

Spread the cake in a serving dish. Cover with the *ovos moles*, warmed up to facilitate absorption, and leave overnight. Decorate with the candied fruit or simply with cinnamon.

Priscos Parish Priest Pudding/Pudim do Abade de Priscos

ENTRE-DOURO AND MINHO PROVINCES
This pudding was created by the Parish Priest of the small town of Priscos, Father Manuel Rebello. He was an extraordinary character, a person of extensive culture in the most diverse subjects. A great-grandniece of his, my good friend, Maria Adosinda, has told me of his ability to know and do almost anything, quite apart from being an excellent, pious and beloved parish priest, to the last days of his very long life (1834–1930). He was a great theatre fan and founded a dramatic society in the town, to the immense delight of his parishioners, and was a splendid photographer – rare hobbies for a priest of his time. His embroidery was perfection itself, and some precious pieces were framed and are still kept by his family. But what brought him fame during his lifetime and immortality now was his culinary talent.

He had a little bag, which he kept well away from curious eyes, where he stored all his secret ingredients, spices and seasonings. Unfortunately it disappeared after his death, and nobody found out what was inside. His art became so well known that he used to be called upon to direct the preparation of great banquets, including some in honour of the Portuguese royal family. On account of his merits he was created Honorary Chaplain of the royal household. This recipe uses fatty bacon, which seems unusual but gives a very special taste to the pudding.

14 oz (390 g) granulated sugar
½ pint (300 ml) water
12 egg yolks, well beaten
2 tablespoons port wine

1½ oz (45 g) bacon fat, without
   rind, very finely sliced
1 stick cinnamon
1 piece lemon rind

Put the bacon slices (which will melt, during cooking), the water, 10 oz (280 g) of the sugar, cinnamon stick and lemon rind in a pan and to the boil, until a syrup is formed. Remove from the heat, cool a little, discard the cinnamon and lemon rind, then add the egg yolks and wine. Beat well and set aside. Prepare the caramel to coat a deep pudding mould about 6–7 inches (15–18 cm) in diameter (see p.151). Pour the prepared mixture into this and bake in the oven, in a bain-marie (p.151), at 246°C/475°F/Gas 9, for nearly an hour or until well set and golden. Allow to cool before taking it out of the mould.
Serves 6 to 8.

Sweet Migas/Migas Doces

BEIRA ALTA
Bread is used in Portugal in the making of puddings as it is almost all over the world. In the two recipes below the bread serves merely as a thickener, being completely disguised with the egg-and-sugar mixture.

7 oz (200 g) granulated sugar
3½ (100 g) fresh white
   breadcrumbs
5 egg yolks

2 oz (60 g) ground almonds
¼ pint (150 ml) water
1 coffeespoon cinnamon

Boil the water with the sugar for a minute, reduce the heat and add the breadcrumbs. Mash well. Mix the ground almonds, stirring all the time over a low flame, until it is homogeneous. Take off the heat and beat in the yolks. Bring the mixture to the heat again, just to boiling point, while stirring. Divide into individual small dessert bowls and sprinkle with cinnamon.
Serves 4.

Variation
From the same province comes a similar bread dessert, using double the amount of fresh white breadcrumbs but no almonds. The bread is soaked in very hot milk (¼ pint/150 ml) and mashed, before adding to the boiling sugar. The rest of the procedure follows as above.

   You can also serve these desserts in a large dish instead of pouring into individual bowls.

Floating Islands/Farófias

ESTREMADURA PROVINCE

This is a very old-fashioned recipe, less popular now but excellent all the same. It is useful to use up whites of eggs which abound in Portuguese kitchens, due to the use of so many yolks. It is a very interesting sweet, consisting of white mounds floating on custard, and lightly dusted with a hint of cinnamon. It is best eaten soon after it has been made (prepare it just before the meal it is intended for), as the whites tend sometimes to flatten a little and thus lose some of their visual appeal – though not the taste, which is delicate and delicious.

3 egg whites, stiffly beaten
3 oz (90 g) granulated sugar
1 pint (600 ml) milk
1 teaspoon custard powder (or the
   egg yolks)

1 piece of lemon rind
cinnamon
pinch of salt

After the whites have been beaten really well, until forming peaks, fold in about a third of the sugar. While you are doing this, have the milk over low heat with a small piece of lemon rind and the remaining sugar in it. When it is boiling, reduce the flame and maintain just a gentle bubbling. Discard the lemon rind. Cook large spoonfuls of the egg-white mixture in the boiling milk. They cook very quickly, puffing up like small castles. Remove each mound as they cook, using a slotted spoon. Keep the *farofias* in a large strainer, to drain off any excess milk. When they are all cooked, put them in a serving bowl and set aside.

Now prepare a custard using the powder (made into a paste with a little cold milk) or the egg yolks, if wanted, and the milk used for cooking the *farofias*. Add also any milk dropped through the strainer and a pinch of salt. Boil gently, to cook the flour, stirring for 2 minutes, and pour into a large serving bowl. Again using a slotted spoon, place the white 'islands' onto the custard, very carefully. Dust with a little cinnamon and serve. All these operations must be done speedily – the *farofias* may collapse a little, if left for too long.

If using the egg yolks for thickening the sauce instead of the custard powder (which is really a short-cut), mix them carefully in the milk, off the heat, bring back to the flame and stir continuously until it thickens, just simmering.

Serves 4 to 6.

Cheese Pudding/Pudim de Queijo

AZORES ARCHIPELAGO
The Azores' own cheese, Queijo da Ilha, (p.30) is used for this recipe. Good Cheddar-type cheese can, however, be substituted.

5 oz (140 g) grated cheese
2 oz (60 g) butter
10 oz (280 g) granulated sugar

4 egg yolks plus 2 whole eggs
a few glacé cherries

Simmer the sugar in a little water, enough to melt it, for 3–4 minutes. Remove from the heat. Beat in the grated cheese and the butter. When cool, add the egg yolks and the whole eggs, beaten. Mix well. Grease and sprinkle with granulated sugar a mould 7–8 inches (18–20 cm) in diameter. Place the cherries around the bottom of the mould and pour in the cheese mixture. Bake for 30–40 minutes in a bain-marie (p.151) in an oven at 190°C/375°F/Gas 5 until golden and set.
Serves 6.

Soft Cheese Pudding/Pudim de Requeijão

ESTRELA MOUNTAIN REGION
This is a rich cheese pudding, including almonds. The original recipe indicates rather a lot of sugar, but I find that reducing it by a third, as indicated below, gives a better result – unless, of course, one is extremely sweet-toothed. One can also make the recipe less expensive by using whole eggs, instead of only yolks. There is no significant loss in flavour or texture by adopting these economical measures.

5 oz (140 g) fresh cheese,
requeijão style (see p.30)
4 oz (110 g) ground almonds

1½ lb (675 g) caster sugar (or 1 lb/450 g)
12 egg yolks (or 6 whole eggs)
1 coffeespoon cinnamon

Combine the sugar with the almonds and the cheese, to obtain a soft paste. Add the eggs, gradually, and the cinnamon. Place in a well-buttered cake tin (about 7–8 inches 17.5–20 cm in diameter) and bake in an oven set to 163°C/325°F/Gas 3 for the first 15 minutes, increasing to 180°C/350°F/Gas 4, until golden (about 30 minutes in all). Take out of the mould only after cooling a little. Serve as a dessert, when cold.
Serves 6.

Walnut Cake/Bolo de Nozes

This is a luxurious cake without flour and could be classified as a pudding or as a most delicious filling for a tart, using *ovos moles* as a topping. Decorate with walnut halves.

7 oz (200 g) walnuts, roughly crushed
7 oz (200 g) caster sugar

4 eggs, separated
filling ovos moles *(variation 2, p.152)*

Mix the walnuts with the sugar and egg yolks, until it is as homogeneous as possible. Beat the egg whites stiffly and fold into the previous mixture. Divide this between two well-buttered cake tins 6 inches (15 cm) in diameter. Bake at 190°C/375°F/Gas 5 for 15–20 minutes or until set. Take out of the tin with great care after cooling a little and join together with the filling. Dust the top with sugar. Serve cold.
Serves 4 to 6.

Dry Sweet Soup/Sopa Seca Doce

MINHO AND DOURO LITORAL PROVINCES
The custom of including meat (especially chicken) in some puddings is still kept up in some northern areas, even though they are prepared mainly for specific rural festivities (grape-picking and weddings). In the Middle Ages, however, the use of sugar and meat was very widespread (see p.7). The recipe below is but one variation of several still in use and can be considered a bread pudding rather than a cake.

½ leg of chicken
4–5 oz (110–140 g) lean beef
1 oz (30 g) fatty bacon
2 tablespoons clear honey
2 sprigs of mint

6–7 oz (175–200 g) white bread, sliced
1 teaspoon cinnamon plus enough for sprinkling
½ teaspoon salt
granulated sugar to taste

Cook the meat in enough water to cover – at least 1 pint (600 ml) – and season with salt and mint. When tender, remove the meat (to be used in some savoury dish) and strain the liquor. Measure about a pint (600 ml) and sweeten it with the honey and sugar to taste, adding the cinnamon. Mix well. Put the slices of bread in a bowl and pour the sweetened liquid over it. Butter a deep fireproof dish about 7–8 inches (18–20 cm) in diameter and sprinkle with sugar and cinnamon. Spoon layers of the soaked break into the dish, alternating with more cinnamon and sugar between each layer. Sprinkle some on top, when all the bread is used up, and cover the dish with foil or greaseproof paper, to prevent burning. Bake for 10 minutes at 190°C/375°F/Gas 5, reducing to 150°C/300°F/Gas 2 for a further

---

15–20 minutes. Remove the foil or paper for the last 5–8 minutes of baking, to produce a golden top. Serve whilst still warm, in the same dish.
Serves 4 to 6.

Straw from Abrantes/Palha de Abrantes

RIBATEJO PROVINCE
From this interesting Roman-founded town comes a well-known egg-yolk-based pudding which, in spite of the name 'straw', is in fact a rich creation in the best Portuguese tradition.

7 oz (200 g) granulated sugar
8 eggs
1 teaspoon cinnamon

Make a portion of 'egg threads' (*fios de ovos*) with half the eggs and the sugar, as explained on p.216. Set aside. Boil the remaining syrup until quite thick (the 'pearl stage', see p.35). Take off the heat and allow to cool a little, before adding the other 4 eggs, very well beaten. Simmer, whilst stirring constantly, until thick. Remove from the heat, beat in the cinnamon and pour the pudding into a glass serving-dish, decorating the top with the egg threads, like straw.
Serves 4 to 6.

Heavenly Food/Manjar Celeste

ESTREMOZ, ALENTEJO PROVINCE
Another celestial title for a sweet, giving away its origin. You guessed: It was a convent, this time the one at Estremoz, founded in the thirteenth century. Estremoz is a lovely old walled town, favoured by the first kings. Vasco da Gama, the famous Portuguese sea-captain in charge of the expedition which braved the first voyage from Europe to Asia (embarking at Lisbon in July 1497), used to live there.

7 oz (200 g) fresh cheese   *7 oz (200 g) granulated sugar*
 (requeijão, p.30)   *4 egg yolks plus 1 whole egg*

Make a light syrup (the 'smooth stage', p.35) with the sugar and a little water (enough to melt it). Add the sieved cheese and beat well by hand or with an electric mixer. Simmer until creamy (5–8 minutes). Remove from heat, cool slightly and add the beaten egg yolks and whole egg. Pour into small earthenware bowls (or small ramekins), previously buttered. Bake at 190°C/375°F/Gas 5 for about 15 minutes or until golden and well set.
Serves 6

Food from Heaven/Manjar Celeste

RIBATEJO PROVINCE
Although this recipe has the same title as the one from
Estremoz, it is in fact a completely different pudding.

3 oz (90 g) soft breadcrumbs (no   2 oz (60 g) ground almonds
  crust)   4 eggs
7 oz (200 g) granulated sugar   ¼ pint (150 ml) 'egg threads'
  plus 2 tablespoons   (p.216)

Make a light syrup ('smooth stage', p.35) with the 7 oz (200 g)
sugar and enough water to melt it. Add the crumbs and
almonds and mix into a paste. Simmer for 4–5 minutes, stirring.
Take off the heat and mix with the beaten eggs, and the 2
tablespoons of sugar, until very fluffy. Bring to simmering
point again and cook for 4–5 minutes or until it thickens. Pour
into a serving dish and decorate with a mound of 'egg threads'.
Serves 4 to 6.

Egg and Cinnamon Pudding, Elvas Fashion/
  Sericá

ALENTEJO PROVINCE
This unusual speciality comes from Elvas, one of the most
interesting walled cities in Portugal. Its Roman-Arabian castle
and the fortress command views of the city and surrounding
landscape. Among all the remarkable constructions in Elvas the
Aqueduct stands out as a masterpiece of the fifteenth and
seventeenth centuries, reckoned the biggest in the Iberian
peninsula and the most beautiful in Europe. Elvas' geogra-
phical position, bordering Spain, gave it great importance as a
meeting-place for kings and nobles from both countries, and at
least two royal weddings, involving both Courts, were
celebrated there – that of a Portuguese princess with the King
of Castile in 1383 and, perhaps more important, that between
the daughter of the Holy Roman Emperor Charles V (himself a
King of Spain as well) and a Portuguese prince in 1552. I am
sure this pudding would do full honours to the banquets that
followed, although the city is renowned for all its cuisine, as
well as its plums and juicy olives.

8 oz (225 g) granulated sugar   2 tablespoons cinnamon
6 eggs, separated   zest of ½ lemon
¾ pint (450 ml) milk   pinch of salt
2½ oz (75g) flour

Mix the flour with the milk, add the egg yolks and sugar and beat well. Bring the mixture to a very gentle simmer, stirring it all the time until it thickens like a cream. Allow to cool. Fold in the stiffly beaten egg whites, add the lemon zest, and spoon into a well-buttered flan mould 8–9 inches (20.5–23 cm) in diameter, criss-crossing the spoonfuls of mixture and sprinkling in between with the cinnamon. Bake at 232°C/450°F/Gas 8 until the surface cracks. Serve lukewarm or cold.
Serves 6.

Egg and Orange Pudding from Madeira/Pudim de Ovos

MADEIRA

6 oz (175 g) caster sugar
½ pint (300 ml) milk
4 eggs, separated
zest of 1 orange

FOR THE CARAMEL
3 oz (90 g) granulated sugar

Beat the egg yolks and sugar until fluffy. Warm the milk slightly and add gradually to the egg mixture. Add the orange zest. Fold in the stiffly beaten egg whites. Bake in a bain-marie (p.151) in a pudding mould (with lid, if possible) lined with the caramel. This is made by boiling the 3 oz (90 g) sugar with a teaspoon of water, until it becomes brownish and runny. Tip into the mould and swirl around, to cover as evenly as possible. Keep the bain-marie in the oven for 35–40 minutes (180°C/350°F/Gas 4) or until the pudding is set, adding more boiling water to the outer tin, as necessary. Take out of the mould only when quite cold.
Serves 4 to 6.

Blancmange/Manjar branco

COIMBRA, BEIRA LITORAL PROVINCE
This is surely one of the most traditional recipes in the Portuguese repertoire. Medieval books cite it as something very delicious and well known.

½ pint (300 ml) milk
½ medium-sized chicken breast,
  cooked until soft
3½ fluid oz (100 ml) liquor from
  the chicken

3 oz (90 g) rice flour
4½ (125 g) caster sugar
zest of ½ orange
pinch of salt

Mince and then pound the chicken breast very thoroughly, until smooth. Add to all the other ingredients, beating well.

Bring to the heat, stirring, and cook until thick. Spoon 4 inch (10 cm) mounds onto buttered trays, and bake at 232°C/450°F/ Gas 8 until brown specks appear on top (20–25 minutes).
Serves 6 to 8.

Chestnut and Milk Jam/Doce de Castanhas

ESTREMADURA PROVINCE
It may sound unusual, but it is an excellent kind of pudding, resembling *marrons glacés*.

½ pint (300 ml) milk   1½ lb (675 g) granulated sugar
2½ lb (1.2 kg) boiled chestnuts   vanilla pod

Sieve the boiled and peeled chestnuts whilst still warm. You may need to sieve this purée twice to make it really smooth, or you could use a liquidizer. Add the milk gradually, beating all the time, or again using a mixer. Make a thick syrup (the 'thread stage', p.35) with the sugar and a little water, adding the vanilla pod. Remove the pod when the syrup is ready. Mix the chestnut purée with the syrup. Beat well again. Bring to the heat, stirring, and allow to come to the boil. Remove from heat and then allow to cool before storing in a jar, under refrigeration. It can also be frozen. This pudding may be served with chocolate flakes, for example, or used as a filling for cakes and tarts. A great winter treat.
Serves 8 to 10.
    Note: A lot of trouble can be saved if canned, unsweetened chestnut purée is available. This would, however, make the mixture wetter, and therefore a third less milk could be used.

Pasta Pudding/Aletria com Ovos

MINHO AND DOURO LITORAL PROVINCES
Pasta (very fine noodles or vermicelli) is used in this recipe for a sweet resembling rice pudding, Portuguese style. It used to be very popular but, perhaps due to so many people watching their waist-lines, it is less so nowadays.

3 oz (90 g) vermicelli, just   2 egg yolks
    crumbled   2 tablespoons butter
4 oz (110 g) caster sugar   cinnamon
½ pint (300 ml) milk   1 piece of lemon rind

First cook the pasta in plain water with a pinch of salt. Drain. Mix with the milk, sugar and lemon rind. Bring to the boil and simmer until creamy. Mix the butter and beaten egg yolks. Bring just to the boil for one second and remove from the heat. Pour into a serving dish and dust with cinnamon (or draw

cinnamon shapes, as one does on the rice pudding, p.147).
Serve lukewarm or cold, on the same day.
Serves 4.

Coconut Pudding/Pudim de Coco

LISBON AREA

Although not strictly a traditional recipe, this luscious pudding
has enough roots and enough devotees to warrant its being
included here. It can be cooked in small patty tins, producing
little puddings or cakes, similar to those sold at many
Portuguese cake-shops.

12 oz (350 g) granulated sugar	*5 egg yolks and 2 whites, well*
7 oz (200 g) desiccated coconut	*beaten together*

Place the sugar in a pan with a little water to melt it and boil
until very thick (the 'pearl stage', p.35). Remove from the heat,
beat in the coconut and finally the eggs. Bake in a buttered
ring mould 6 inches (15 cm) in diameter, at 180°C/350°F/Gas 4,
for 20–25 minutes or until set.
Serves 6 to 8.

Variation
Make individual puddings putting the mixture in well-buttered
patty tins. They are wonderful eaten lukewarm or cold, for tea.

Golden Spaghetti Squash/Doce Dourado de Chila

OPORTO

This magnificent dessert was created by nuns at an Oporto
convent. It is very sweet, and you may consider reducing the
given amount of sugar. Otherwise its chewy texture and
luscious taste make it a memorable pudding.

8 oz (225 g) spaghetti squash jam (p.213)	*1 piece of orange rind (or some orange water)*
6–7 oz (175–200 g) stale sponge cake (see recipes for pão de ló, *p.203)*	*1 tablespoon candied citron or lemon peel*
10 egg yolks	*5 oz (140 g) roughly ground almonds*
1 lb (450 g) granulated sugar	*1 teaspoon cinnamon*

Slice the cake and place it on a platter. Set aside. Make a syrup
with the sugar and some orange water or with plain water and
the orange rind. Boil until thickish and pour some over the
sliced cake, just to soak it. Mix the jam and candied peel with
the remaining syrup and simmer for 1–2 minutes. Add the

almonds, mix well, boil for another minute. Remove from the heat and allow to cool a little. Then beat in the egg yolks and simmer again, whilst stirring, to thicken. Pour this mixture over the sliced cake and when cold sprinkle with the cinnamon.
Serves 6 to 8.

Baked Apples/Maçãs Assadas

Baked apples are a common pudding offered at Portuguese homes and restaurants. The apples used are large russets, very fleshy and extremely good. In *The Sin of Father Amaro* Eça de Queiroz refers to baked apples: ' "Marvellous!", said the Canon, as Mrs Janeira brought a large platter full of baked apples to the table. "I'll have some of those. I never refuse anything as delectable as baked apples!" '

4 large russet apples (or English   *4 heaped tablespoons caster or*
Coxs)   *granulated sugar*
                                                                 4 teaspoons butter

Wash well but do not core or peel the apples (the pips actually impart a good flavour). Place them in a buttered baking tin. Melt the butter and brush the apples. Sprinkle with the sugar. Bake at 180°C/350°F/Gas 4 for 35–40 minutes or until tender and brown.
Serves 4.

Variations
1 Sprinkle the apples with 4 teaspoons of port wine, after brushing with butter. Dust with the sugar and bake as above.
2 Mix a little cinnamon and/or powdered cloves with the sugar.

Peaches in Wine and Other Fruit Salads/Pessego com Vinho e Saladas de Fruta

> At dinner, last night, I told her [Ana] how fond of peaches my cousin Gonçalo is, especially when they are steeped in wine, so she decided to send you this basket full of peaches …
> Eça de Quieroz, *The Remarkable House of Ramires*
> (*A Ilustre Casa de Ramires*)

Peaches steeped in wine and sugar are truly something from Heaven, but the Portuguese make beautiful fruit salads anyway, adding wine (port, generally) or liqueur, for more flavour. When not using wine, citrus juices (lemon, orange, mandarin) are added, for a subtle aroma. In order to bring out the full flavours, the salad must be made a few hours before the meal or even the previous day if kept in the fridge – in which case some of the ingredients, such as sliced bananas, will be added only just before serving.

There are no rules for fruit salad ingredients. They depend on the season and on taste – also on the occasion. A grand dinner may include a fruit salad among the desserts (there will be more than one dessert at a grand dinner), and this salad will itself reflect the care put into that meal, so it will probably include a great variety of fruits, among them pineapple (fresh, of course), peaches, pears and so on.

Choose a glass bowl, mix in it the various fruits of your choice (except any soft fruits, such as strawberries and those which will discolour, such as banana, which are added just prior to serving) and dust generously with sugar. If using wine, mix a few spoonfuls of white wine and a liqueur glass of port or equivalent. Taste for sweetness and leave aside, preferably under refrigeration, until needed. Before serving, add the soft fruits, using some of them as decoration. Dust the top with sugar. For a simpler salad, without wine, add citrus juices of your choice and sugar to taste.

Sweet Maize Porridge/Papas de Milho Doces

NORTHERN PROVINCES

This is a really 'heavy' pudding, intended as part of a winter meal for very hungry people. It is served hot. It is also good as a hot cereal for breakfast. Think of it as a kind of porridge – and very nice, too.

6 oz (175 g) cornmeal (p.25)	*cinnamon (optional)*
1 pint (600 ml) liquid (only water or half milk/half water)	*½ coffeespoon salt*
4 oz (110 g) granulated sugar	*1 teaspoon vegetable oil, if milk is not used*

Mix the cornmeal with the chosen liquid (and oil, if used) and bring to the boil, stirring all the time. Cook over a gentle heat for 12–15 minutes. Stir frequently. Add the salt and sugar towards the end. Add more liquid and/or sugar, according to taste. Serve whilst still warm, with a sprinkling of cinnamon, if liked. Instead of sugar, honey or treacle (or a mixture of sugar and one of these) can be used.
Serves 4 to 6.

Sweets

Marzipan Sweets, Algarve Style/Doces de Amendoa

Even in the Algarve, where almonds grow in abundance, these sweets tend to be expensive, due to the labour involved in preparing them, but nobody would dare return from a visit there without bringing back a frilled box full of almond sweets. They are quite delicious and beautiful to look at, as they are made in various dainty shapes (fruit, fish, vegetables) and decorated accordingly by hand. They are normally filled with *ovos moles* (p.152) or *fios de ovos* (p.216), producing a mouth-watering soft centre which distinguishes these marzipan sweets from the harder ones made with ordinary almond paste and available in many countries.

7 oz (200 g) granulated sugar
7 oz (200 g) finely ground almonds
3 tablespoons water

Boil the sugar and water very gently until thick (see the 'pearl stage', p.35) over a gentle heat. Add the almonds. Mix well and boil, whilst stirring, until quite dry. Let the paste cool completely (overnight, if possible). It should now be hard enough to allow moulding (with slightly wet fingers). If not, it will have to be boiled again for a little while, to get rid of any excess moisture. Cool once more and mould in your favourite little shapes, about 1 inch (2.5 cm) in diameter, introducing some egg filling in the middle, as described above. Leave aside for one day and then paint carefully with vegetable dye and decorate to taste. Place each sweet in a paper case and serve on a platter, as you would serve chocolates, to end a meal.

A very pretty shape to make is a nest, with eggs the size of a pea inside (also moulded with the almond paste). The 'straw' is achieved with some 'egg threads'. A darker nest can be made by adding some powdered chocolate to the paste.
Makes about 24 sweets.

Egg Sweets from Viseu/Bolos de Ovos de Viseu

BEIRA ALTA PROVINCE
Egg sweets appear in every corner of Portugal, but Viseu seem to be particularly skilful in making them and has become famous for it. Apart from eating egg sweets, however, Viseu calls for a leisurely visit. Romans, Swabians, Visigoths and Arabs claimed it, and later the Christians walled it, to protect

this precious town from neighbouring Castilians, and transformed it into an important cultural centre. But while preserving its interesting past, Viseu is also one of the most forward-looking and well planned of Portugal's northern cities.

7 oz (200 g) granulated sugar
14 egg yolks

Add a little water to the sugar, just to melt it and boil until a thick syrup is formed (see the 'thread stage', p.35). Remove from the heat and add 13 of the egg yolks, previously beaten. Combine vigorously and bring to a gentle simmer, stirring all the time until it thickens. Cool the mixture completely (you can speed this up by leaving it in the fridge for a while). With floured hands, mould small shapes – 1 inch (2.5 cm) balls, cylinders, pyramids, etc, and coat them in the remaining egg yolk, well beaten with a drop of water. Place under a hot grill for a minute or two, to burn the tops slightly. Put them in paper cases, after rolling in sugar. Serve two days later, to allow the sweets to dry and firm up a little.
Makes about 24 sweets.

Walnuts Cascais Fashion/Nozes de Cascais

Romans and Moors had their eyes on Cascais, and so have many people today. Cascais is an extremely pretty little town near Lisbon, favoured by deposed kings, expatriates, tourists and commuters. Its beaches, gardens, quaint old streets and even the new ones attract them all but, in spite of that, Cascais keeps its serene air of quiet elegance and intimacy. Restaurants with marvellous fish dishes abound, and old patisseries still produce Cascais' main sweet specialities. *areias* ('sand' – small biscuits, see p.198) and these crackling walnut sweets, shiny and delicious, with a coat of caramel, like toffee apples.

3 oz (90 g) granulated sugar
4 oz (110 g) ground almonds
4 tablespoons water
9 walnuts, in perfect halves (18)
5 egg yolks

For the crackling caramel
    coating
4 oz (110 g) granulated sugar
3 tablespoons water
2 drops lemon juice

Make a thick syrup with the water and sugar. Remove from the heat and mix in the beaten egg yolks, adding them gradually to the syrup. Then mix in the almonds. Simmer, stirring, until thick. Pour onto a plate and leave for a few hours. Then shape 1 inch (2.5 cm) balls with this paste. Place half a walnut on top of each and set them aside.

Make a syrup with the water and sugar allowing it to turn into *light-coloured* caramel. Watch over this carefully. When reaching this point, take off the heat, add the 2 drops of lemon juice, stir and immediately submerge each walnut cake in it, using a fork. Place the coated cakes on a large oiled platter (to prevent sticking) and leave them until the following day. Pare any excess caramel from the sides (with sharp scissors) and place in paper cases. If the caramel dries up half way through the coating operation, add a drop of water to it and bring again to the heat, to restore its fluidity.
Makes about 18 sweets.

Breeze from the Lis River/Brisas do Lis

LEIRIA, ESTREMADURA PROVINCE

These small cake-like sweets are as delicious as the town they come from. Leiria was, however, the scene of bloody fighting between Christians and Moors until, at the final battle in 1134, the Christians won. Later kings built a splendid palace there, which they used on many occasions.

The typical and appreciated little brisas from Leiria, are prepared as follows:

2 oz (60 g) ground almonds
7 oz (200 g) caster sugar
4 large eggs, beaten

Combine all ingredients and bake in small, well-buttered patty tins, in an oven set to 200°C/400°F/Gas 6, for 20 minutes or until golden and set. Serve in frilled paper cases, for tea or with liqueurs or port.
Makes about 1 dozen brisas.

Angel's Breasts/Papos de Anjo

MIRANDELA, TRÁS-OS-MONTES PROVINCE

Anything called 'angel's breasts' must surely be delectable and sweet. Old convents in the Azores, Beja, Amarante and Viseu have different confections under this name. The recipe below is, however, from a convent in Mirandela, a lovely town which is of Roman origin and has a beautiful Roman bridge, rebuilt during the sixteenth century.

12 oz (350 g) granulated sugar
6 eggs plus 4 yolks, all beaten up together

2 tablespoons thick jam, any flavour
1 teaspoon cinnamon

Make a thick syrup (see the 'thread stage', p.35) with the sugar and a little water, to melt it. Remove from the heat and beat in

the jam. Boil again over a low flame, to thicken again. Cool it down a little and add the beaten eggs and cinnamon, stirring vigorously. Butter really well small patty tins and half fill them with the mixture (the sweets rise a lot, on baking). Bring them to a preheated oven (200°C/400°F/Gas 6) until set and golden. Dust with icing sugar before serving, when cold.
Makes 24 to 30 sweets.

Dom Rodrigo Sweets/Bolos de Dom Rodrigo

THE ALGARVE

These sweets are sold wrapped in foil, with the ends twisted upwards, in the middle, to keep any loose syrup inside. They are delicate and very sweet. One can cope with only one at a time, but what a heavenly thing they are!

Egg threads (p.216)   *4 oz (110 g) granulated sugar*
3 egg yolks, slightly beaten   *cinnamon*
3 oz (90 g) ground almonds   *sugar*

Make the egg threads described on p.216 and keep them wet with a little of the syrup left over. Keep the rest of the syrup for later.

Make more syrup (to the 'thread stage', p.35) with the 4 oz (110 g) sugar and a little water to cover it. Mix in the ground almonds and cook gently for 2 minutes. Remove from the heat and add the beaten yolks. Mix well and bring just to the boil, to cook them. Remove from the heat again and sprinkle with a little cinnamon.

Divide the egg threads into 8–10 little mounds, and make a well in the centre of each. Fill each well with the almond-and-egg mixture, and cover this filling with the threads, bringing them over it, so that you have 8–10 balls of filled threads. Bring the left-over syrup to the boil (adding just a little water) and cook the 'balls' in it, a few at a time, for only one moment. Take them out with a slotted spoon. When they are all ready and cool, wrap them in squares of foil, as explained above.
Makes 8 to 10 Dom Rodrigos.

Fig Lord/Morgado de Figo

THE ALGARVE

This is the fig-and-almond paste used in the Algarve for moulding all kinds of small shapes, served as sweets or to be made into a large cake, to cut in small sections only when needed, as it will keep almost indefinitely.

8 oz (225 g) very good-quality
   dried figs
8 oz (225 g) granulated sugar
8 oz (225 g) ground almonds

1 teaspoon cinnamon
2 teaspoons powdered cocoa
grated rind of 1 large lemon

Cut up the figs (discarding the little stems) into very small pieces, using scissors, which facilitates this tedious work. Set aside. Bring 6 tablespoons of water to the heat, add the sugar, cinnamon, lemon zest and cocoa, and boil until a thick syrup is formed. Add the almonds, mix and allow to boil again for 2–3 minutes. Then add the figs and boil for a further 4–5 minutes, stirring, always over a low flame. Remove from the heat and cool until you can handle the mixture. Place it on a sugared surface and press firmly, using your hands and a spatula, to mould the paste.

If the cake shape is what is wanted, it is now ready for decoration with icing sugar and/or little motifs made of almond paste. Otherwise, break off pieces and mould shapes to your taste, with the help of a little sugar. Place them in paper cases. Keep in boxes, to avoid their drying too much.

Makes about 36 small sweets.

Sweet Potato Cakes/Fartes de Batata

MADEIRA
The sweet potato is grown in Madeira (and in the Algarve, too – see Ingredients, p.28), so one would expect to find local specialities made with this heavy, floury and quite delicious variety of potato. These exquisite sweets from Madeira are very easy to make.

14 oz (400 g) mashed sweet
   potato, cooled
12 oz (350 g) granulated sugar
1 tablespoon flour
2 eggs

1 oz (30 g) butter plus 2
   tablespoons melted butter for
   brushing
3 oz (90 g) ground almonds
3 oz (90 g) mixed glacée fruit
2 tablespoons orange juice

Mix the sugar with the 1 oz (30 g) butter and the eggs. Add the mashed potato, flour, almonds, juice and fruit (previously cut into small pieces). Beat thoroughly. Then bring to the boil over low heat, until all moisture disappears, whilst stirring, to prevent sticking. When very thick, take the mixture off the heat and turn it onto a floured board. Shape into 1 inch (2.5 cm) squares and place in greased tins. Brush the tops with melted butter and bake at 190°C/375°F/Gas 5, for 10–15 minutes, or

until golden brown. When baked, brush again with melted butter and dredge with sugar.
Makes about 36 sweets.

Little Egg and Bread Sweets, Bragança Fashion/ Bolos de Ovos e Pão de Bragança

TRÁS-OS-MONTES PROVINCE
A rich mixture, using bread and lots of eggs yolks, as one would expect in traditional recipes.

7 oz (200 g) stale bread, crumbled	*14 oz (400 g) granulated sugar*
7 oz (200 g) ground almonds	*1 teaspoon cinnamon*
14 egg yolks	*2 tablespoons orange water*

Mix the breadcrumbs and ground almonds. Set aside. Make a syrup with the sugar and a little water. Boil until thick (the 'pearl stage', p.35). Remove from the heat and mix in the bread and almonds. Combine the egg yolks into this and beat very well. Add the cinnamon and orange water (or plain water, failing this) if the mixture is too thick. Bring to the heat and simmer, whilst stirring, for 2–3 minutes, to cook the eggs and acquire a smooth consistency. It must become almost solid, but not dry. Leave until the following day and shape small cakes, rolling them in sugar. Put them in paper cases, to savour later, slowly and in peace, as if you were looking at the vast, tranquil horizons enjoyed from Bragança's belvedere, beside St Bartholomew's Chapel.
Makes about 36 sweets.

Lorvão Sweets/Pasteis de Lorvão

BEIRA LITORAL PROVINCE
This is one of the recipes dreamed up by nuns or monks, and the fact that in Lorvão there was at least one important monastery, of the Cistercian Order, may have something to do with these traditional sweets.

7 oz (200 g) granulated sugar	*1 tablespoon flour*
2 oz (60 g) ground almonds	*½ teaspoon cinnamon*
6 egg yolks	*zest of ½ lemon*
1 egg white	*¼ pint (150 ml) water*

Boil the sugar and water until a thick syrup is formed (see the 'thread stage', p.35). Take off the heat, stir the almonds and flour and bring to a gentle boil again, stirring all the time. Cool it down before adding the egg yolks, well beaten, the white of

egg and remaining ingredients. Mix well and bake at
163°C/325°F/Gas 3 in patty tins previously buttered and floured,
until set and slightly browned on top – about 25 minutes. When
baked, dredge the little sweets with sugar and put them in
paper cases.
Makes 24 small pasteis.

Potato Delights/Delícias de Batata

BENAVENTE, RIBATEJO PROVINCE
Mashed potato gives an interesting texture to sweets, as these
'delights' from Roman Benavente show.

3 oz (90 g) ground almonds
3½ oz (100 g) mashed potato
7 oz (200 g) granulated sugar
1 tablespoon fine cornflour
1 tablespoon butter

2 eggs
3 tablespoons water
icing sugar and cinnamon for
  sprinkling

Mix the water with the sugar and boil to make a light syrup (see
p.35). Add the mashed potato and almonds. Boil until thick,
over a low flame, stirring. Set aside until almost cold. Add the
eggs and flour and beat well. Bake this mixture in well-buttered
patty tins, at 210°C/425°F/Gas 7 for 20 minutes or until golden
brown. Take out of the tins carefully, before the *delícias* are
completely cold, and dust with a mixture of icing sugar and
cinnamon.
Makes 12 to 16 delícias.

Little Oranges/Laranjinhas

SETÚBAL REGION, SOUTH OF LISBON
These sweets originate from the Setúbal area, where oranges
grow. Make the *laranjinhas* a few days before they are to be
served, to get firmer.

4 large carrots
fresh skin (and pith) of 3 oranges
7 oz (200 g) granulated sugar

Cut the carrots in half – not in small pieces, so they do not
absorb too much water. Boil the carrots with the orange peel
(with all its pith, to avoid too much bitterness), until tender.
Drain very thoroughly and dry again in a clean cloth. Mash and
sieve. Bring the sugar to the boil for 2–3 minutes with 2
tablespoons water, until thick (see the 'pearl stage', p.35). Add

the purée. Boil again, stirring with wooden spoon. Allow the mixture to dry, without burning (this needs a really low flame throughout and a very watchful eye). Spread the resulting paste on a plate and leave until completely cold. Shape small balls 1 inch (2.5 cm) in diameter. Roll them in sugar and place in paper cases. Leave them untouched to dry, for 2 or 3 days. You can make these little oranges more realistic by sticking a small stem and leaf on top.

Makes about 24 laranjinhas.

Candied Orange Peel/Casca de Laranja Cristalizada

SETÚBAL, SOUTH OF LISBON

Setúbal was founded by the Celts and later developed by the Romans, who worked its famous salt-pits which, together with the fishing, fruit-growing and wines of the region, contributed to the continuous development of the city. Nowadays various industries in and near Setúbal also give it prosperity.

Oranges are one of the crops around Setúbal, and the region is renowned for its orange *compôte* and candied orange peel. The latter is not too difficult to make at home, and many Portuguese housewives like to keep some homemade candied peel to use in cakes and to eat as a snack.

orange peel – any amount
the same weight of granulated sugar

When eating oranges, save the peel and ask your family to do the same. Most of the pith must be left, when peeling the oranges, otherwise the peel is too bitter. It will keep in the fridge for a couple of days. Then soak it for 24 hours, changing the water several times, to get rid of the bitterness. Cut the peel into strips ½ inch (12 mm) wide and place them in a pan containing boiling water. Bring to the boil again and remove at once. Drain and put the parboiled peel in a clean cloth, to absorb all moisture. When it is as dry as you can get it, weigh it. Using the same amount of sugar, make a syrup with just the minimum of water, boiling until thick (see the 'pearl stage', p.35). Add the peel and stir it around, to get well coated with the syrup. Do this over very low heat and being careful not to break the peel. Allow the mixture to become quite dry, but without burning it. Pour on a tray and separate the strips immediately with a knife. Allow to cool overnight.

If the peel is not perfectly dry at this stage, it might go mouldy very quickly, so either boil it again with great care, in order to finish drying, or leave it spread out over a tray or board for a day or so, turning now and then. Store in jars in a cool larder.

Chocolate Salami/Salame de Chocolate

LISBON AREA
This is a very popular sweet in some Portuguese households, not needing baking or cooking. Its appearance and taste make it suitable for birthday parties.

3 oz (90 g) drinking chocolate (the powdered variety)
3 oz (90 g) butter
3 oz (90 g) caster sugar

5 oz (140 g) crumbed biscuits (petit-beurre, digestive or any kind of plain biscuits)
1 egg

Mix the butter with the sugar, then add the chocolate, egg and, finally, crumbed biscuits. This will provide a stiff paste, which you will shape like a very thick sausage (hence the name 'salami'). Wrap it in slightly oiled foil and refrigerate overnight to harden. Cut just before it is needed, slicing it thickly. You can also shape small balls with the paste, roll them in powdered chocolate and put in paper cases.
Serves 4 to 6.

Pastries

Cream (or Belem) Tarts/Pasteis de Nata or Pasteis de Belém

LISBON
These cakes were first made popular in a very ancient shop in the Belém district of Lisbon. It is still open, and its many rooms, with walls covered in well-preserved Portuguese tiles, are constantly full of people eating the cakes, with coffee. The shop is not far from the splendid Belém Tower, one of the most famous and lovely of Lisbon landmarks, built in the sixteenth century on the spot from which the caravels used to come and go, during the maritime era. *Pasteis de Nata* (custard tarts with a difference) are nowadays available everywhere in Portugal and are perhaps the most popular of all small pastries. They can be extremely good or simply good, according to who prepares them. Generally they are bought readymade, as the homemade ones do not, somehow, come out as shapely as the bought ones, although they are still very good to eat.

PUFF-PASTRY DOUGH
9 oz (250 g) flour
9 oz (250 g) unsalted butter
squeeze of lemon juice
pinch of salt

FILLING
5 oz (140 g) single cream
4 egg yolks
2½ oz (75 g) caster sugar

Prepare the filling, beating the egg yolks and sugar until thick. Add the cream gradually, beat well and bring to the heat. Simmer, while stirring, until a very thick custard is obtained. Set aside to cool down.

For a good puff-pastry, the ingredients should be very cool and the oven quite hot. Sieve the flour and put it into a basin. Make a well in the centre, add a pinch of salt and enough iced water to form the dough. Add the water gradually and squeeze in a little lemon juice as well, as this helps to make a light pastry. Work the dough until it is elastic and really smooth. Shape into a ball, cover and place in the fridge for 15 minutes, to cool it again. Then roll it into an oblong. Divide the cold butter into 3 equal portions. Cut the first one into little bits, and place them along the rolled-out pastry, without reaching the edges. Fold in three, with the first flat away from you and the second towards you. Turn this square half-way round, press the edges and cool it again in the fridge for a few minutes. Roll out as before, and repeat the procedure until the butter is finished, and again twice, after that. It is said that puff pastry needs seven of these turns, to trap enough air between the various layers formed while turning and rolling. But do try to complete at least the five turns indicated here.

Then roll the pastry out thinly, cut it into rounds to line the patty tins, pressing it well around, fill with a tablespoon of the prepared custard and bake in a hot oven (250°C/475°F/Gas 9) until the custard is browned on top and the pastry very golden.

The tarts should be eaten on the day they are baked, otherwise they lose some of their appeal, which resides in the wonderful crunchiness of the pastry and softness of the cream inside. If there are any left the following day, it is advisable to warm them up for a few minutes. They are, incidentally, very nice whilst still warm.

Traditionally they are dusted with cinnamon mixed with icing sugar, but most people nowadays prefer them without.
Makes 12 to 16 tarts.

Cheese tartlets Sintra-style/Queijadas de Sintra

Sintra is a very old town, near Lisbon, its ancient castle, perched high on a mountain, bearing striking evidence to the former presence of the Moors. Portuguese kings and queens loved Sintra and built many magnificent palaces in and around the town, which is enveloped in thick woods. Sintra is little changed: delightful and noble, of exquisite and enduring charm. Lord Byron wrote of it, artists surrender to it. *Queijadas* are made exclusively there but are available in the best Lisbon patisseries.

DOUGH
10 oz (280 g) flour
1½ tablespoons butter
salt

FILLING
12 oz (350 g) fresh cheese
    (requeijão – see p.30)
2 oz (60 g) grated hard cheese,
    Cheddar type
7 oz (200 g) caster sugar
5 tablespoons flour
3 egg yolks plus 1 whole egg
½ teaspoon cinnamon

The cases in which the cheese filling is cooked are thin and crunchy, rather like very thin water-biscuits. The dough is generally prepared well in advance, preferably the previous day. Put the flour in a basin, make a well in the centre, add the softened butter and a little salt. Mix with the tips of the fingers, and add tepid water very gradually while kneading thoroughly. The dough must be elastic and smooth but rather on the dry side, and should not stick to the basin. Cover with a dry cloth and then with a damp one. Set aside to rest until the following day, or at least for a few hours.

Meanwhile prepare the filling. Sieve the fresh cheese, and mix well with the grated cheese, until a smooth paste is obtained. Add the sugar and then all the other ingredients, little by little, beating between additions.

Roll out the dough really fine (the thickness of 3 sheets of paper, put together) on a floured board. Cut out small rounds, 3 inches (7.5 cm) in diameter, and line buttered patty tins with them, cutting 4 snippets to adjust the dough into the tins. Fill with the cheese mixture and bake in a hot oven (210°C/425°F/ Gas 7) for about 15 minutes or until brown.

When cold, join the tartlets in pairs, placing a small piece of greaseproof paper between them. Keep in tins, to prevent drying.
Makes 24 to 30 queijadas.

Bean Tarts/Pasteis de Feijão

TORRES VEDRAS, NEAR LISBON
Torres Vedras was an important copper-mining centre in 2000 BC. Nowadays it is a bustling town, with excellent wine, and

particularly interesting for its many historical associations and architectural remains. Nearby, the fortress of St Vincent testifies to the presence of British troops under the Duke of Wellington, when fighting to help the Portuguese repel the Napoleonic invaders, led by General Masséna. The impregnable 'Lines of Torres Vedras' built by Wellington successfully halted the advance of the French troops.

The bean tarts, which are supposedly a Torres Vedras creation and still sold as a local speciality (in boxes of 6), are truly exquisite, and the bean purée gives them a texture all their own.

PASTRY	FILLING
7 oz (200 g) flour	8 oz (225 g) granulated sugar
3 tablespoons butter (or butter and lard)	4 oz (110 g) puréed haricot beans
	4 oz (110 g) ground almonds
water	5 egg yolks
salt	

Mix the pastry ingredients with a little tepid water to form a soft and pliable dough. Set aside, covered, while preparing the filling.

Make a syrup with the sugar and 3 tablespoons of water. Boil until thick (see the 'pearl stage', p.35). Add the sieved bean purée and cook for a couple of minutes. Mix in the almonds and boil again. Set aside, until almost cold. Add the egg yolks and bring again to the boil, then remove from the heat and allow to cool. Roll out the dough quite thinly and line small buttered patty tins. Divide the filling between them. Bake at 218°C/425°F/Gas 7 for about 20 minutes or until a golden crust is formed.
Makes 24 tarts.

Rice Patties from the Azores/Pastéis de Arroz dos Açores

DOUGH	FILLING
7 oz (200 g) flour	8 oz (225 g) rice
1 tablespoon sugar	12 oz (350 g) granulated sugar
1 tablespoon butter	5 egg yolks
1 egg yolk	1½ oz (45 g) ground almonds
	pinch salt

Prepare the filling a day in advance, to allow it to cool and thicken. Cook the rice until mushy in 3 times its volume of water, adding a little salt. Sieve the soft rice and set aside.

Prepare a thick syrup with the sugar and enough water to melt
it. Add the rice and boil gently for 5 minutes, stirring. Add the
ground almonds and cook again for 2–3 minutes. Add the
beaten egg yolks, mix over the heat and remove from it at once.
Keep this mixture until the following day, when it should be
very thick.

For the dough, mix the flour with the other ingredients and a
little water to obtain a smooth consistency. Knead. Leave to
rest for 20–30 minutes. Roll out quite thinly (little more than the
thickness of paper), cut rounds 4 inches (10 cm) in diameter
and divide the filling among them. Fold in half-moon shapes,
pressing the edges. Put in buttered baking tins and bring to the
oven (163°C/325°F/Gas 3) for 15 minutes, to dry out without
actually getting browned. Dust with icing sugar when ready.
Makes 24 pasteis.

St Clara Turnovers/Pasteis de Santa Clara

COIMBRA, BEIRA LITORAL PROVINCE
Never missing the opportunity of settling at beautiful spots, at
the time when they dominated most of Europe, the Romans
founded the town of Aeminium, now Coimbra, on the banks of
the Mondego river. There are still important Roman remains in
the city, especially at nearby Conimbriga (from which Coimbra
derives its present name). Coimbra can also claim one of the
oldest universities in Europe (dating from 1308) and to have
been the first capital of the country, for over a century, chosen
by Afonso Henriques, who became Portugal's first king in 1140.
Historically and culturally Coimbra is quite remarkable, and it
is still one of the most important and interesting Portuguese
cities. From its many monasteries and convents came various
original recipes, which have been preserved to this day, like
these delicious turnovers.

PASTRY
7 oz (200 g) flour
4 oz (110 g) chilled butter
1 beaten egg for brushing

FILLING
7 oz (200 g) granulated sugar
4 oz (110 g) ground almonds
7 well-beaten egg yolks

Use the rubbing-in method (with fingertips) to mix the flour
with the chilled butter, adding a little very cold water, until a
pliable dough is obtained. Cover and keep in a cool place or
fridge while you prepare the filling.

Melt the sugar in a little water and boil until thick. Add the
ground almonds and yolks, mix very well and simmer, while
stirring, until very thick. Cool.

Roll out the pastry to ⅛ inch (3 mm) thickness, cut into

rounds of about 3 inches (7.5 cm) diameter and divide the filling between them, placing it in the middle of each round. Wet the edges and fold, pressing firmly, to form a half-moon shape. Brush with the beaten egg and bake in greased trays at 200°C/400°F/Gas 6 until golden. When ready, dredge with sugar.

Makes 12 to 16 turnovers.

Turnovers from Vila Real/Pasteis de Vila Real

TRÁS-OS-MONTES PROVINCE

Vila Real, one of the main inland northern cities, was the birthplace of Diogo Cão, a distinguished sailor who in 1482 began his travels along the African coast and initiated the custom of marking these lands with stone monuments (*padrões*) testifying that the Portuguese had been there: 'Here have arrived the ships of the learned King of Portugal.' The monuments erected beside the Zaire river waterfalls signalled the first European contacts with the Congo.

Closer to our time, in 1895, a hydro-electric power station was built on the beautiful gorges of the Corgo river, near Vila Real, making this city the first in Portugal to be provided with electricity.

The turnovers described below originated, predictably enough, at a convent. They can be fried or baked, and among the various existing versions this one is particularly delicate.

DOUGH	FILLING
8 oz (225 g) flour	*6 oz (175 g) granulated sugar*
1 egg	*3 egg yolks*
2½ oz (75 g) butter, lard or margarine	*1 medium apple, grated*
	2 oz (60 g) ground almonds
½ teaspoon salt	*½ teaspoon cinnamon*
	1 thin slice fresh white bread (if needed)

To prepare the dough, mix the flour with the fat using the tips of your fingers. Then add the beaten egg, some cold water and salt. Knead well, adding a dusting of flour if it is sticky. It should become very elastic and smooth. Form a ball with this dough and set it aside in a cool place for an hour or so.

Meanwhile, prepare the filling. In a pan bring the sugar to the boil with some water, to melt it, and make a thickish syrup (the 'thread stage', p.35). Add the apple and almonds, mix well and boil until very thick. Cool and add the yolks, one by one, and the cinnamon. Bring to the heat again, stirring , and allow to thicken. Should the mixture be slightly wet, add the fresh breadcrumbs (a slice of bread finely crumbled). Work everything together again. Set aside.

Roll out the pastry on a floured board to a thickness of ⅛ inch (3 mm) and cut rounds about 3 inches (7.5 cm) in diameter, using a pastry cutter. Share the filling between all the rounds (about 2 teaspoonfuls each), fold in half, press the edges with the help of a fork and bake in greased tins in a moderately hot oven (200°C/400°F/Gas 6) until golden. Dredge with sugar immediately after baking.

You can also fry the turnovers but baking makes them less likely to burst.

Makes 12 to 16 turnovers.

Cheese Tartlets Beira Style/Queijadas da Beira

Most Portuguese regions have their own cheese tartlets, made with fresh *requeijão* or similar fresh cheese.

7 oz (200 g) caster sugar	*4 eggs*
7 oz (200 g) fresh requeijão (p.30)	*2 oz (60 g) cornflour*

Mix the sieved cheese very thoroughly with the sugar and eggs. Add the flour. Beat well. Divide this paste between some small tartlet moulds or patty tins, which must be well buttered. Bake in a hot oven (200°C/400°F/Gas 6) for about 20 minutes or until golden brown. Take them out carefully after cooling a bit.

Makes 24 to 30 queijadas.

Cheese Tartlets Pereiro Style/Queijadas do Pereiro

BEIRO PROVINCE

DOUGH	FILLING
8 oz (225 g) flour	*7 oz (200 g) fresh cheese,*
1½ tablespoons melted butter	*requeijão style (p.30)*
½ coffeespoon salt	*7 oz (200 g) caster sugar*
	5 egg yolks

Make a well in the centre of the flour and add some lukewarm water, the salt and the melted butter. Knead well and add some more water, if needed, to form a smooth dough. Set aside, covered, for 45–60 minutes. In the meantime mix the cheese, egg yolks and sugar to a soft paste. Roll out the dough quite

thinly, about ⅛ inch (3 mm) and line fluted patty tins, which must have been well buttered. Fill them with the cheese mixture and bake at 200°C/400°F/Gas 6, for 15–20 minutes, or until golden brown. Take them out of the tins when lukewarm. Serve cold, with tea or coffee.
Makes about 24 small tartlets.

Custard Tarts from the Azores/Covilhetes de Leite

PASTRY
7 oz (200 g) flour
2 tablespoons butter
1 tablespoon lard
pinch salt
water

FILLING
1 pint (600 ml) milk
8 oz (225 g) granulated sugar
4 egg yolks plus 2 whole eggs
1 tablespoon flour
1 teaspoon cinnamon

Prepare a dough with the flour, making a well in the centre, adding the fats and salt and then enough tepid water to obtain a smooth consistency. Mix very well and set aside, to rest.

Meantime, boil the milk with the sugar for a while, to reduce by a third. Remove from the heat and allow to cool. Add the cinnamon, egg yolks and 2 whole eggs, as well as the flour, mixed with a little milk. Beat well. Roll out the dough quite thinly (⅛ inch/3 mm) and line greased patty tins. Fill with the prepared mixture and bake in a preheated oven to 190°C/375°F/Gas 5 for 20–25 minutes or until golden brown. Serve the tarts when cold.
Makes 24 tarts.

Fluffy Cakes, from Faial/Fofas do Faial

AZORES ARCHIPELAGO
These choux-type pastries can be filled with custard or Chantilly cream but are also very nice just by themselves. They are traditionally made in the Azores for the Carnival season.

12 oz (350 g) flour
1 oz (30 g) granulated sugar
½ pint (300 ml) liquid – half milk, half water
3½ oz (100 g) butter

10 eggs
1 coffeespoon salt
2 tablespoons aniseeds (or fennel seeds)

In a large pan bring the liquid to the boil with the butter, sugar, seeds and salt. When boiling, mix in the flour, all at once, reduce the heat and stir until the paste is smooth and no longer sticks to the sides of the pan. Remove from the heat and allow

to cool. Then mix in the eggs, one at a time, beating vigorously until all the moisture is absorbed, before adding the next egg. It should have the consistency of a thick meringue paste. If you arrive at this consistency before adding all the eggs, do not add any more. If, on the other hand, it is still too stiff after the last egg has been beaten in, mix in another one – although this should not be necessary. Beat well again and bake in small mounds (the size of a ping-pong ball) in buttered trays, until puffy and golden in an oven preheated to 210°C/425°F/Gas 7. After cooling they can be filled with sweetened whipped double cream, Chantilly or a thick custard.
Makes 30 to 36 fofas.

Almond Tart/Tarte de Amendoa

ESTREMADURA
This is a lovely dessert, served sometimes in Portuguese restaurants and at parties.

DOUGH
6 oz (175 g) flour
3 oz (90 g) softened butter
1 egg
3 oz (90 g) caster sugar
pinch of salt

FILLING
3½ oz (100 g) peeled almonds,
  cut into pieces lengthwise
3 oz (90 g) sugar
4 tablespoons milk
3 oz (90 g) butter

Mix the flour with the other ingredients rapidly and spread over the bottom of a buttered tart mould. Bake blind for about 15 minutes at 200°C/400°F/Gas 6 or until golden brown.

In the meantime mix all filling ingredients and bring to the boil, to thicken a little. Pour into the baked base, spread evenly and bake at 210°C/425°F/Gas 7 to dry up the top slightly (about 5 minutes).
Serves 6 to 8.

Apple Tart with Custard/Tarte de Maçã e Creme

LISBON AREA
This tart is a nice addition to any party table or special meal.

PASTRY
6 oz (175 g) flour
3 oz (90 g) butter
pinch of salt

FILLING
1 lb (450 g) russet apples (or
  Cox's)
½ pint (300 ml) milk
4 tablespoons caster sugar
2 eggs
1 tablespoon flour

Prepare the pastry first by swiftly mixing the flour with the butter, salt and enough cold water to make a soft, non-stick dough. Leave in cool place for half an hour. Meanwhile core and peel the apples (in Portugal this is made with *reinetas*, which are very similar to russets but can be substituted by good Cox's). Cut the apples into very thin slices. Roll out the pastry and cover a buttered flan mould with it. Fill the pastry case with the sliced apples, placing them in neat rows all round. Bake at 180°C/350°F/Gas 4 for about 25 minutes. Remove from the oven and pour over the apples a mixture made with the eggs, milk, flour and sugar, all beaten up. Return the tart to the oven again and bake for a further 20 minutes or until golden and well set. Serve cold or whilst still warm, with or without cream.

Serves 6 to 8.

Small Cakes

'Bowlful' from Abrantes/Tigeladas de Abrantes

RIBATEJO PROVINCE
Abrantes is no longer famous for its silk production, as it was in the eighteenth and nineteenth centuries but it is renowned for these custard cakes baked in the oven. It is possible to buy them outside Abrantes, in good pastry-shops.

¾ pint (450 ml) milk	*2 oz (60 g) flour*
6 eggs	*pinch salt*
7 oz (200 g) caster sugar	

Beat all the ingredients very thoroughly by hand for at least 25 minutes, or use an electric mixer for 8 minutes or so. Whilst you are doing this, prepare the small earthenware bowls in which this should be baked, which are like deep saucers (or use ramekin dishes), warming them in the oven, set to 200°C/400°F/Gas 6. (You do not need to butter the bowls.) Put the bowls inside a large baking tin or on a tray, so that you do not burn yourself when pulling them out to fill with the egg mixture. Use a ladle to do this. Bake for 15 to 20 minutes until solid and with brown specks on top. Take them out of the bowls immediately. Serve cold. The *tigeladas* are eaten as cakes with tea or coffee.

Makes 24 tigeladas.

St Gonçalo Cakes/Bolos de S. Gonçalo

DOURO LITORAL PROVINCE

Many popular saints' days are celebrated at times coinciding with ancient fertility rites. St Gonçalo is one such saint, nobody seems to know why. He was an architect who in the thirteenth century built the elegant bridge which bears his name and still stands at Amarante, a delightfully picturesque town founded by the Romans. Both here, at the end of the first week in June and on 11 January, in Gaia (opposite Oporto, and famous for the port wine cellars that line its main streets) Christian-cum-pagan festivals celebrate Gonçalo as a saint who finds husbands for old maids. A pilgrimage, a noisy fair, dancing, singing and eating (of suggestive-looking cakes) are all part of the feasts.

7 oz (200 g) caster sugar
7 oz (200 g) flour
6 oz (175 g) butter
1 tablespoon of liqueur (or
   brandy)

5 eggs, separated
1 teaspoon baking powder
pinch of salt

Mix the sugar with the egg yolks, then add the softened butter and the liqueur and beat until fluffy. Add the stiffly beaten egg whites and finally the flour mixed with the baking powder and salt. Bake this paste in well-greased patty tins in an oven preheated to 190°C/375°F/Gas 5, for about 25 minutes or until golden. The real St Gonçalo cakes should have a phallic shape, which would demand elongated tins, but obviously any patty tins will do.

Makes about 24 cakes.

Rotten Cakes for Christmas/Bolos Podres do Natal

RIBATEJO PROVINCE

In Portugal there are various recipes of so-called 'rotten cakes'. Their unglamorous title refers only to their dark and generally heavy texture; they are always rich in spices and as a rule contain olive oil and either honey or dark sugar. This one is a kind of scalded dough, so the resulting consistency is similar to that of a pudding.

1 lb (450 g) flour
7 oz (200 g) soft brown sugar
8 fluid oz (225 ml) olive oil
5 tablespoons water

1 teaspoon ground aniseed
1 teaspoon cinnamon
icing sugar for sprinkling

In a pan mix the water, oil and spices. Bring to the boil and pour over the flour, already mixed with the sugar. Mix well and shape little pyramids with a 1½ inch (4 cm) base and about 2½ inches (6.5 cm) high. Bake in an oven preheated to 210°C/425°F/Gas 7 for 15 minutes. When cold, dust the cakes with sifted icing sugar.
Makes 36 cakes.

Variation
Use the same recipe but adding ½ coffeespoon of ground cloves to the dough and putting a peeled whole almond on top of each pyramid, before baking.

Christmas Cakes from Bombarral/Broas de Bombarral

ESTREMADURA PROVINCE
Bombarral was founded in the twelfth century and is remarkable for the tiles in its churches and public buildings. *Pão-de-ló* (sponge cake) is one of its specialities, but these *broas* can be claimed as the best cakes in town.

1 lb (450 g) maize flour (medium-
   coarse)
1 lb (450 g) granulated sugar
1½ lb (675 g) sweet potato purée
1 tablespoon cinnamon
grated rind of 1 lemon
1 tablespoon powdered aniseed
pinch of salt
beaten egg for brushing

Make a thick syrup with the sugar and enough water to dissolve it (see the 'pearl stage', p.35). Mix with sweet potato purée made by boiling sweet potatoes in water then mashing and weighing the amount needed. Boil together, stirring, to thicken. Set aside.

In a basin mix the flour, salt and spices and add the hot mixture. Beat well and cover, leaving it until the following day.

Then with floured hands mould little oval cakes, measuring approximately 1 inch (2.5 cm) on the widest part. Flatten to ½ inch (12 mm) and pinch the ends, to give the cakes the shape of leaves. Brush with beaten egg. Put in tins brushed with cooking oil (not necessarily olive oil). Bake at 210°C/425°F/Gas 7 for 15 minutes, or until golden brown.
Makes about 48 broas.

Castle Cakes/Broas Castelares

ESTREMADURA PROVINCE

These are small oval cakes made for the Christmas period. These delicious *broas* are sold all over Lisbon and Estremadura province, both before and well after the season.

4 oz (110 g) ground almonds
4 oz (110 g) caster sugar
7 oz (200 g) sweet potato purée
1 large egg
2 tablespoons flour

2 tablespoons fine maize flour
grated rind of 1 small orange
grated rind of 1 small lemon
beaten egg for brushing

Make a sweet potato purée by boiling sweet potatoes in plain water then peeling and mashing, weighing the amount needed. Mix the purée, almonds and sugar. Bring to the heat, stirring, to dry up a little. Remove from the heat, add the remaining ingredients and beat well. Cool the mixture and shape small oval cakes, measuring 1 inch (2.5 cm) on the widest part. Pinch ends, to make them look like leaves. Flatten to ½ inch (12 mm). Brush with beaten egg. Bake in a hot oven (210°C/425°F/Gas 7) for 15 minutes or until golden brown.
Makes 16 to 20 broas.

Coconut Cakes/Bolos de Coco

7 oz (200 g) desiccated coconut
7 oz (200 g) caster sugar

1 teaspoon flour
3 large eggs

Mix all the ingredients thoroughly. Shape small round cakes, about 1½ inches (3.5–4 cm) in diameter. Place in well-buttered and floured baking tins and bake at 210°C/425°F/Gas 7 for 10–12 minutes or until golden.

These cakes can also be baked in little mounds or pyramids, instead of round shapes.
Makes about 24 cakes.

Fried Cakes

Dreams/Sonhos

Sonhos are fried cakes like small doughnuts, but much lighter in texture. There are many variations on the same theme all over Portugal. Generally speaking, fried cakes are intended for the Christmas season but, being so good and popular, *Sonhos* are made at other times as well, and some specialist patisseries sel'

them freshly made on a daily basis. The recipe below is
flavoured with orange.

5 oz (140 g) flour
4 eggs
6 oz (175 g) granulated sugar
¼ pint (150 ml) water

1 tablespoon butter
juice of 3 medium oranges
pinch salt
oil for deep frying

Bring the water to the boil, together with the butter and pinch
of salt. Add the flour and stir thoroughly with a wooden spoon,
to form a ball. Take off the heat and place it in a basin. After
cooling a little, beat with a quarter of the orange juice and the
eggs, one by one. Continue beating, to air the dough. When
ready, deep-fry spoonfuls in hot oil, until golden. Set aside, on
kitchen paper. Prepare a syrup with the sugar, the remaining
juice and ¼ pint (150 ml) water. Boil over *low heat* for 2 minutes.
Allow to cool. Serve the *Sonhos* after dipping them in this
syrup.
Makes 24 sonhos.

Variation
The *Sonhos* can be coated with a mixture of caster sugar and
cinnamon, instead of the syrup, just after frying.

Pumpkin Cakes/Bolinhos de Jerimu de Viana

MINHO AND DOURO LITORAL PROVINCES
Although *abóbora* is the Portuguese for pumpkin, in some
northern regions it is also known as *jerimu*. These little cakes
are a Christmas speciality and were created in the beautiful city
of Viana do Castelo (Minho), a paradise for arts and crafts
treasure-hunters. Its gastronomic traditions are as rich as its
filigree jewellery, local costumes, embroidery, ceramics and
architecture.

10 oz (280 g) pumpkin purée
1 lb (450 g) granulated sugar
4 eggs
1 tablespoon flour

cinnamon stick
½ teaspoon salt
oil for deep frying

Cook some peeled pumpkin, drain thoroughly, pat dry with a
cloth and purée it, weighing enough for the recipe. You can use
any left-over purée in vegetable soups. Mix the pumpkin purée
with the flour, salt and eggs and beat very well, until fluffy.
With the help of two dessertspoons, shape the cakes and go on
placing them in the hot oil. Fry until golden brown, turning

once. As they dry, put them aside. When they are all ready, make a syrup with the sugar and a little water to melt it, boiling with the cinnamon for one minute. Remove the cinnamon, place the cakes in the syrup and bring again to simmering point for a minute. Drain the cakes with a slotted spoon and put them in a serving bowl, until cold. If there is any syrup left, pour it over the cakes afterwards, to keep them moist. They are better after a few days, so if you are preparing them for Christmas, make them the week before.
Makes 24 bolinhos.

Variation
Same as before, but omitting the syrup and sprinkling the cakes very liberally with a mixture of sugar and cinnamon.

Sweet Potato Turnovers/Recheios or Azevias de Batata Doce

These are delicacies for the Christmas table and, like so much of the food of that season, they are fried. Sweet potato makes a most unusual but glorious filling; it can also be eaten alone as a dessert or be used as a filling for tartlets.

DOUGH	FILLING
12 oz (350 g) flour	*1 lb (450 g) sweet potatoes*
½ oz (15 g) butter	*10 oz (280 g) granulated sugar*
1 oz (30 g) lard	*1 cinnamon stick*
½ coffeespoon salt
oil for deep frying
	sugar and cinnamon for sprinkling

Prepare the filling first. Cook the sweet potatoes in their jackets, until tender. Drain, peel and sieve. Mix with the sugar. Bring to the boil, with the cinnamon stick. Cook gently, stirring, until really thick. Remove the cinnamon and set aside to cool.

Meanwhile, prepare the dough, a type especially suitable for frying. Combine the fats with the flour with finger-tips. Make a well in the centre and add the salt and enough water to make a smooth dough. Knead thoroughly for 15 minutes. Form a ball and cover with a cloth. Place a damp cloth on top. Allow to rest for 45–60 minutes, before rolling out to ⅛ inch (3 mm). Using a pastry wheel, cut rounds off the dough 4 inches (10 cm) in diameter. Place a tablespoon of filling in the middle of each round; fold and press the edges.

When all half-moons are done, deep-fry them, 3 or 4 at a

time, according to the size of frying pan, turning once, for an overall golden colour. Place in kitchen paper to absorb excess fat and then sprinkle liberally with a mixture of ⅔ sugar to ⅓ cinnamon.

These turnovers are delicious accompaniments for tea or coffee and, although at their best on the same day, they will still be nice one or two days afterwards – if allowed to be left around that long!
Makes 30 turnovers.

Chickpea Turnovers from St Clara Convent/
Pasteis de Grão do Convento de Santa Clara, Évora

ALENTEJO PROVINCE
Romans, Swabians, Visigoths, Moors and many Portuguese kings have left their mark on Évora. Today, with its old monuments, convents and monasteries, splendid buildings and Roman remains (such as the Temple to Diana), Évora is still one of the most attractive, learned and important of Portuguese cities.

DOUGH
7 oz (200 g) flour
1 egg yolk
1 tablespoon olive oil
pinch salt
oil for deep frying

FILLING
3 oz (90 g) ground almonds
7 oz (200 g) granulated sugar
5 oz (140 g) chickpea purée
2 oz (60 g) butter
5 egg yolks
½ teaspoon cinnamon

To prepare the dough, first make a well in the centre of the flour, add the salt, egg yolk, oil and about 2 fluid oz (0.5 ml) tepid water. Knead until smooth, mixing more water if needed. Cover and allow to rest for 45–60 minutes.

For the filling, make a light syrup (see p.35) with the sugar and just enough water to melt it. Take off the heat and mix in the sieved chickpea purée, ground almonds, butter and cinnamon. Bring to simmering point and cook for 5 minutes, whilst stirring. Remove from the heat and combine the beaten egg yolks. Simmer again for a minute. Stir the mixture all the time. Allow to cool, when ready.

Then roll out the dough thinly (⅛ inch/3 mm) and cut rounds of about 4 inches (10 cm). Divide the filling among them, fold in half and press the edges with a fork, to seal. Lift each turnover carefully and deep-fry, turning once, until golden. Place in

kitchen paper to absorb excess fat. Serve lukewarm or cold, sprinkled with sugar, with tea or coffee.
Makes 18 pasteis.

Christmas Fried Cakes/Filhós de Natal

There are scores of fried cake recipes from all over Portugal, especially for the Christmas season. *Filhos* are among the most traditional.

2 lb (1 kg) flour
1 lb (450 g) pumpkin
4 tablespoons brandy or
    equivalent
½ oz (15 g) fresh yeast
1 teaspoon baking powder

1 coffeespoon cinnamon
grated rind of 1 small lemon
oil for frying
mixture of caster sugar and
    cinnamon for sprinkling (or
    honey syrup)

Peel the sliced pumpkin and boil until tender (use a minimum of water and do not overcook). Drain. Keep the water. Put the flour in a basin and make a well in the centre. Put the mashed pumpkin in this and mix to a dough, using also some pumpkin water. Add the yeast, baking powder and all other ingredients. Work this dough very thoroughly for at least 30 minutes until it is light and fluffy. You may need to add a little more tepid water to obtain an elastic, smooth consistency. Cover with cloth and blanket and put aside in a warm place, to rise. When it doubles its volume, heat the oil in a deep frying pan. With two spoons shape egg-sized cakes and drop them one by one in the oil. Fry until golden brown. When ready, dust them liberally with the sugar and cinnamon mixture (⅔ sugar for ⅓ cinnamon). Some people prefer them soaked in a light honey syrup (honey diluted to taste with some water and boiled for a minute).
Makes about 48 filhós.

Christmas Fried Cakes, Ribatejo Fashion/Filhós de Natal do Ribatejo

1 lb (450 g) flour
10 oz (280 g) white bread dough
3 eggs
3 oz (90 g) caster sugar
12 oz (350 g) pumpkin

1½ oranges (juice and zest)
2 tablespoons brandy
cinnamon and sugar for
    sprinkling
oil for frying

Mix the bread dough with the sugar, brandy and puréed pumpkin (see previous recipe). Make a soft dough, adding some of the pumpkin liquor. Add the flour, alternating with the eggs and the other ingredients, until everything is mixed. Add more liquid if necessary, but only very gradually, although this is a softer dough. Beat very hard for 30 minutes at least, until fluffy. Cover with a blanket and keep in a warm place until it doubles in volume. Heat the oil and fry spoonfuls of dough until golden brown. Sprinkle with the sugar/cinnamon mixture. *Makes 36 to 48 filhós, according to size.*

Abbot's Ears/Orelhas de Abade

NORTHERN PROVINCES

Very plain and easy to make, this is typical Christmas fare in the northern provinces of Trás-os-Montes and Alto Douro. Referring to all the delicious fried sweets made there during that season, Ramalho Ortigão mentions in *As Farpas* (*The Arrows*) '... the "abbot's ears" had come out of the frying pan and were placed on big platters, forming pyramids.'

7 oz (200 g) white bread dough
caster sugar and cinnamon for sprinkling
oil for frying

Have the bread dough prepared in advance and ready, when you want to fry the ears. Knead it again. Roll out small portions of dough very thinly with the rolling pin, over a floured board. Spread the pieces further, pulling with the fingers. Cut out ear-shaped bits of rolled-out dough and fry in preheated oil to 182°C/360°F, until golden, turning once. Place on kitchen paper to absorb excess fat, then dip each ear in a mixture of ⅔ caster sugar to ⅓ cinnamon. They are best eaten the same day. *Makes 24 orelhas.*

Fried Sweet Potato/Fritos de Batata

MADEIRA

A very common sweet, served in Madeira as a snack or dessert. It is equally good hot or cold.

1 lb (450g) cooked sweet potato
¼ pint (150 ml) light beer
3 oz (90 g) flour
1 large beaten egg
caster sugar and cinnamon for sprinkling
pinch of salt
oil for frying

Boil or bake the potatoes (in their jackets), until tender. Peel and cut into thick slices. Set aside. Prepare a batter with the flour, beer and egg. Beat until foamy. Mix the slices of potato into this batter. Warm up the oil to 182°C/360°F and fry by the spoonful, until golden, turning once. Place in kitchen paper, to absorb excess fat, and sprinkle with a mixture of sugar and cinnamon, to taste.

Makes about 18 sweets.

Golden Slices/Fatias Douradas or Rabanadas

Golden Slices seem to have originated in the Minho province though they are now prepared and greatly enjoyed all over the country. There are variations, of course. Some are finished just with a good sprinkling of sugar and cinnamon, others are dipped in syrup or honey, and so on. One thing they all have in common is a delicious richness.

On Christmas Eve Fatias Douradas form a centrepiece for the array of desserts following the traditional late meal. They are best eaten the day they are made but I still have yet to see any being thrown away, even after they have lost their first appeal.

Júlio Diniz vividly illustrates the importance of Fatias Douradas at Christmas in his *Morgadinha dos Canaviais* (*Lady of the Reeds*), in which Henrique, the central male character, wishing to help make the *rabanadas*, approaches the lady who is busy pouring honey over some fresh ones: ' "Well," she said. "Are you not aware that *rabanadas* are the very essence of Christmas supper? How could I entrust them to you?" ' How, indeed. Nobody would entrust that work to a mere helper, however willing.

14 oz (400 g) day-old thickly sliced white bread (close textured)	oil for frying caster sugar and cinnamon (2 parts of sugar for one of
½ pint (300 ml) milk	cinnamon), for sprinkling – or
5–6 eggs	syrup, or honey
pinch salt	

Never use bread which is too soft or the 'cotton-wool' type, as it would become too mushy and bland. Have one bowl with the milk and another with the beaten eggs, with the salt.

Mix 4–5 oz (110–140 g) caster sugar and a tablespoon of cinnamon, to start with, as you can always prepare some more later, if needed. It all depends on how generous you are with the sprinkling, but it is a good idea to be quite generous. Alternatively you can make a light syrup with 7 oz (200 g) granulated sugar and twice its volume of water, boiling both for a couple of minutes. Or make a honey syrup by warming up ¼ pint (150 ml) clear honey and the same amount of water, mixing both very well over low heat. Set aside whatever sweetener you have decided upon, to be used after the slices have been fried.

Soak each slice of bread in milk, transferring it immediately to the bowl of beaten egg. Allow it to become well coated on both sides and deep fry until golden, turning once. Remove from the oil with a slotted spoon or slice, and place in platter. Two or three slices can be fried at once, depending on the size of the pan. When ready, and still very warm, sprinkle the slices with the cinnamon mixture or use one of the given syrups; making sure that each slice gets its share of sweetener. Serve soon after they have been made, or when cold.
Serves 8.

Variations
1 An old recipe, still in use in various parts of the country, indicates red wine (¾ pint/450 ml) for the syrup, sweetening it by boiling it with enough sugar and honey to taste, and a little cinnamon. Use as before.

2 A so-called rich version of *rabanadas* uses a light sugar syrup like the one made as a sauce, in the main recipe (flavoured with a cinnamon stick and lemon rind) to cook the egg-coated slices, for 2 minutes each side, instead of frying them in oil. Add a little hot water to the syrup now and then to prevent its thickening too much. Any remaining syrup is poured over the slices, when they are all ready.

Biscuits

S-Shaped Biscuits, Peniche Fashion/SS de Peniche

ESTREMADURA PROVINCE
Perhaps someone in the lovely fishing town of Peniche was thinking of the intricate lace typical of the area and wanted to reproduce its twists and turns in the form of biscuits. Whatever the reason, a long time ago it was decided to call them 'S-shaped biscuits'. They have the advantage of using up left-over egg whites (always something to be considered when cooking Portuguese style, which demands so many yolks), but they are really very tasty and delicate, keep well and are ideal for tea.

10 oz (280 g) caster sugar   *2 tablespoons butter*
10 oz (280 g) ground almonds   *5 egg whites, stiffly beaten*
3½ oz (100 g) flour

Place the sugar, butter, almonds and beaten egg whites, well mixed together, in a pot over a low flame. Stir and allow to come to the boil. Remove from the heat, cool a little and add the flour. Beat well. Bring to the boil once more. Stir and cook gently until stiff but pliable. Cool and shape the biscuits with sugared hands in the form of two Ss together. Bake in buttered and floured tins, in an oven preheated to 190°C/375°F/Gas 5 until golden (approx 10 minutes). Handle with care when removing from the tins, using a spatula.
Makes about 30 biscuits.

Sand from Cascais/Areias de Cascais

These are small biscuits of the shortbread type, typical of the beautiful small town of Cascais, near Lisbon.

11 oz (310 g) flour
4 oz (110 g) granulated sugar
6 oz (175 g) lard

1 tablespoon butter
½ coffeespoon cinnamon
grated rind of ½ small lemon

Work the fats into the flour with the tips of your fingers, then mix in the sugar and flavourings. Shape small biscuits, the size of a walnut, with floured hands. Bake on greased and floured trays at 190°C/375°F/Gas 5 until just golden. When ready (about 10–15 minutes) roll them in caster sugar, to give the impression they are covered with sand. Store in tins, after cooling.
Makes about 36 areias.

Pine-seed Biscuits/Bolos de Pinhões

BEIRA LITORAL PROVINCE
Pine trees grow all over Portugal, and therefore pine-seeds are abundant. These cakes make use of them, although more often than not pine-seeds are eaten by themselves, rather than being used in cooking.

5 oz (140 g) fine cornflour or
   arrowroot flour
3 oz (90 g) flour
7 oz (200 g) pine-seeds, roughly
   ground, leaving some whole

3 oz (90 g) melted butter
5 oz (140 g) caster sugar
4 medium eggs
½ coffeespoon cinnamon
pinch salt

Mix all the ingredients, except a handful of whole seeds. Shape the biscuits between hand and spoon. Place a few whole seeds on top of each and bake 12–15 minutes at 210°C/425°F/Gas 7 in buttered and floured baking tins, until golden brown.
Makes 36 small biscuits.

Buns

Buns from Coimbra/Arrufadas de Coimbra

BEIRA LITORAL PROVINCE

No one should go to the old university city of Coimbra without buying its best-known speciality, these lovely buns, eaten all the year round.

1½ lb (675 g) flour   *6 oz (175 g) caster sugar*
½ oz (15 g) fresh yeast   *4 tablespoons tepid milk*
3 oz (90 g) softened butter   *1 teaspoon cinnamon*
3 large eggs   *pinch of salt*

Mix the flour with the yeast, which must have been dissolved in the tepid milk. Add the sugar, cinnamon, salt and beaten eggs. Knead, add the butter, knead again, very thoroughly. If the dough is too hard, add a little more tepid milk. It should resemble a bread dough. Cover and leave in a warm place until the following day. Prepare baking tins lined with greased greaseproof paper. Mould round cakes 2½ inches (6.5 cm) in diameter. Allow to rest for ½ hour. Then brush with milk and bake in an oven preheated to 210°C/425°F/Gas 7, until golden brown.

Makes about 18 arrufadas.

Sweet Buns, Pombal Fashion/Fogaças Doces de Pombal

BEIRA LITORAL PROVINCE

These buns are made with a yeast dough and keep very well. There are many regional variations under the name of fogaças, including savoury versions, like the one given on p.132 but all of them are meant for religious festivals. These sweet *fogaças* come from Pombal (south of Coimbra), a town of remote origin.

The story is told of a rich woman, whose surname was Fogaça, who asked the Holy Virgin to rid the town of a plague of locusts (a confirmed happening in the twelfth century) which was destroying crops. As the locusts disappeared, she prepared cakes as a thanksgiving and offered them to the priest. The recipe later acquired her own name and has been perpetuated ever since. Despite the tradition, it is possible that the word had already been introduced into Portuguese in Roman times, for Italians still have *focaccia*, a kind of flat, quite tasteless bread made during the Christmas season.

1 lb (450 g) flour
½ oz (15 g) fresh yeast
.3 large eggs
¼ pint (150 ml) milk
1 tablespoon powdered aniseed

2 oz (60 g) caster sugar
2 oz (60 g) lard
3 oz (90 g) butter
pinch of salt
beaten egg for brushing

Prepare the yeast dough first. Mix a third of the flour with the crumbled yeast and half the milk (lukewarm). Cover and set aside.

Put another third of the flour in a basin, make a well in the centre and add the softened butter and lard, salt, milk, aniseed and sugar. Mix thoroughly. Add the yeast dough. Knead really well for 8–10 minutes. Start adding the eggs, one by one, alternating with the remaining flour and kneading well between additions. The dough should not stick to the sides of the basin, when ready. Form a ball with it, cover with a cloth, then a blanket and leave in warm place, to rise.

When it is ready, roll it out to a 1 inch (2.5 cm) thickness and mould handfuls into rounds and horseshoe shapes. Brush with beaten egg and leave again in a warm place for a while (45–60 minutes) on buttered baking trays. Bake in an oven preheated to 190°C/375°F/Gas 5 for 35–40 minutes or until golden brown. *Makes about 18 fogaças.*

Sweet Buns/Regueifas

MINHO PROVINCE

A yeast dough, enriched with eggs and the popular cinnamon, makes these buns always found at country festivities, as they keep well for the several days they are needed.

4 oz (110 g) caster sugar
1¼ lb (560 g) flour
½ oz (15 g) fresh yeast
2 oz (60 g) melted butter
2 whole eggs, plus 3 egg yolks

½ coffeespoon saffron
1 coffeespoon cinnamon
1 coffeespoon baking powder
pinch of salt
butter for brushing

Mix the saffron and cinnamon in a little tepid water. Set aside. Crumble the yeast, add tepid water, salt and baking powder and mix with 4 oz (110 g) flour. Combine well and leave in a warm place, covered, for 1½ hours. Mix the butter, sugar, eggs and yolks with the spices. Beat well. Put 1 lb (450 g) flour in a bowl, make a well in the centre and place the yeast dough in it. Add the egg mixture. Combine well and knead until smooth. Leave in a warm place, covered, to double in size. Then, with floured hands, mould buns in various shapes to your taste. Leave again for a while, to rise. Bake until golden (the time

depends on the size of your buns) at 210°C/425°F/Gas 7. Brush the tops with butter, once ready, and whilst still warm.
Makes 18 medium-sized buns.

All Saints' Day Buns/Bolos dos Santos

BEIRA BAIXA PROVINCE
All Saints' Day (1 November) is celebrated all over Portugal with family gatherings, especially in rural areas, when cakes and chestnuts are eaten. A little sadness creeps in, as on the following day, 2 November, families visit cemeteries and remember the departed.

1 lb (450 g) flour	1 tablespoon cinnamon
1 oz (30 g) fresh yeast	1 tablespoon powdered aniseed
3 eggs	pinch of salt
2 oz (60 g) melted lard	beaten egg for brushing
3 oz (90 g) caster sugar	sugar for topping

Place the flour in a warm basin and make a well in the centre. Pour into this the crumbled yeast, already dissolved in 4 tablespoons of warm water, with a pinch of salt. Mix and add all other ingredients, moistening with more tepid water, if needed, to form a smooth, bread-like dough. Cover and leave in a warm place to rise for 45–60 minutes. Then shape buns 2 inches (5 cm) in diameter and place them on buttered baking sheets. Leave to rest in a warm place for 10–15 minutes. Brush with beaten egg, top the centre with a little mound of sugar and bake at 210°C/425°F/Gas 7 for 15–20 minutes or until nicely browned.
Makes 12 to 18 buns.

All Saints' Day Buns/Bolinhos dos Santos

BEIRA LITORAL PROVINCE

1 lb (450 g) maize flour	2 tablespoons olive oil
8 oz (225 g) flour	1 orange (juice and zest)
1 oz (30 g) fresh yeast	1 lemon (zest only)
8 oz (225 g) brown sugar	3 tablespoons brandy (or
2 eggs	equivalent)
2 lb (1 kg) pumpkin	1 tablespoon powdered aniseed
6 oz (175 g) dried fruit (mixed	1 tablespoon cinnamon
nuts, sultanas etc to taste)	1 coffeespoon salt

Prepare the yeast with a little of the flour and tepid water. While it rests, cook the pumpkin in just a drop of water; drain and absorb any excess moisture in a cloth. Place the maize flour

in a warm basin and add the cooked pumpkin, still hot. Work both together. Add the flour and the yeast dough. Knead well. Add all other ingredients except the dried fruits, and knead again until you have a really elastic, light dough. Mix in the fruit, previously cut into rough pieces, cover the basin and leave in a warm place, to double in size. Butter baking sheets and shape cakes 1½–2 inches (3.5–5 cm) in diameter. Allow to rest for 15–20 minutes and bake at 210°C/425°F/Gas 7 for 15–20 minutes or until golden brown.
Makes about 30 buns.

Easter Buns/Bolos de Páscoa

TRÁS-OS-MONTES PROVINCE
After the rigours of the Lent period – which, in remote areas, can still be a reality in this day and age – good things to eat are very welcome, when Easter finally arrives.

12 oz (350 g) caster sugar
9 eggs
¼ pint (150 ml) olive oil
¼ pint (150 ml) milk
enough flour for the dough
1½ oz (45 g) fresh yeast

½ teaspoon baking powder
1 tablespoon brandy (or
  equivalent)
1 heaped tablespoon cinnamon
1 coffeespoon salt

Crumble the yeast and mix with a little tepid water. Add the salt, baking powder, milk, brandy, cinnamon and olive oil. Beat well. Set aside for a moment while you beat the eggs with the sugar and heat them to blood temperature, stirring all the time. Combine this with the previous mixture and pour into a large basin. Add flour gradually until a smooth dough is formed (the amount of flour depends on local varieties). The consistency of the dough should be similar to that of bread, and it should not stick to the sides of the basin. After kneading thoroughly, cover the basin with a blanket and leave in a warm place until the following day.

Next day knead again for a little while and mould small balls out of this dough (the size is up to you, but a diameter of 2 inches 5 cm would be adequate). Place the cakes in buttered baking tins and leave for another hour before baking until golden in an oven set to 180°C/350°F/Gas 4. Brushing them with a mixture of beaten egg and milk before baking will improve their appearance.
Makes 24 to 30 buns.

Large Cakes

Sponge Cake/Pão-de-ló

The best-known versions are from some northern provinces, such as Minho, Douro and Beira Alta, but there are various other recipes of *pão-de-ló* all over the country. Many northern villages and towns boast their own special *pão-de-ló*, and any Portuguese household worth its salt will produce a good one. This has been, and perhaps will always be, one the best loved cakes, to eat on its own when fresh and, when it becomes hard, as a basis for puddings. In Portuguese patisseries and good grocers *pão-de-ló* is sold in its traditional shape, baked in a ring-mould, and wrapped in strong white paper, which is used to line the mould, when prepared in commercial ovens. Home-made *pão-de-ló* will always be a little different from the bought one, on account of the oven, if not the recipe. Nevertheless, whatever oven is used, this cake is always a good bet for tea. The secret for a good texture lies in the thorough whipping.

5 eggs	*5 oz (140 g) caster sugar, free*
2½ oz (75 g) finest white	*from any lumps*
self-raising flour, sifted	*pinch of salt*

If you are not prepared to whip hard by hand, use an electric mixer. With it you can halve the times indicated here.

Whip the eggs with the sugar for 20 minutes, then add the flour and whip again for another 15 minutes. Bake in a ring-mould 7–8 inches (18–20.5 cm) in diameter, lined and greased with butter, in an oven preheated to 190°C/375°F/Gas 5, for about 20 minutes or until golden brown and springy to the touch. Check it with a cake-tester.
Serves 4 to 6.

Variations
1 A very light and nicely textured *pão-de-ló* is obtained with the following recipe:

5 eggs, separated	*4½ oz (approx. 130 g) fine rice*
7 oz (200 g) caster sugar	*flour*
	1 teaspoon baking powder

Beat the yolks with the sugar very hard (at least 10 minutes), until they become whitish. Carefully add half the stiffly beaten egg whites. Then mix in the flour (sifted with the baking

powder), trying to achieve a smooth texture without actually beating. Finally fold in the remaining egg whites. Bake as for the previous cake.
Serves 6.

2 This recipe is a simpler, homely version – one that I use often with good results:

4 *eggs, separated*
7 *oz (200 g) caster sugar*
5 *oz (140 g) fine plain flour*

1 *teaspoon baking powder*
4 *tablespoons cold water*

Mix the yolks with the sugar as in variation 1. Then add the water, little by little, beating well between additions. Mix in the flour (sifted with the baking powder) and finally fold in the whipped egg whites. Bake as before.
Serves 6.

Sponge Roll, Viana Fashion/Torta de Viana do Castelo

MINHO PROVINCE
This delicious sponge roll is but one of the many specialities typical of Viana do Castelo. 'The Princess of the Lima', as Viana is called, stands at the mouth of that river and offers superb views from St Luzia hill and its interesting basilica. A few miles away is Ponte do Lima, another lovely old-world town on the banks of the river.

7 *oz (200 g) caster sugar*
3 *oz (90 g) flour*
3 *large eggs, separated*

Filling – any good jam or ovos moles (p.152)

Grease a swiss roll-type baking tin, about 9 × 13 inches (23 × 31 cm) and line it with buttered greaseproof paper. Cream the egg yolks with the sugar. Beat the whites until stiff and add to the yolks, folding and alternating with the sifted flour. Do not beat the mixture. Bring to the oven in the prepared tin and bake at 232°C/450°F/Gas 8 until just golden (only 7–10 minutes). Do not overcook, or it will dry and break when rolling. Turn it into a sugared tea-towel, spread the filling swiftly and roll up carefully, with the help of the tea-towel. Trim the edges and cool on a cake-rack.
Serves 4 to 6.

Rich Molasses Cake/Bolo Rico de Mel

MADEIRA

Although it is commonly known as 'honey cake', it should really be called 'molasses cake', as the 'honey' used comes from the cane, not the hive. This is a very old recipe, evolved from the times when spices and raw sugar first came to Madeira, following the navigators' loaded caravels from the East and Africa. Madeira itself started cane-sugar production from its early days as Portuguese territory. Molasses cake is the most traditional and irresistible of Madeira's sweet specialities. It is intended as a Christmas treat, though it is eaten all the year round and now exported to Lisbon, where it is sold in great quantities. Molasses cake keeps well for at least a year, and even when dried up and old it is still pure delight, with its rich and spicy flavours lingering in the mouth.

1 lb (450 g) flour
8 oz (225 g) crushed walnuts
3 oz (90 g) lard
7 oz (200 g) butter
8 oz (225 g) sugar (the darker, the
  better)
2 oz (60 g) candied peel
4 oz (110 g) stoned prunes
8 fluid oz (225 ml) molasses
grated rind and juice of 1
  medium-sized orange
grated rind of 1 medium lemon

5 oz (140 g) ground almonds
1 teaspoon each of powdered
  aniseed, mixed spices, clove,
  nutmeg
1 tablespoon cinnamon
1 teaspoon salt
½ oz (15 g) fresh yeast and 4 oz
  (110 g) flour to mix it with
1 teaspoon baking powder
1 handful of whole peeled
  almonds, for decoration

To prepare the yeast dough, first make a well in the centre of the 4 oz (110 g) flour, add the crumbled yeast and enough tepid water to form a soft dough. Sprinkle with flour and leave to rise in a warm place, covered with a cloth, until the following day. In a large basin place the flour, mixed with the sugar and baking powder, and make a well in the centre. Add the yeast dough and mix. Gradually add the warmed molasses and the melted fats, the juice and grated rind of the orange, the lemon rind, crushed walnuts, ground almonds, cut-up prunes and spices, alternating the various ingredients while combining and kneading everything very thoroughly, until it no longer sticks to the basin. Cover with a cloth, then a blanket, and leave to rise in a warm place with a constant temperature for three days.

Preheat the oven to 190°C/375°F/Gas 5. In the meantime divide the dough into four portions and grease generously round baking tins 7 inches (18 cm) in diameter. The cakes do

not rise much while baking and their thickness can be gauged when distributing the dough: about 1½ inches (4 cm). Flatten the top of the cakes and decorate with almonds, in a circle. Bake for 40–45 minutes or until a cake-tester comes out dry. To ensure that the cakes are completely cold before storing, leave until the following day. Then wrap in greaseproof paper or foil and keep in tins.
Serves 10 to 12.

Fruit Cake/Bolo de Frutas

MADEIRA
Like the dark (almost black) and richly spiced Molasses Cake (p.205), this one is a Christmas treat in Madeira, containing all the traditional dried fruits and nuts common to so many recipes for that season, the world over.

7 oz (200 g) flour
7 oz (200 g) sugar
¼ pint (150 ml) milk
4 oz (110 g) butter
3 oz (90 g) lard
3 large eggs
1 tablespoon cinnamon
2 tablespoons runny honey
3 oz (90 g) raisins (free from seeds) or sultanas

2 oz (60 g) candied mixed peel
2 oz (60 g) almonds (flaked)
2 oz (60 g) dried plums
3 tablespoons sweet madeira (or port)
grated rind of 1 small lemon
½ coffeespoon nutmeg
1 tablespoon baking powder

Mix well all the nuts and spices, rind and dried fruits with the flour, baking powder, sugar and wine. Add the milk and beaten eggs. Melt the fats and honey and beat in the mixture. Bake in a buttered round cake tin about 8 inches (20 cm) in diameter in an oven preheated to 180°C/350°F/Gas 4 for 40–45 minutes or until firm and golden brown. Try the cake-tester.

This cake keeps well but in Madeira it is generally eaten within one or two days of baking.
Serves 6 to 8.

Christmas Cake/Bolo de Natal

AZORES ARCHIPELAGO
In spite of its name, this cake is also used for celebrations other than Christmas, such as birthdays and weddings, decorated accordingly. It keeps well and should in fact be made two or three weeks in advance.

14 oz (400 g) flour
2 teaspoons baking powder
7 oz (200 g) butter
11 oz (310 g) caster sugar
3 tablespoons molasses
4 large eggs, separated
14 oz (400 g) glacé fruits and
  candied peel

grated rind of 1 lemon (or orange)
2 tablespoons brandy (or
  equivalent)
2 tablespoons port wine (or
  equivalent)
3 oz (90 g) walnuts

Sprinkle some flour onto the fruit, to prevent it sinking, and set aside. Cream the butter with the sugar and egg yolks, and add the flour gradually (previously mixed with the baking powder) alternating with the molasses, wine, brandy and grated rind. Fold in the stiffly beaten egg whites and finally the fruits. Bake in a large mould, 8–9 inches (20–23 cm) in diameter, at 180°C/350°F/Gas 4 until a cake-tester comes out clean (45–50 minutes). Decorate only when completely cold, or leave it as it is. *Serves* 12.

Rotten Cake/Bolo Podre

ALENTEJO PROVINCE
The so-called 'rotten' cakes owes its name to its dark, rough appearance. It is one of those tasty and homely cakes that makes people come back for more.

12 oz (350 g) wholemeal flour
1½ teaspoons baking powder
½ pint (300 ml) olive oil
½ pint (300 ml) dark honey
4 eggs

3 tablespoons brandy (or
  equivalent)
½ coffeespoon ground cloves
1 tablespoon cinnamon
handful of whole peeled almonds,
  for decoration

Mix all ingredients except the flour and the almonds, and beat until it thickens. Using an electric mixer saves effort. Gradually add the flour and baking powder. Beat again. Leave to rest until the following day.

Pour the mixture into a large, well-buttered cake tin 8–10 inches (20–25.5 cm) in diameter or use two smaller tins. Decorate the top with the almonds and bake at 180°C/350°F/Gas 4 for 45 minutes or until a cake-tester comes out clean. *Serves 8.*

Honey Cake/Bolo de Mel

RIBATEJO PROVINCE
A simple cake for any occasion. The flavourings can be varied, to give it different guises (try mixed spices and grated orange rind).

7 oz (200 g) flour　　　　　　¼ pint (150 ml) dark honey
1 teaspoon baking powder　　　2 oz (60 g) dark sugar
6 eggs, separated　　　　　　　2 teaspoons cinnamon
2 tablespoons softened butter　 1 teaspoon powdered aniseed
4 tablespoons olive oil　　　　　pinch of salt

Cream the egg yolks with the sugar and the butter. Add the oil, honey and spices. Mix in the flour with the baking powder, gradually. Fold in the stiffly beaten egg whites. Bake in a well-greased tin 8 inches (20.5 cm) in diameter at 190°C/375°F/ Gas 5 until a cake-tester comes out clean – about 40 minutes. *Serves 6.*

King's Cake/Bolo Rei

ESTREMADURA PROVINCE
Ever present in enormous quantities, in all patisseries and good grocers, from the start of December well into January and sometimes at other occasions, too (increasingly, during the Easter celebrations). As the name implies, though, it really belongs to Twelfth Night (Epiphany), a day which, until recently, was a Bank holiday in Portugal and which is still very much a part of the Christmas celebrations. Generally, it contains a small prize inside (a little heart, an owl or something, wrapped up in paper) and also a dried broad bean. The person who eats the slice where the broad bean or the prize is, soon finds out. When the prize is found, a great cheer is given, but whoever gets the broad bean is meant to buy the King's Cake the following year.

1½ lb (675 g) flour　　　　　　　6 tablespoons port wine (or
1 oz (30 g) fresh yeast　　　　　　　equivalent)
5 oz (140 g) caster sugar　　　　　grated rind of 1 lemon and 1
5 oz (140 g) butter　　　　　　　　orange
5 oz (140 g) mixed nuts and dried　1 teaspoon salt
　fruit　　　　　　　　　　　　　1 beaten egg, for brushing
5 oz (140 g) mixed glacé fruit and　1 dried broad bean and 1 small
　candied peel　　　　　　　　　　souvenir (optional)
3 large eggs

Steep the dried fruits in the wine, to swell up. Crumble the yeast into a little warm water (enough to dissolve it) and add it to about 4 oz (110 g) of the given flour. Mix well and set aside for 20 minutes in a warm place, to rise.

Beat the eggs with the sugar, the softened butter, salt and grated rind. Mix in the yeast dough and then the flour, gradually. Knead really well, until it becomes elastic and

smooth. Mix in the fruit with the wine and knead again. Gather the dough into a ball and sprinkle with flour. Cover and keep in warm place for 5–6 hours, to double in volume. With floured hands, shape one large or two smaller King's Cakes into a ring. Brush the cake or cakes with the beaten egg and stick the glacé fruits and candied peel on top, all round. Bake at 210°C/425°F/Gas 7 for 20–25 minutes or until golden brown. After cooling, put the cakes in tins or wrap in foil, to keep them moist.
Serves 10 to 12.

Fancy Bread

Plain Cake/Boleima

ALENTEJO PROVINCE
This plain cake is a variety of 'fancy bread', and it does help if one has already some bread dough prepared. Weigh it and add the other ingredients in the proportions indicated below.

1 lb (450 g) white bread dough
1 teaspoon baking powder
4 oz (110 g) lard
2 tablespoons butter
10 oz (280 g) caster sugar
3 eggs

2 tablespoons brandy (or equivalent)
grated rind of 1 orange (or lemon)
1 teaspoon cinnamon mixed with 2 tablespoons sugar

Add all the ingredients except the cinnamon mixture to the bread dough and mix very well. Put into a well-buttered baking tray (8 × 12 inches/20 × 30 cm) and sprinkle with the sugar/cinnamon mixture. Bake at 190°C/375°F/Gas 5 for 20–25 minutes or until golden brown.
Serves 8 to 10.

Fancy Bread for Easter/Folar de Páscoa

ESTREMADURA PROVINCE BUT USED COUNTRYWIDE IN SIMILAR FORM
Fancy breads eaten during the Easter period are very attractive loaves with one or two boiled eggs stuck on top, as decoration, secured by a trellis made of dough. They remain excellent to the very end, and the traditional flavourings of aniseed and cinnamon make them a most welcome companion for tea or coffee.

Folares can also be eaten at other times apart from Easter.

14 oz (400 g) flour
½ oz (15 g) fresh yeast
1½ oz (45 g) caster sugar
3 oz (90 g) butter
1 large egg
½ pint (300 ml) milk
1 teaspoon powdered aniseed

1 teaspoon cinnamon
½ teaspoon salt

FOR DECORATION
2 hard-boiled eggs, shelled
1 beaten egg for brushing

In a warm bowl combine the crumbled yeast with a quarter of the given flour and a third of the milk (which should be warm). Mix in half the sugar. Make a dough with these, then cover and leave in a warm place to rise, for about half an hour. Meanwhile, beat the egg with the remaining milk and sugar, salt and spices. Add the flour gradually and work the dough for a few minutes. Add the softened butter and work again. Mix the yeast dough and knead really well. When ready, it should not stick to the sides of the bowl. Cover and set aside in a warm place, for about three hours, to rise. Then with floured hands shape one big or two smaller loaves (round or slightly egg-shaped) and place the boiled eggs on top, half buried and secured with two strips of dough, crossing each other. Brush the *folar* with beaten egg and bake in a hot oven (210°C/425°F/Gas 7) until nicely brown.
Serves 8 to 10.

Buttery Bola/Bola de Manteiga

BEIRA ALTA PROVINCE
Some regions adopt the name of *bola* for *folar*, but all these recipes are basically a fancy bread and can be made with bread dough itself – such as this very rich version of *bola*.

1 lb (450 g) white bread dough
7 oz (200 g) caster sugar
3 tablespoons cinnamon

7 oz (200 g) butter plus 1
tablespoon for brushing the top
after baking

Grease well a square cake mould or deep baking tin about 8–9 inches (20.5–23 cm) in diameter. Divide the bread dough into five more or less equal parts. Roll out two pieces and spread one over the bottom of the tin and the other over the sides, thus forming a container of dough. Divide the butter and sugar into three equal parts. Pour a third of the butter (previously melted) over the first layer of dough, then sprinkle with a third of the sugar and a tablespoon of cinnamon. Cover this with another rolled-out piece of dough and again spread the melted butter, sugar and cinnamon over it, then again to the final layer. The

last one is a dough lid, on top. With a sharp knife mark the *bola* into squares, coming down half way through the assembled layers. Bake at 210°C/425°F/Gas 7 for 25–30 minutes or until golden brown, then brush the top with a tablespoon of butter. Take it out of the tin when you can handle it, and cool it on a wire rack.
Serves 8 to 10.

Jams and Jellies

Light-Coloured or 'White' Quince Cheese/
Marmelada Branca

I imagine that the name 'cheese' has been given to this jam, in English, because it becomes so hard after drying that it can be cut with a knife. However, even when one does not manage to achieve this perfection – for which you need strong sunshine, quince jam is always quite thick and suitable to eat either on its own or with bread, biscuits or cheese as the Portuguese do.

2½ lb (1.2 kg) quinces (gamboas or marmelos pp.28–29)
2 lb (1 kg) granulated sugar

The secret for keeping quince cheese light in colour is to avoid oxidizing the fruit. Therefore no metal spoons or knives must touch it. To do this, cook them whole, unpeeled (but very thoroughly washed and free from the 'fur' which normally covers part of the skin) in enough boiling water just to half cover them (you can turn them over half way through). They will be tender in 10–12 minutes. Try not to overcook them. Drain very well and peel, after cooling enough to handle. Do not use a knife but your fingers not only to peel the cooked fruit but also to open it and take out the pips. Mash and sieve the flesh (keep the pips and all the bits and pieces you have put aside at this stage, including the skin, if you want to make some jelly). The pulp must be smooth, and if you think it isn't, sieve it again.

Meanwhile, put the sugar in a large pan and add a little water or use some of the liquid in which the fruit has been cooked (keep the remainder also, for the jelly). Use the minimum of liquid, though, otherwise it will take ages to dry up the jam. Boil the sugar and liquid until they make a 'soft ball' syrup (p.35). All you really want is a syrup as thick as possible, before it actually gets too hard.

Add the prepared pulp and stir into the syrup with a wooden spoon. When it is well mixed, bring it to the boil over a gentle heat, stirring, and let the jam dry as much as you can, without burning. (Protect your hand from splashes with a cloth or thick glove.) The longer the jam boils, the more danger there is of its becoming reddish, so the idea is to go through all these operations fairly quickly.

Take the pan off the heat as soon as a 'parting' is formed at the bottom of the pan when you stir with the wooden spoon. Beat it energetically for a little while after finishing cooking, until it cools down. Pour into bowls or trays, to harden.

Traditionally, the *marmelada* is dried in the sun. This is where a warm climate comes in handy. The containers are set outside, in some protected spot, covered with a net to prevent flying insects having a go at them, and allowed to dry until a crust is formed on top. This may take several days, so one takes the *marmelada* out every morning and brings it in again in the afternoon for, say, 4 or 5 days, then it should be ready to store in a damp-free place (a cool larder, for example), covering the surface with cellophane. I find that, in the absence of strong enough sun shining reliably for that length of time over my *marmelada*, it is a good idea to bring it to a cool oven (121–135°C/250–275°F/Gas ¼–½) for several hours. A crust will thus be formed on top. I pour the *marmelada* into fireproof containers, of course. The trouble with this procedure is that the resulting *marmelada* will never be quite as light in colour as was intended. However, I actually prefer the reddish version, which to me looks much richer, even though the taste is about the same.

Variation
For the 'red' version (*Marmelada Vermelha*), use the same amounts of fruit and sugar as before. The idea, in this case, is to oxidize the quinces as much as one can, so make free use of metal knives and spoons. Peel and cut the quinces before cooking (quartering them and keeping the cores with the pips, and skins, for jelly) and bring to the boil until tender, as before. Drain and follow exactly the same procedure. The remaining water (after cooking the fruit) is used to cook all the bits set aside, for 10–15 minutes. Drain and keep the liquor, which at this stage will be full of wonderful pectin for a fragrant jelly.

Quince Jelly/Geleia de Marmelo

This is of course a must, when making *marmelada*, as it would be a great pity to waste the richly flavoured skins and cores of the quinces. It does not really differ from other fruit jellies, so all you do is to use the liquid in which the fruit was cooked, boil it with any skins and cores that have been put aside, so as to extract as much flavour and pectin as possible, then strain it thoroughly and measure the resulting liquor. The general rule is to use the same amount of sugar as of liquid, so you have to calculate this yourself, according to how much you have. Then mix both ingredients and boil (take off scum if necessary but do not stir) until a jelly is obtained 10–12 minutes after you first start boiling it. Test this by putting a teaspoonful of jelly on a cold plate. Push with fingertips – it will wrinkle, if ready. Store in jars.

Grape Jam/Doce de Uvas

This is a delightful light jam-cum-jelly with a very delicate taste. It is not made as often now as it used to be (which is a pity) but I remember a dear aunt of mine, from the Ribatejo province, having jars of white grape jam every year, after the gathering of ripe grapes in the vineyard.

2 lb (1 kg) cleaned grapes
2 lb (1 kg) granulated sugar

Bring the grapes and sugar to the boil. Some of the skins will rise to the surface, and it is easy then to skim them off with a slotted spoon. Place them in a sieve, press with a spoon, to extract all the juice and flesh, and return this to the pan. Continue simmering until set – test a drop in a saucer. It should not, however, take too long (12–15 minutes, perhaps). Bottle in prepared jars.

Spaghetti Squash Jam/Doce de Chila

Spaghetti squash is a gourd which, when cooked, becomes like thin spaghetti – hence the name. The threads are then made into a jam, which is very popular all over Portugal, to eat by the spoonful or to use as a filling for tartlets and cakes. It has a very characteristic texture, at once fleshy and crunchy, different from anything else. Spaghetti squash is not available everywhere, but sometimes it is imported into the countries where it does not grow. It looks like an elongated pale yellow melon.

1 lb (450 g) spaghetti squash (after having cooked it) – buy about twice
   this amount uncooked
1 lb (450 g) granulated sugar

In order to keep the jam very pale in colour, one must not use a knife when cutting the gourd. The classic way of breaking it is to throw it on the floor. The pieces are then picked up, washed and freed from seeds and from the yellow mushy centre, by hand.

Put all these pieces (skin and all) in a roomy pan with boiling water and cook until the skin comes apart. Remove from the heat and place in cold water. Working with your hands, separate the skin from the flesh, and discard any seeds that have emerged during cooking. Then put the clean flesh in a container, making it all into threads, with your fingers. Cover with water and a little salt and leave to soak until the following day.

Then drain the threads and wash them in clean water, using a sieve under the tap. Drain well. Meanwhile make a syrup with the sugar and ½ pint (300 ml) water, until thickish. Add the prepared threads and boil again until thick, stirring now and then. This will now look like fine cooked spaghetti, shiny with the sugar. Pour into bowls, to store and cover with cellophane.

This jam can be used for filling cakes as it is or mixed with egg yolks, bringing it just to the boil, to cook the yolks, before using. Add two yolks for each 5 oz (140 g) of jam. Try this to fill turnovers either baked or fried, and also in recipes calling for 'egg threads'.

Friar John's Delight/Delícia do Frei João

ALCOBAÇA MONASTERY, NORTH OF ESTREMADURA PROVINCE
Although nuns were known for their inventiveness in regard to sweets, and monks for their wines, this does not mean that monks could not create some sweet concoctions of their own. The one below is a jam made with all (or most) fruits in season (Alcobaça is rich in fruit) mixed with walnuts. The jam is a real speciality of the Benedictine monks.

The monastery was founded in 1178 and inaugurated during the reign of the first Portuguese king. Alcobaça became an important cultural centre, the monks contributing greatly to its splendour, with historical works set on their own printing-press in the sixteenth century. The abbot was a very powerful man, with many titles, including that of 'lord of the water and wind', referring to the wind- and watermills on the Order's extensive estates. Unfortunately, much of the riches accumulated by the monks over seven centuries (silver and precious books) were pillaged during the Napoleonic invasions and the remainder confiscated at the abolition of the religious orders, in

1834. But Alcobaça's noble ancestry is still much in evidence today.

2 lb (1 kg) mixed ripe fruit (half peaches and the remaining weight made up of seeded and peeled muscat grapes, sweet melon, pears, apples, quince etc)

1½ lb (675 g) granulated sugar
2 oz (60 g) very good quality walnuts, roughly crushed

Wash, peel and core the fruit. Cut it into small pieces. Add the sugar and boil gently, in a roomy pan, until a thick jam is formed. Stir the mixture carefully most of the time, and be careful not to let it burn. When a thick consistency is reached, add the walnuts, boil for another minute, remove from the heat and bottle.

Pumpkin Jam/Doce de Abóbora

This is an excellent jam very useful for filling tarts and cakes or as a dessert, mixed with toasted almonds or crushed walnuts. If mixed with a couple of egg yolks and simmered, it can be used for fillings where *ovos moles* (p.152) are called for.

1 lb (450 g) cooked pumpkin
1¼ lb (560 g) granulated sugar
1 teaspoon cinnamon

Peel and clean the pumpkin and cook in water until tender, adding just a pinch of salt. Place in a sieve to drain it as much as possible while pressing it lightly to extract the liquid trapped inside. Mash and sieve, to obtain a very smooth purée. Mix with the sugar and boil, stirring with wooden spoon until it thickens. Take off the heat and stir in the cinnamon. Pour into a glass bowl and sprinkle with just a hint of cinnamon.

Tomato Jam/Doce de Tomate

This jam is made in most Portuguese households whenever there is a tomato glut. Tomatoes make a tasty, thick jam of a rich dark red colour. The flavour is definitely 'different' from that of any other jam.

ripe tomatoes (big, ripe, and pulpy, if possible)
granulated sugar

lemon juice
1 vanilla pod or 1 stick cinnamon

Peel, deseed and cut tomatoes. Drain excess juice. Weigh the pulp and mix with an equal amount of sugar. Boil with the vanilla pod (or cinnamon stick) over a low heat, stirring from time to time with a wooden spoon. When a small amount of jam resembles jelly when dropped in a saucer, the tomato jam is ready. At the last minute add the juice of ½ lemon (for each 2 lb/1 kg) tomatoes. Pour into sterilized jars. Serve with bread and butter or as a filling for cakes.

If you prefer a smoother jam, liquidize the pulp before adding the sugar, but to my way of thinking it is better to find little 'chunks' of tomato when eating this jam by the spoon.

Tomato Jam/Doce de Tomate

There is a version using unripe tomatoes, less common than the ripe alternative, but useful as a standby and also when you want to use up unripe tomatoes.

2 lb (1 kg) unripe tomatoes (still green in colour)
1½ lb (675 g) granulated sugar

1 medium lemon
1 vanilla pod or cinnamon stick
1 clove (whole)

Wash the tomatoes and slice them very thinly. Add the lemon, also thinly sliced, the sugar and the spices. Let this mixture stand for 24 hours. Remove the spices and boil over a gentle heat, without a lid, for 1½–2 hours. Bottle as usual. This can be eaten by the spoonful in small amounts or with bread and butter, or can be used as a decoration and filling for cakes.

Fillings

Egg Threads/Fios de Ovos

This is another way of preparing egg yolks and sugar (Portugal's favourite taste) for sweets. Egg threads look rather like mounds of yellow noodles and, like *ovos moles* (p.152) are served as a garnish to cakes and puddings or to fill Algarvean almonds cakes.

Most people buy egg threads at sweetshops, when wishing to prepare something special at home. They are a little troublesome to make, and professional cooks have a funnel with various narrow openings to make the egg yolks drop in fine threads over the boiling sugar. Failing a special funnel, one must of course use an ordinary one, but the operation becomes much more precarious, and success does not always ensue. Nevertheless, do not dismay, because any egg yolk dropped unevenly over the syrup will still be edible, though less pretty to look at than the proper yellow noodle-like threads.

7 oz (200 g) granulated sugar
1 whole egg plus 4 egg yolks, beaten lightly, together
3 fluid oz (scant 100 ml) water

Boil the sugar and water, until thickish (see the 'thread stage' p.35). Reduce the heat, but keep the syrup at boiling point. Drop half the egg mixture into the syrup through the funnel, rotating it to form the threads and allowing them to cook for a couple of minutes. Remove with a slotted spoon and place on a damp plate. Repeat the procedure with the remaining eggs, after adding a drop of water to the syrup, to prevent its becoming too hard. Separate the cooked threads with the help of two forks, so that they do not remain stuck together. Use the same day. The syrup can be left for some other sweet.

Chantilly Cream, Portuguese Style

Nowadays Chantilly cream is widely used in Portugal to fill cakes and to decorate all kinds of sweets sold at the many patisseries. It can be bought ready made at good delicatessens in Lisbon and other cities (not so much in small towns), but to ensure freshness it is always better to prepare it at home.

¼ pint (150 ml) double cream   *1 oz (30 g) icing sugar (sifted, to*
1 egg white, stiffly beaten   *avoid lumps)*
                                                      1 or 2 drops vanilla essence

Whip the cream (do not overdo it, or it will turn to butter), flavour with the vanilla, add the egg white and sweeten with the sugar. Do not, however, add all the sugar at once unless you prefer the cream sweeter. Place in the refrigerator until needed. It will keep for a couple of days.

Variations
1 I find that the real Portuguese Chantilly taste is achieved quite well using half double cream and half good soured cream. Beat well as before, add sugar to taste and a drop of vanilla. If you want to bulk it up, add the stiffly beaten egg white.
2 Whip double cream as in the recipe above, then add a tablespoon of plain yogurt, vanilla and sugar to taste. Again use the egg white if you want, but you do not need to do so.

Chestnut Filling

*10 oz (300 g) chestnut purée
    (made with sieved, boiled
    chestnuts – or use from a tin of
    unsweetened purée)
3 oz (90 g) icing sugar*

*3 tablespoons milk
3 oz (90 g) butter
¼ pint (150 ml) double cream
    (whipped)
4 drops vanilla essence*

Mix the cold chestnut purée with the sugar, vanilla, softened butter and milk. Beat very hard until smooth. Fold in the whipped cream. Taste for sugar.

This filling can be used for tartlets, topping or filling cakes, but it is also a good dessert by itself, after it has been in the refrigerator for a while. Decorate with cream and/or chocolate vermicelli.

Coffee Cream for Fillings

*4 oz (110 g) butter at room
    temperature
icing sugar – to taste*

*1 egg yolk
1½ tablespoons instant coffee (or
    very strong real coffee)*

Beat the butter until it is soft, add the yolk, the coffee and enough sugar to sweeten. Beat well and use for filling cakes or as a topping.

Variation
Add a handful of broken walnuts to the cream.

Butter Cream for Fillings, Portuguese Style

*7 oz (200 g) butter
2 egg yolks
6 oz (175 g) icing sugar, sifted*

*Flavouring (vanilla essence/
    lemon rind/etc – to taste)*

Mix the sugar with the butter and yolks. Beat well. Add the flavouring. Beat well again. It must be thoroughly creamy. Use as a filling for sponge cakes (p.203), as a topping for small or large cakes or to sandwich biscuits.

Custard for Fillings, Portuguese Style

*½ pint (300 ml) milk
2 large eggs (separated)
1 tablespoon cornflour*

*3 oz (90 g) granulated sugar
flavouring – to taste*

Mix the cornflour to a paste with some of the milk. Beat in the yolks, add the remaining milk, the sugar and chosen flavouring. Bring to the boil, stirring all the time and cook very gently until it thickens. Set aside while you beat the egg whites stiffly. Fold them into the custard. Use for filling sponge-type cakes, puff-pastry cases and mille-feuilles. It can also be served as a sauce for puddings and cooked or preserved fruit, in which case you can omit the tablespoon of cornflour.

Drinks

Portuguese Wines

> Nothing filled him with more enthusiasm than the Tormes [Minho region] wine, poured from the green jug – a crisp, light, fragrant wine, with more soul and more soul-giving than many a poem or sacred book.
>
> Eça de Queiroz, *The City and the Mountains*

Maybe palaeontologists are right in saying that the vine existed well before man. Certainly references to wine appear even in the oldest of documents, and it seems that the cultivation of vines and the making of wine were associated with the greatest civilizations of the past. Little wonder, then, that an old country like Portugal has such deep traditions in this respect.

Even though the long Moorish presence in the country had the effect of hindering the making of wine and the cultivation of vines (due to their laws prohibiting the use of alcoholic drinks), there were always places free from their domination, where those practices continued. And as the process of reconquest proceeded, so too the cultivation of vines gained impetus, and soon practically the whole country had some kind of wine-producing going on. The Church – through the many religious orders – helped protect and develop this activity, being instrumental in the selection of better strains of vine and in the making of delicious liqueurs, some of which are being produced to this day.

It is said that it was the Crusaders who encouraged the first wine exports from Portugal. When stopping to help the Portuguese repel the Moors, they were impressed by the quality of the local wines and soon word got around. Nothing like a personal recommendation of this kind! Even Chaucer the English poet (c.1340–1400) had something to say on the subject of Portuguese wines.

By the reign of King Fernando (1367–83), exports were already well established, albeit on an irregular basis. By the fifteenth century it was common practice to send to England wine from around Lisbon and the Minho region, long before the port wine trade as such had even been born.

From the beginning of the sixteenth century Portugal held a monopoly on the sale of spices and other precious merchandise from Brazil and the East. This forced foreign traders to visit Lisbon and Oporto to purchase these products, and consequently Portuguese wines became better known, especially among the English, who were the most assiduous in their commercial dealings with Portugal. This eventually caused English merchants to establish themselves in the Lisbon and Oporto areas and later to concentrate their efforts on the export of wine to England, once the profitable trade in spices had been diversified to countries other than Portugal.

At a later stage, the addition of brandy to some of the wine grown in the Douro region – a practice initially intended to make it smoother and more durable – led to the creation of port wine (which is credited by some to the enterprise of English wine merchants in Oporto, to meet English taste), and hence to the export of this wine to England and later also to France and many other countries (port wine being dubbed 'the best Portuguese ambassador').

The long Alliance (600 years now) between England and Portugal, particularly through the Treaty of Methuen of 1703, helped consolidate the wine trade (though it had its ups and downs) and to establish the reputation of Portuguese wines and port. It is not within the scope of this book to enlarge on this, but it would be worthwhile reading elsewhere about England's fascinating involvement with Portugal through wines throughout the centuries.

In order to protect Portuguese wine and establish codes of practice and quality standards, the Marquis of Pombal (King José's reign, 1750–77) ordered the demarcation of the Douro region, the first to attain this status. The code was gradually extended to other areas, and today there are ten main demarcated regions, each with very specific characteristics, and seven others, including the Azores, where outstanding wines are also produced which, though not fully demarcated, are equally protected.

There is no doubt that this care has benefited the industry, which nowadays employs about 235,000 workers. Notwithstanding its small size, Portugal is a major wine producer (the sixth in the world), although exports account for only about a quarter of the wine produced, the rest being consumed by the Portuguese themselves.

White *vinho verde* ('green' wine – the name does not reflect the colour and was given on account of its youth) may have been 'discovered' outside Portugal only a few years ago, but locally it has been appreciated for centuries. There is also red *vinho verde*, but it tends to be drunk only within the region.

Grapes have been cultivated since Roman times in the area, following a characteristic method of free growth, above the ground (the vines either cling to trees or are supported by stone pillars). The soil (schist and granite), the type of cultivation and the climate all contribute to produce a fresh wine which has the advantage of being quite low in alcohol content. In our times of fierce campaigns against 'drinking and driving' (and quite rightly so), this is an added bonus in its favour. Due to its high quota of lactic acid, it has a very good 'anti-thirst', zesty quality, provided it is served cool.

The wild valleys of the Douro have seen vineyards planted in narrow terraces since the Roman era. It is the land where the port comes from, though the amount of wine to be fortified and made into port is strictly controlled, the remainder being sold as 'Douro', excellent whites and reds, for the table. The region is extremely hot and dry during summer but very cold in winter. Growing grapes or anything else is far from easy in that part of the country, and achieved only through the endurance of its people. The soil is rich in potassium but poor in organic matter. It contains clay and a great deal of schist.

Dão shares with Douro the climate and type of soil, though with its own winemaking traditions, producing distinctive wines, which are considered among the best full-bodied Portuguese table wines. They should be allowed to age, to accentuate their splendid bouquet and fruity quality. They can be red or white, both excellent.

Bairrada is the region north of Coimbra, where so much rich food comes from – the wine being just the right complement for it. Bairrada wines have long-held traditions, being more 'French' in quality than other Portuguese wines. Perhaps it is the red clay soil or the fact that they grow along a coastal strip, in good agricultural land. They have a good quota of fruitiness and tannin and, although well known in Portugal, only recently have they been noticed abroad. They can be red or white, the latter being in great part made into 'champagne type' sparkling wines, from sweet to dry.

The Estremadura province embraces various wine-producing regions, of which Carcavelos, Colares and Bucelas are the most outstanding, though Torres Vedras, and, above it, the Obidos, Caldas and Alcobaça areas are also worth mentioning.

Colares is still considered by many as the best (red) Portuguese table wine, the white being also very good and both medium-dry, with a rich bouquet and at their best when old. The proximity of the sea makes Colares very susceptible to the maritime winds, hence the special protection given to the vines with canes, in this sandy soil.

Bucelas is also believed to have been introduced by the Romans. Its qualities, now perhaps considered 'old-fashioned', centre on the characteristic vanilla bouquet it acquires when old (as it should be). It is said that it was the Duke of Wellington who made Bucelas known outside Portugal. When he was in the country, fighting the French during the Peninsula Wars, he is reported to have sent Bucelas wine back home, to the British Court. It seems that both the gesture and the wine were well appreciated, and the export of Bucelas wine to Britain followed suit.

Carcavelos has long been a good wine-producing area, and history books tell us that King Jose sent wines from the nearby Oeiras estate (belonging to the Marquis of Pombal, his minister) to the Chinese Court in the year 1752. Carcavelos wine is sweet, aromatic and smooth. But obviously Carcavelos, Bucelas, Colares and other wines grown near the Lisbon area are under increasing threat, due to the tremendous expansion of the capital and its suburbs.

South of Lisbon, Palmela offers excellent wines, but Setúbal is actually a demarcated region, for its Muscat wines, unique in the country. The older the muscatel gets, the richer it becomes, without losing the freshness of its luscious aroma. This is sweet dessert wine of the highest quality, worth taking for its own sake at any time.

The Algarve demarcated region extends for most of the strip situated along the coast, concentrating on the agricultural land with privileged climate where almonds, figs, carob, soft fruit and vegetables grow, together with grapes. But the main areas are those around Lagoa, Lagos, Portimão and Tavira. Red wines from the Algarve acquire a rich topaz colour when old. They are light, fruity and smooth. The whites are delicate and rather high in alcohol content, being used partly for making generous wines and to produce muscatel types, when muscat grapes are also added.

Finally, the Madeira demarcated region, where the famous wine of the same name grows. The Portuguese did not waste time in taking advantage of the island's climate, soon after it was discovered, in 1418. Prince Henry himself ordered the planting of special strains of vine (and sugarcane), on the rich, sun-drenched slopes of the island. The vines came from Greece (Malvasia), and the idea was to compete with the Genoese and Venetian markets. Thanks to the law passed in England in 1665 by Charles II, it became forbidden to export goods from Europe to the West Indies and America save for those transported in English ships. But there was an exception: Madeira wine. This favoured the wine to an extraordinary degree at that time, making it extremely popular. English ships made a point of stopping at Madeira to load wine, when going and returning from the Americas. Gradually Madeira wine became fashionable not only on the other side of the Atlantic but also in Europe, and it was very much in demand at the most refined European Courts, from England to Russia. Some say that many noble-women used Madeira to scent their handkerchiefs, so fragrant was this wine.

Legend also said that in 1478 George, Duke of Clarence, brother of Edward IV of England, was drowned in a butt of malmsey (Madeira) wine.

Many more strains of grapes have of course been introduced in Madeira, apart from the initial malvasia, and this is reflected by the great variety of madeiras available, from dry to very sweet, but all of them extremely fragrant. Dry white madeira, like dry white port, is excellent as a choice aperitif.

The remaining districts within the limits of demarcated regions also produce wines of remarkable quality and variety. They are divided into several main areas, where the diversity of ecological conditions, strains of grapes and methods of culti-vation and vinification are reflected by marked differences between the wines.

The following are deserving of special mention, though this is not an exhaustive list, by any means:

Trás-os-Montes region, with great wines within the Vila Real and Bragança districts (some of which are the *rosé* kind), and including Mogadouro, Miranda do Douro, Macedo de Cavalei-ros, Mirandela, Chaves and Valpaços.

Lafões area (between the demarcated Vinhos Verdes and Dão).

Beira region (inland), including Pinhel, Figueira de Castelo Rodrigo, Trancoso, Belmonte, Covilhã, Fundão and Castelo Branco.

The so-called 'western' area, comprising part of Estremadura and including the wines from Alenquer and Torres Vedras (both of which were greatly appreciated by the English six centuries ago), Óbidos, Caldas da Raínha, and Arruda dos Vinhos.

Ribatejo province, with splendid wine traditions for many centuries, including areas like Abrantes, Azambuja, Cartaxo, Rio Maior, Santarém, Almeirim, Alpiarça, Chamusca and Salvaterra de Magos, all producing wines widely appreciated.

Some areas of the Alentejo province, not very extensive in spite of the size of the region (whose agricultural characteristics make it more suited to cereal growing), nevertheless include distinctive wines from Reguengos de Monsaraz, Vidigueira, Granja, Portalegre, Redondo and Borba.

The islands of Pico and Graciosa, in the Azores archipelago, which, since 1439, when the Portuguese sent there the first settlers, have produced various high-quality wines (thanks to the special climate). A blend made from the *verdelho* and *arinto* strains produces an internationally renowned wine, which, incidentally, used to be greatly favoured by Russian tsars.

Having heard just a little of the vast subject of Portuguese wines, how are we to use them? A few hints regarding the best-known regions may help, although one must remember that, for the sake of price and reasons to do with marketing, a large amount of the wine available is the result of blending, according to different labels.

Very dry white: Vinho Verde, Lafões, Vale de Varosa – suitable for shellfish and served very cool (but not iced).

White dry (with more bouquet): Bucelas, Colares, Dão, Bairrada, Trás-os-Montes, Alcobaça – suitable for cold fish dishes. Serve cool.

White medium-dry (aged, with more body and smoother to the palate): Palmela, Ribatejo, Algarve and Alentejo – suitable for hot fish dishes. Serve cool.

Heavier whites (with more bouquet): Bucelas, Colares, Dão, Bairrada, Trás-os-Montes, Alcobaça – as well as:

   Rosé wines from Trás-os-Montes, Bairrada, Dão, the Algarve and

   Lighter reds from Alcobaça, Dão, Covilhã

– suitable for hot or cold smoked meat dishes. Serve cool but less so than the previous ones.

Lighter reds: Colares, Bairrada, Dão, Reguengos de Monsaraz, Ribatejo – suitable for all kinds of poultry. Serve at room temperature.

Medium-body reds: Covilhã, Colares, Dão, Ribatejo, Alentejo – suitable for all white meats. Serve at room temperature.

Full-bodied reds: Bairrada, Ribatejo, Palmela – suitable for red meats, stews and roasts. Serve at room temperature.

Very old reds, fully matured: Bairrada, a few from Dão, Ribatejo, Reguengos – suitable for game. Serve at room temperature.

Very old reds, from all regions – Suitable for cheeses eaten *before* sweet desserts. Serve at room temperature.

Sweet and fortified wines, in general: Suitable for cheeses eaten *after* sweet desserts. Serve at room temperature.

Sparkling wines, sweet or dry (Champagne type), as well as all sweet generous wines (whites, Rosé or others): Suitable for desserts. Serve the whites and *rosé* chilled and the others at room temperature.

However, one's own taste is the only sure guide. As will be seen, each region comprises a great variety of types, and the label will be of help in choosing the right kind for particular requirements. For those who are not experts in these things, sometimes any kind of *good* wine is all right with anything, provided the quality itself is creditable and the temperature correct. This is an important point: generally speaking, whites should be cool and red at room temperature (though some perfectionists go to the extreme of warming them up slightly).

Note: All the white wines – especially the dry ones and the vinho verde – are suitable as aperitifs. Serve them cool.

A few pearls of popular wisdom, regarding wines:

'Cheer up, belly – wine is coming!'
'Better to get drunk than to catch a cold.'
'Those who are old and eat soup with wine become young again.'

But also a word of warning:

'Run away from a bad neighbour and from excess of wine.'
'More men get drowned in a glass than at sea.'
'When drink comes in, wisdom gets out.'

Port

'A wine aged ninety.' ... 'My grandfather inherited it.' ... 'Senatorial port!' we say. We cannot say that of any other wine. Port is deep-sea deep. It is in its flavour deep; mark the difference. It is like a classic tragedy, organic in conception. ... Port is our noblest legacy!' ... 'I will say, that I am consoled for not having lived ninety years back, or at any other period but at present, by this one glass of your ancestral wine.

George Meredith, *The Egoist* (1879)

The above quotation endorses, in no uncertain terms, the

accepted view that in the past port was considered 'the Englishman's drink'. Although less so, at present, vintage port is still kept as a valuable heirloom or reserved for special auctions held at the best world market, namely London.

Port is highly protected and regulated by Portuguese law, to prevent adulteration, and the growers have a vested interest in adhering to the rules. As a fortified wine, it follows traditional methods and, according to the colour of the grapes, sugar content, amount of brandy added, time allowed for maturing, the kind of wood utilized for the casks and other factors, it is divided into several types: vintage, tawny, ruby and white (the dry kind, used as an aperitif).

Mulled Wine/Vinho Quente

MINHO AND DOURO PROVINCES

'I have already chosen my task,' said the councillor, grabbing a spoon from Christina's hands, while she was preparing the mulled wine, that national punch which it would have been disastrous not to have included in that very special meal [at Christmas].

Júlio Diniz, *The Lady of the Reeds* (*A Morgadinha dos Canaviais*)

½ pint (300 ml) port	7 oz (200 g) sugar
½ pint (300 ml) light red wine	6 eggs
½ pint (300 ml) madeira	1½ pints (900 ml) water

Bring the water to the boil in a large pan. Add the madeira and the light red wine, and allow to reach boiling point. Using a separate container, beat the eggs vigorously with the sugar. Add some of the hot wine to the egg mixture, beat again, then add this to the rest of the hot wine. Bring once more to the boil, stirring, and once this point is reached remove from the heat. Now add the port and mix very well. It should be sweet enough, but you can add more sugar to taste. Strain and put aside until it is time to serve the punch.

To serve, warm it up in a bain-marie (p.151). For this, put the pan containing the wine mixture inside a bigger pan which must contain boiling water, put this over a low flame to keep a gentle bubbling until the punch is hot enough. The bain-marie method is necessary to avoid curdling the eggs, but do stir the mixture now and then, while reheating. Pour into cups with a ladle. Some people take this drink with small pieces of bread dipped into it.

Serve to round off Christmas Eve supper, after Midnight Mass.

Mulled Port/Porto Quente

OPORTO REGION
This rather grand recipe uses only port and brandy, which may
be excused, as this is intended for Christmas Eve supper as well
as New Year's Eve. If it is cold outside, this special brew will
put life into any wavering soul.

¾ *pint (450 ml) good sweet port*
1 *tablespoon brown sugar or good*
  honey

3 *tablespoons raisins without*
  seeds (or sultanas)
1 *cinnamon stick*
2 *tablespoons brandy*

Soak all the ingredients for half an hour in a saucepan. Then
bring to the boil and simmer for 2 minutes, serving immediately in cups, with a ladle.

Liqueurs and Fortified Drinks

Since alcoholic drinks are so important to complement
Portuguese meals, it is customary to serve a liqueur with the
coffee as the perfect finish to a special meal. But often the
liqueur will be served just to the ladies, for the men may prefer
something stronger, such as *aguardente* or *bagaceira*. All those
alcoholic drinks thought to help the digestion of rich food are
classified in Portugal as *digestivos* and are a readily forgiven sin.

Liqueurs may also be served at any time during the day
(instead of port) with small cakes, sweets and/or nuts, as a
snack, to anyone calling at the house. They are also used to
flavour and impart fragrance to fruit salads and confectionery.

Almost every household in Portugal will have some
homemade liqueur speciality, based on absolutely pure alcohol
(which can be bought at Portuguese chemists, over the
counter) or on *aguardente* or *bagaceira*, popular spirits available
at any grocer's or tavern all over Portugal, at a very reasonable
price.

Aguardente is spirits obtained from the distillation of wine.
The same name can be applied to fermented fruits and cereals –
sugarcane, wheat and even potato can be used. An exceedingly
good *aguardente* is made with pears, but normally it derives
mostly from wine. *Aguardente* has the same appearance as
brandy and, when good, is very similar to it, even though some
class it as 'crude brandy'. The making of *aguardente* is well
rooted in Portugal, and the rules for its ageing and marketing
are defined by law.

Bagaceira or *bagaço* is a transparent drink (like gin) distilled directly from the fresh left-overs of pressed grapes, after extracting their juice for winemaking. One could call it a kind of brandy extracted from the husks of grapes. It is very strong and fragrant.

Apart from alcohol, *aguardente* and *bagaceira*, the other ingredients for homemade liqueurs are sugar and flavourings, in which Portuguese imagination excels; fruit of all kinds, peppermint, milk, cocoa, coffee, aniseed and even mixed flavours which resemble and often are just as good or even surpass famous label liqueurs.

Some religious orders have for centuries produced 'secret recipe' liqueurs. One such is the monastery of Singeverga in the North of Portugal, which markets a liqueur made with spices. It has an exquisite taste and is on a par with any world-famous liqueur. Another excellent Portuguese liqueur (not made by monks) is the Beirão from the Lousã Mountain, in the Beiras region, also made with herbs and spices. It almost reaches the heights of the Singeverga. They are both sold in handsome bottles.

If you would like to try some of the recipes for liqueurs that follow and cannot find pure alcohol, *aguardente* or *bagaceira*, brandy can be substituted.

When the recipe indicates clarification, it is better to go through this procedure, to guarantee a transparent liqueur, although this is not always strictly necessary, if the ingredients do not cloud the mixture.

After the given time for maceration or infusion, pour into the bottle the white and crushed shell of 1 egg. Shake really hard, to mix well and then leave to stand for 2–3 days. By that time a sediment will have formed at the bottom. Without disturbing this too much, filter the liquid into another container, using a proper paper filter (generally obtainable at stores selling wine-making equipment). Stand for another day. Filter again, if necessary. Now the liqueur will be clear and ready to be put in a liqueur bottle with a tight-fitting glass top or, failing this, in any ordinary bottle with a good cork.

Morello Cherry Liqueur/Ginjinha or Ginja em Aguardente

Ginjinha is widely made at home in Portugal, but it is also made commercially and sold at every wine bar and restaurant. 'Ginjinha' is the popular name for 'Ginja em Aguardente' – the Portuguese are very fond of using the diminutive for anything they like or which is dainty or homely. Ginjinha is perhaps the most traditional Portuguese liqueur, even mentioned in popular songs. If morello cherries are available, it is possible to make ginjinha outside Portugal without any difficulty (using brandy if not *aguardente*, see p.229).

1 lb (450 g) very sound morello cherries	1 cinnamon stick (optional)
7 oz (200 g) caster sugar	enough spirits to cover the fruit, about ¾ pint (450 ml)
1 clove (optional)	

Wash the cherries, dry them and discard the stems but do not stone them. Place the fruit in a liqueur bottle (with a widish mouth), cover with the sugar, the spices (if used) and the chosen spirits. Put in a suitably sized cork or the bottle's own stopper, very carefully, to ensure that no air at all gets into the bottle. Put it in a dark place, shaking daily for the first week. Then leave to stand. It will be ready in 3 months but it is much better if left for nearly a year. A few cherries are served inside each glass of ginjinha.

Milk Liqueur/Licor de Leite

This is a rich, thick and spicy liqueur, of which there are two main versions.

1 pint (600 ml) spirits (aguardente or brandy)	¼ vanilla pod, cut into small pieces
1 pint (600 ml) milk (cold)	1 medium lemon, thinly sliced (with the rind) – wash it first
1 lb (450 g) caster sugar	1 tablespoon ground almonds
1 clove	

Discard any pips from the lemon slices (but use all the juice that may drop while slicing it). Place all the ingredients in a wide-mouthed bottle or jar and cover very tightly. Leave it to macerate for 8 weeks, shaking the bottle twice a week. Clarify and filter as indicated on p.229 before bottling and corking well.

1 pint (600 ml) cold milk	1 vanilla pod, cut in pieces
1 pint (600 ml) spirits, as above	1 whole nutmeg
10 oz (280 g) caster sugar	1 lemon, cut in pieces

Proceed as above. After 6–8 weeks it will be ready to filter and bottle.

Cocoa Liqueur/Licor de Cacau

Another popular liqueur made by Portuguese housewives.

*½ pint (300 ml) spirits (pure
  alcohol/aguardente/brandy)*
10 oz (280 g) caster sugar
½ pint (300 ml) water

*3½ oz (100 g) powdered pure
  cocoa*
½ vanilla pod, cut into pieces

Place the sugar, water and vanilla in a pan. Bring to the boil for just a minute. Whilst still warm, add the spirits and the cocoa. Mix well and put in a bottle to macerate for two weeks. Clarify (p.229), filter and bottle.

Aniseed Liqueur/Licor de Erva-Doce

This aromatic liqueur is a favourite of mine. My mother used to be a great specialist at it. It improves with age, like most liqueurs, and if well made it is just like any very good bought liqueur.

12 oz (350 g) caster sugar
*½ pint (300 ml) spirits (pure
  alcohol/aguardente/or brandy)*

½ pint (300 ml) water
½ oz (15 g) aniseed, crushed

Place the spirits in a jar or bottle with the aniseed, cover tightly and leave for 3–4 days, to draw all the flavour. Then prepare a syrup with the water and sugar, until it thickens a little (about 2–3 minutes, over low heat). When the syrup is almost cold, pour it into the bottle, mix well with the spirits and seeds and leave for 3–4 weeks, shaking it during the first 3–4 days only. Clarify (p.229), filter and bottle.

Coffee Liqueur/Licor de Café

Another popular liqueur, at least in more old-fashioned households.

4 fluid oz (120 ml) water
*¾ pint (450 ml) spirits
  (aguardente or brandy)*
1 lb (450 g) caster sugar

*2 tablespoons of very aromatic
  freshly ground coffee (not the
  instant variety!)*

Place the spirits in a bottle or jar and mix in the coffee, which must have been ground just prior to using. Leave for 2 weeks, shaking the bottle 3 times a week. Prepare a syrup with the water and sugar, boiling just for a minute. Cool and add to the

bottle. Shake well. Leave to stand again for 2 or 3 days. Clarify,
filter (p.229) and bottle.

Variation
This is a somewhat weaker version of this liqueur:

¾ pint (450 ml) water	*6 oz (175 g) caster sugar*
3 tablespoons freshly ground	*½ pint (300 ml) spirits*
coffee	

Make a strong coffee using the freshly ground coffee beans and
half the water. With the remaining water, make a syrup with
the sugar, boiling both for 3–4 minutes over a low flame. Cool.
Add to the coffee, mix and place in the bottle, with the chosen
spirits. Cover and leave for 3–4 weeks, shaking 3–4 times
during the first week. Clarify and filter (p.229) and bottle.

Tangerine Liqueur/Licor de Tangerina

Wonderfully fragrant, this liqueur is also excellent for
flavouring cakes, puddings and fruit salads, and as an aid to
digestion (hence very appropriate to serve after a meal).

1 pint (600 ml) spirits (pure	*juice of 3 of the fruits used*
alcohol, aguardente,	*(strained)*
bagaceira or brandy)	*1¼ pints (750 ml) water*
rind of 6 medium-sized tangerines	*1½ lb (675 g) caster sugar*
(or clementines or mandarins)	

Macerate the rind, juice and spirits for 3 weeks. After that add a
syrup made with the water and sugar, boiled for 2–3 minutes
and cooled. Mix well. Leave to stand for 2–3 days. Filter and
bottle.

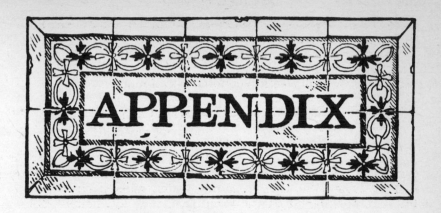

Vegetarian Recipes

The following are recipes which are strictly vegetarian:

Soups

Chickpea Soup/Sopa de Grão and Variation (pp.50–1)

Bean and Cabbage Soup/Sopa de Feijão (p.51)

Vegetable Purée/Sopa de Legumes (p.52)

Tomato, Egg and Bread Soup/Sopa de Tomate com Ovo e Pão (pp.52–3)

Green Bean Soup with Tomato/Sopa de Feijão Verde com Tomate and Variation (pp.53–4)

Dried Chestnut Soup/Sopa de Castanhas Piladas (p.54)

Maize Porridge/Papas de Milho (pp.54–5)

Bread Dishes

Bread-Pap/Açorda (pp.58–9)

Coriander Bread Soup/Açorda Alentejana (p.61)

Açorda Madeira Style/Açorda Madeirense (pp.61–2)

Migas Ribatejo Style/Migas do Ribatejo (p.62)

Migas Beira Litoral Style/Migas à Moda da Beira Litoral (p.63)

Garlic Dry Soup/Sopa Seca de Alho (p.66)

Gaspachos (pp.67–8)

Sauces

Tomato Sauce/Molho de Tomate (p.135)

Villain Sauce/Molho de Vilão (p.136)

Mayonnaise (p.138)

Beirão Style Sauce/Molho Beirão (p.138)

Other Dishes

Little Fish from the Garden/Peixinhos da Horta (p.139)

Black-eyed Beans Salad/Salada de Feijão Frade and Variation (p.140)

Stewed Green Beans/Feijão Verde Guisado (p.141)

Green Mousse/Esparregado and Variation (pp.141–2)

Tomato Rice/Arroz de Tomate and Variations (p.146)

Rich Broad Beans/Fava Rica (p.143)

Broad Beans with Coriander/Favas com Coentros (pp.144–5)

Broad Beans with Yellow Sauce/Favas com Molho Amarelo (p.145)

Broad Beans with Olive Oil/Favas com Azeite (pp.145–6)

All Sweet Things recipes (p.147 to p.219) except
Priscos Parish Priest Pudding/Pudim do Abade de Priscos (p.158), Dry Sweet Soup/Sopa Seca Doce (p.162) and Blancmange/Manjar Branco (p.165)

These recipes may be successfully adapted to vegetarian dishes as indicated below:

Soups

Green Broth/Caldo Verde and Variations (pp.39–40) – omitting chouriço slices

Broad Bean Soup/Sopa de Favas (p.51) – omitting ham

Pea Soup/Sopa de Puré de Ervilhas (p.52) – omitting ham

Bread Dishes

Migas Beira Baixa Style/Migas à Beira Baixa (p.63) – omitting pork meat

Other Dishes

Bean Stew/Feijoada (p.102) – omitting pork meat

Peas with Smoked Sausage/Paio com Ervilhas (p.116) – omitting the pork meat

Stewed Wild Mushrooms/Cogumelos Guisados (p.142) – omitting bacon

Broad Beans Lisbon Fashion/Favas à Moda de Lisboa (pp.143–4) – omitting pork meat

Index

Accompaniments and vegetables, 139-46, *see also* individual names
Açordas (bread-pap), 58-62
  coriander, Alentejo style, 61
  Madeira style, 61
  Portuguese style, 58-9
  salted cod, 59
  seafood, 60
Alcoholic drinks, 220-32
  liqueurs and fortified drinks, 228-32
  wines, 220-8
Alheiras, 24
Almeida, Fialho de, (Portuguese writer), 3, 5, 132
Almond(s), 26
  fried, 14
  sweets (marzipan), Algarve style, 170
  tart, 186
Aniseed liqueur, 229
Apple(s)
  baked, 168
  tart, with custard, 186-7
  in turnovers from Vila Real, 183-4

Bacon, 24
Bain-marie, 33
Bean(s), broad, 142-3
  Lisbon fashion, 143-4
  Ribatejo fashion, 144
  rich (*fava rica*), 143
  soup, 51-2
  with coriander, 144-5
  with olive oil, 145-6
  with yellow sauce, Bairrada style, 145
Bean(s), dried
  black-eyed, salad, 140-1
  and cabbage soup, 51
  and coriander rice (variation), 146

stew, Portuguese style (*feijoada*), 103
  tarts, 180-1
Beans(s), green
  little fish from the kitchen garden, 138-9
  in soup (variation), 40
  stewed, Portuguese style, 141
  and tomato soup, 53-4
Beef
  in boiled meat and vegetables, Portuguese style (*Cozido à Portuguesa*), 100-1
  in festival soup
  soup, 43
  steak, 97-8
    with egg on horseback, 98-9
    Marrare fashion, 99
    with onion, 99-100
  stew, 101
  stock soup, 42-3
Beverages
  coffee, 18
  lemon, 18
  liqueurs, 228-32
  mineral water, 18-19
  tea, 17
  wines, 220-8
Biscuits
  pine-seed, 198
  sand from Cascais (*areias*), 198
  s-shaped, Peniche fashion, 197-8
  see also Cakes
Blancmange (*manjar branco*), 165-6
Blood stews (*sarrabulho/cabidela*), 116-19, 124, 128
  Bairrada fashion, 118
  Beira Alta fashion, 117
  chicken, 124
  Estremadura fashion, 118
  giblets with rice, 128
  pig's offal, 119
  rice, 119

nIndex37

suckling pig, 112

Branco, Camilo Castelo (Portuguese writer), 27, 76

Bread
dough, 33, 69-70
maize, 57-8

Bread dishes, 56-7, see also Açordas, Dry Soups, Ensopados, Fancy bread, Gaspachos, Migas, Pies

Broth
beef, 42-3
chicken, 41
green (caldo verde), 39-40

Buns
All Saints' Day, 201-2
from Coimbra (arrufadas), 199
Easter, 202
sweet (regueifas), 200-1
sweet, Pombal fashion (fogaças), 199-200
See also cakes

Butter, 21
cream filling, Portuguese style, 218
savoury, 15

Cabbage and bean soup, 51

Cake(s)
fried
Abbot's Ears, 195
chickpea turnovers from St Clara Convent, 193-4
Christmas cakes, 194
Christmas cakes, Ribatejo fashion, 194-5
dreams, (sonhos), 190-1
Golden Slices (Fatias Douradas/ Rabanadas), 196-7
pumpkin, 191-2
sweet potato, 195-6
sweet potato turnovers, 192-3
large
Christmas, 206-7
fruit, 206
honey, 207-8
King's (Bolo Rei), 208-9
rich molasses, 205-6
Rotten, 207
sponge (pão-de-ló), 203-4
sponge roll, Viana fashion, 204
walnut, 162
small
Bowlful from Abrantes (tigeladas), 187
Castle (Broas Castelares), 190
Christmas cakes from

Bombarral (broas), 189
coconut, 190
Rotten, for Christmas, 188
St Gonçalo, 188
See also Biscuits, Buns, Pastries and Turnovers

Caldeirada (fish stew), 32, 81-3
eel, Aveiro style, 81-2
rich, 82-3
sardine, 82

Caramel
crême (flan), 151
for puddings, 36

Cataplana, 37

Chantilly cream, Portuguese style, 217

Cheese(s), 29-31
in Heavenly Food, 163
pudding, 161
with salted cod, 77
soft, pudding, 161
tartlets, Beira style, 184
tartlets, Sintra style (queijadas), 179-80
tartlets, Pereiro style, 184-5

Chestnuts, 27
filling, 218
dried, soup, 54
and milk jam, 166

Chicken
in blancmange, 165-6
blood stew (cabidela), 124
in boiled meat and vegetables (cozido), 100-1
celebration pastics (fogaças), 132-3
consommé (variation), 41
in dry sweet soup, 162-3
fricassée, 124-5
jugged or in deep pot (Frango na Púcara), 123-4
pies, Alentejo style (empadas), 130-1
in pies (variation), 69-70
rice, Portuguese style, 125
soup, 41

Chickpea(s)
with boiled cod (Meia Desfeita), 75-6
in dry soup, Minho fashion, 44
rice (variation), 146
soup, 50-1
turnovers from St Clara Convent, 193-4

Chinese leaves in soup (variation), 40

Chocolate
mousse, 151-2
salami (sweet), 178

Chouriço, 23-4
Christmas dishes
  cake, 206-7
  cakes, Bombarral (*broas*), 189
  Christmas Eve cod, 72-3
  Christmas Eve Golden Soup, 157-8
  Christmas Eve menu, 11
  fried cakes (*filhós*), 194
  fried cakes, Ribatejo fashion, 194-5
  Golden Slices (*Fatias Douradas*),
    196-7
  lunch menu, 11
  Rotten Cakes, 188-9
  stuffed turkey, 121-2
Cider, 25
Cinnamon and egg pudding, 164-5
Citrus fruits, 25-6
  drinks, Lemon, 18
  Orange
    with duck and rice, 126
    and egg pudding, from Madeira,
      165
    peel, candied, 177-8
    roll, 155
Clams, 26
Cockles, 26-7
  Bulhão Pato fashion, 92
  in *cataplana* pan, 92
  in seafood *açorda*, 60
  soup (Algarve), 49
  soup, Minho fashion, 50
Cocoa liqueur, 229
Coconut
  cakes, 190
  pudding, 167
Cod (salted, dried), 21-2, 31-2
  açorda, 59
  boiled with chickpeas (*Meia Des-
    feita*), 75-6
  Brás fashion, 74-5
  cakes (*pasteis de Bacalhau*), 76-7
  with cheese, 77
  Christmas Eve, 72-3
  dry soup, 67
  Gomes de Sá fashion, 73-4
  pie, 77-8
  rice, 78-9
Coffee, 18
  cream filling, 218
  liqueur, 229-30
Cold meats, 15
Condiments, 20
Cooking fats and oils, 21
Cooking methods *see* Methods of
  cooking

Coriander, 20
  and bean rice (variation), 146
  bread soup, Alentejo style, 61
  in broad beans, Lisbon fashion,
    143-4
  in broad beans, Ribatejo fashion,
    144
  with broad beans, 144-5
  in villain sauce, 136
Cornmeal *see* Maize
Cream tarts (*Pasteis de Nata*), 178-9
Custard
  with apple tart, 186-7
  egg (*leite-creme*), 149-50
  for fillings, Portuguese style,
    218-19
  tarts from the Azores, 185
Cuttlefish
  with ink, 95
  (or squid) stewed, 94-5

Desserts, *see* Apples, Biscuits, Buns,
  Cakes, Fancy breads, Pas-
  tries, Pies *and* Puddings
Diniz, Julio, Portuguese writer, 196,
  227
Dough
  bread, 33
  maize bread, 57-8
  pastry for frying, 34
  pies, 69-70
  puff-pastry, 179
Dry soups
  garlic, 66
  Minho fashion, 44
  Minho style, 66
  salted cod, 67
Duck
  with rice, 125-6
  with rice and orange, 126

Easter dishes
  buns, 202
  fancy bread, 209-10
Eel stew, Aveiro style, 81-2
Egg(s)
  and bread sweets, Bragança style,
    175
  and cinnamon pudding, 164-5
  custard, 149-50
  and orange pudding from Ma-
    deira, 165
  and smoked sausage, 115-16
  soft (*ovos moles*), 152
  with steak, 98-9

stuffed, 14-15
sweets, from Viseu, 170-1
threads (*Fios de Ovos*), 216-17
tomato and bread soup, 52-3
Ensopados (bread dishes)
fish, 65
kid, 64-5
Equipment, 36-7
Everyday menus, 16

Fancy bread
buttery, 210-11
for Easter (*folar*), 209-10
plain, 209
See also Pies *and* Buns
Farinheiras, 24
Fats and oils, 21
Fatty bacon (*toucinho*), 24
Fig lord (*morgado*), 173-4
Fillings (for cakes and puddings)
butter cream, Portuguese style, 218
Chantilly cream, Portuguese style, 217
chestnut, 218
coffee cream, 218
custard, Portuguese style, 218-19
egg threads (*Fios de Ovos*), 216-17
pumpkin jam, 215
soft eggs (*ovos moles*), 152
spaghetti squash jam, 213-14
sweet potato compote, 192
Fish, 26-7,1 32, 71-2, 87-8
baked, 85
butter, 15
ensopado, 65
grilled red mullet Setúbal fashion, 85-6
hake with everything (*Pescada com Todos*), 84-5
in seafood *açorda*, 60
soup
Alentejo fashion, 48-9
chowder type, Algarve fashion, 49
Madeira style, 48
trout (cold), Beira Alta style, 86-7
see also Caldeiradas (fish stew), Cod, Lampreys, Sardines, Seafood, Shellfish *and* Tuna
Flavourings, 20
Fortified drinks and liqueurs, 228-32
Fresh yeast, 31
Fried cakes *see* Cake(s)
Fruit(s)
cake, 206

citrus, 18, 25-6, 126, 155, 165, 177-8
salad, 168-9

Game *see* Duck, Hare, Partridge *and* Rabbit
Garlic, 20
dry soup, 66
marinade with wine, 32-3
Garrett, Almeida, Portuguese writer, 5, 155
Gaspacho
Alentejo style, 67-8
Algarve style, 68
Goat stew, Bairrada style (*chanfana*), 102
Grape jam, 213
Green mousse (*esparregado*), 141
Greens, in soup (variation), 40

Haggis
Beira Baixa style, 120-1
Beira Litoral style, 121
Trás-os-Montes style, 120
Hake with everything (*Pescada com Todos*), 84-5
Hare (or Rabbit)
grilled, 127
soup, 44-5
Herbs, 20
Honey cake, 207-8
Hors-d'oeuvres, 14

Jams and jellies
chestnut and milk, 166
Friar John's Delight, 214-15
grape, 213
pumpkin, 215
quince, 28-9
cheese (*marmelada*), 211-12
jelly, 212-13
tomato
ripe, 215-16
unripe, 216

Kale, in green broth (*caldo verde*), 39-40
Kid
Beira Alta style, 105
ensopado, 64-5
Ribatejo fashion, 104-5
roast, 104

Lamprey(s), 87-8
rice, 88-9

Large cakes *see* Cakes
Lemon drinks, 18
Linguiça, 23
Liqueurs
  aniseed, 229
  cocoa, 229
  coffee, 229-30
  milk, 230
  morello cherry (*ginjinha*), 229-30
  tangerine, 232
Liver
  in blood stews, 116-19
  with Them (potatoes) (*iscas*), 114-15
Lobster
  in seafood *açorda*, 60
  stewed, 91

Madeira wine, 25, 224
  in mulled wine, 227
Maize
  bread, 57-8
  flour, 25
  porridge
    savoury, 54-5
    sweet, 169
Marinade, 32-3
Marzipan sweets from Algarve, 170
Mayonnaise, 138
Meats(s)
  cold, 15
  goat stew, Bairrada style (*chanfana*),
    102
  pasties, celebration chicken (*foga-
    ças*), 132-3
  tripe, Oporto style, 107-8
  turkey, stuffed for Christmas, 121-2
  see also Beef, Chicken, Haggis, Kid,
    Pies, Pork *and* Veal
Menus
  Christmas Eve, 11
  Christmas lunch, 11
  everyday, 16
Meredith, George, English writer, 226
Methods of cooking
  bain-marie, 33
  bread dough, 33
  fish stews (*caldeiradas*), 32
  marinade, 32-3
  refogado, 31
  salted cod, 31-2
  salt the fish, 32
  syrup (stages of), 35-6
Migas (bread dishes)
  Alentejo style, 64
  Beira Baixa style, 63-4

Beira Litoral style, 63
  Ribatejo style, 62-3
  sweet, 159
Milk
  and chestnut jam, 166
  liqueur, 230
Mineral water, 18-19
Molasses, rich cake, 205-6
Morcelas, 24
Morello cherry liqueur (*ginjinha*),
    229-30
Mullet, grilled, 85-6
Mushrooms (wild), stewed, 142
Mussels, 26-7, 46-7

Octopus with Rice, 95-6
Offal, in blood stew, 119
Oil(s), 21
  olive, 21
    broad beans with, 145-6
Onion, 20-1
  in *refogado*, 31
  with steak, 99-100
Orange, 25-6
  with duck and rice, 126
  and egg pudding, 165
  peel, candied, 177-8
  roll, 155
Ortigão, Ramalho, Portuguese
    writer, 10

Paio, 24
Partridge
  cold, 130
  soup, 46
  with villain sauce, 129-30
  with vinegar sauce, 129
Pasta
  in beef stock soup (variation), 43
  in chicken soup (variation), 41
  pudding (*aletria*), 166-7
Pasties, celebration chicken (*fogaças*),
    132-3
Pastries
  almond tart, 186
  apple tart with custard, 186-7
  bean tarts, 180-1
  cheese tartlets (*queijadas*)
    Beira style, 184
    Pereiro style, 184-5
    Sintra style, 179-80
  cream tarts (*Pasteis de Nata*), 178-9
  custard tarts from the Azores, 185
  fluffy cakes from Faial, 185-6
  rice patties from the Azores, 181-2

St Clara turnovers, 182-3
Turnovers from Vila Real, 183-4
see also Cakes
Peaches in wine (salad), 168-9
Peas
 with rice (variation), 146
 with smoked sausage, 116
 soup, 52
Pies (*folares/bolas*)
 bread and meats, 68-70
 chicken, Alentejo style, 130-1
 salted cod, 77-8
 Veal, Castelo Branco fashion, 131-2
Pine-seed biscuits, 198-9
Pork, 22-4, 109-11
 Alentejo style, 114
 bacon, 24
 in boiled meat with vegetables (*cozido*), 100-1
 crisp, Trás-os-Montes style, 113
 crisp, Viana style (Rojões), 112-13
 liver
  in blood stews, 116-19
  with Them (potatoes), 114-15
 offal, in blood stew, 119
 presunto, 22-4
 sausages, 23-4
  smoked, with eggs, 115-16
  smoked, with peas, 116
 stews with pig's blood (*sarrabulho/ cabidela*), 116-17
  Bairrada fashion, 118
  Beira Alta fashion, 117
  Estremadura fashion, 118
  offal, 119
  suckling pig, 113
  rice, 119
 suckling pig
  Bairrada style (*leitão*), 111-12
  blood stew (*cabidela*), 113
Porridge, maize
 savoury, 54-5
 sweet, 169
Port, 25, 226-7
 mulled, 228
 sauce, 137
Potato, sweet *see* Sweet potato
Potato, as thickener, 40
Poultry *see* Chicken *and* Turkey
Prawns
 in chowder, 46-7
 rissoles, 90-1
 in salad, 14
 in seafood *açorda*, 60
Presunto, 22-4

Puddings
 Bacon from Heaven (*Toucinho do Céu*), 153-4
 baked apples, 168
 blancmange, 165-6
 cheese, 161
 chestnut, and milk jam, 166
 chocolate mousse, 151-2
 Christmas Golden Soup, 157-8
 coconut, 167
 crême caramel, 151
 custard (*leite-creme*), 149-50
 dry sweet soup, 162-3
 egg
  and cinnamon, 164-5
  and orange, from Madeira, 165
 Floating Islands (*farófias*), 160
 Food from Heaven, 164
 fruit salads, 168-9
 golden spaghetti squash (*chila*), 167-8
 Heavenly Food, 163
 Nun's Belly (*Barriga de Freira*), 155-6
 orange roll, 155
 pasta (*aletria*), 166-7
 peaches in wine, 168-9
 Priscos Parish Priest (*Pudim do Abade de Priscos*), 158-9
 Rice (*arroz doce*), 146-7
 slices, Tomar style (*Fatias de Tomar*), 156
 soft cheese, 161
 soft eggs (*ovos moles*), 152-3
 Straw from Abrantes (*Palha de Abrantes*), 163
 sweet maize porridge, 169
 sweet *migas*, 159
 walnut cake, 162
 see also Cakes
Pumpkin
 in Christmas fried cakes, 194-5
 jam, 215
 in vegetable purée soup, 52

Queiroz, Eça de, Portuguese writer, 19, 40, 104, 112, 116, 142, 147, 157, 168, 220
Quince(s), 28-9
 cheese (jam), (*marmelada*), 29, 211-12
 jelly, 212-13

Rabbit
 (or hare), grilled, 127-8
 hunter's, 127

in pies (variation), 69-70
(or Hare), (wild), soup, 44-5
Refogado, 31
Reminders, 37
Requeijão (cheese), 30
Rice
   in blood stew, 119, 128
   chicken, Portuguese style, 125
   with duck, 125-6
   lamprey, 88-9
   octopus, 95-6
   in the oven, 108-9
   in patties, from the Azores, 181-2
   pudding, 146-7
   with salted cod, 78-9
   tomato, 146
Ricotta (cheese), 30
Runner beans *see* Beans, green

Salad
   black-eyed beans, 140-1
   fruit, 168-9
   prawns (or lobster), 14
   vegetable, 15
Salpicão, 24
Salted cod *see* Cod
Sardines, 79
   canned, 14-15
   charcoal grilled, 79-80
   fresh, 79-80
   stew, 82
Sauces
   Beirão style, 138
   mayonnaise, 138
   port wine, 137
   tomato, Portuguese style, 134-5
   vinegar, 137
      from the Algarve (*escabeche*), 136-7
   villain, 136
   yellow, 145
Sausages, 23-4
   smoked, with eggs, 115-16
   smoked, with peas, 116
Seafood, 94
   açorda, 60
   cuttlefish (or squid), stewed, 94-5
   cuttlefish with ink, 95
   octopus with rice, 95-6
   see also shellfish
Shellfish
   lobster, stewed, 91
   in seafood açorda, 60
   see also Cockles, Prawns, Shrimps
Shrimps

in chowder, 46-7
in rissoles, 90-1
in salad, 14
soup, 47
Snails, Portuguese style, 93
Soups, 38-9
   bean and cabbage, 51
   beef, 42-3
   broad bean, 51-2
   chicken (*canja*), 40-1
   chickpea, 50-1
   chowder type, 49
   cockle, 49-50
   dried chestnut, 54
   dry, 44, 66-7
   festival, 43-4
   fish, 48-9
   gaspacho, 67-8
   green bean with tomato, 53-4
   green broth (*caldo verde*), 39-40
   maize porridge, 54-5
   partridge, 46
   pea, 52
   prawn (or shrimp) and mussel chowder, 46-7
   shrimp, 47
   stone, 41-2
   tomato, egg and bread, 52-3
   vegetable purée, 52
   wild rabbit (or hare), 44-6
Spaghetti squash (*chila*)
   golden dessert, 167-8
   jam, 213-14
Spinach in green mousse, 141
Sponge cake (*pão-de-ló*), 203-4
Steak, 97-8
   with egg on horseback, 98-9
   Marrare fashion, 99
   with onion, 99-100
Stew
   beans (*feijoada*), 102-3
   beef, 101
   with blood (*sarrabulho/cabidela*) *see* Blood stews
   cuttlefish, 94-5
   fish, 32, 81-3
   goat, 102
   green beans, 141
   lobster, 91
   wild mushrooms, 142
String beans *see* Beans, green
Suckling pig
   Bairrada style, 111-12
   Blood stew, 113
Sweet potato, 28

cakes, 174-5
  in Castle cakes (*broas*), 190
  in Christmas cakes (*broas*), 189
  delights, 176
  fried, 195-6
  turnovers, 192-3
Sweets
  Angel's Breasts, 172-3
  Breeze from the Lis river, 172
  candied orange peel, 177-8
  chocolate saiami, 178
  Dom Rodrigo, 173
  eggs, from Viseu, 170-1
  fig lord (*morgado*), 173-4
  little egg and bread sweets, Bragança fashion, 175
  little oranges, 176-7
  Lorvão, 175-6
  marzipan, from the Algarve, 170
  potato cakes, 174-5
  potato delights, 176
  walnuts, Cascais style, 171-2
  see also Buns, Cakes, Pastries *and* Puddings
Syrup (stages of), 35-6

Tangerine liqueur, 232
Tarts *see* Pastries
Tea, 17
Tomato
  egg and bread soup, 52-3
  and green bean soup, 53-4
  jams, 215-16
  rice, 146
  sauce, Portuguese style, 134-5
Toucinho, 24
Tripe, Oporto style, 107-8
Tuna
  canned, 14-15
  steaks, 87

Turkey, stuffed for Christmas, 121-2
Turnip-tops, 27-8
  in green broth (variation), 40
  in green mousse, 141
Turnovers
  chickpea, from St Clara Convent, 193-4
  dough (for frying), 34
  rice, from the Azores, 181-2
  St Clara, 182-3
  Sweet Potato, 192-3
  Vila Real, 183-4

Veal
  Barrosã fashion, 106
  pies, Castelo Branco fashion (*empadas*), 131-2
  in pies (variation), 69-70
  spit-roast (*Vitela no Espeto*), 106-7
Vegetable salad, 15
Vegetable purée soup, 52
Vegetables and Accompaniments, 139-46
  see also individual names
Vegetarian recipes, 233-5

Walnut(s)
  cake, 162
  Cascais fashion, 171-2
Watercress, in soup (variation), 40
Water (mineral), 18-19
Wild mushrooms, stewed, 142
Wild rabbit (or Hare) soup, 44-6
Wine, 24-5, 220-6
  in fruit salad, 168-9
  in marinade, 32-3
  mulled, 227

Yeast, fresh and dried, 31